RECONSTRUCTING THE ROMAN REPUBLIC

RECONSTRUCTING THE ROMAN REPUBLIC

AN ANCIENT POLITICAL CULTURE AND MODERN RESEARCH

KARL-J. HÖLKESKAMP

Translated by Henry Heitmann-Gordon
Revised, updated, and augmented by the author

PRINCETON UNIVERSITY PRESS

PRINCETON AND OXFORD

The original edition was published under the title *Rekonstruktionen einer Republik. Die politische Kultur des antiken Rom und die Forschung der letzten Jahrzehnte* © 2004 by Oldenbourg Wissenschaftsverlag GmbH, München

English translation copyright © 2010 by Princeton University Press
Published by Princeton University Press, 41 William Street, Princeton, New Jersey 08540
In the United Kingdom: Princeton University Press, 6 Oxford Street, Woodstock, Oxfordshire OX20 1TW

Library of Congress Cataloging-in-Publication Data
Hölkeskamp, Karl-Joachim.
    [Rekonstruktionen einer Republik. English]
    Reconstructing the Roman republic : an ancient political culture and modern research / Karl-J. Hölkeskamp ; translated by Henry Heitmann-Gordon, revised, updated, and augmented by the author.
        p. cm.
    Includes bibliographical references and index.
    ISBN 978-0-691-14038-4 (cloth : alk. paper)
    1. Rome—Politics and government—265–30 B.C. 2. Rome—History—Republic, 265–30 B.C. I. Heitmann-Gordon, Henry. II. Title.
    DG241.2.H6515 2010
    937'.02072—dc22   2009046995

British Library Cataloging-in-Publication Data is available

This book has been composed in Sabon

Printed on acid-free paper. ∞

press.princeton.edu

Printed in the United States of America

10 9 8 7 6 5 4 3 2 1

CONTENTS

FIGURES

PREFACE TO THE ENGLISH EDITION

A S THE ORIGINAL EDITION, published in German in 2004, this book has a history of its own—and in a way, although this may seem paradoxical, this history goes back far beyond that date, namely to my years in Cambridge, which were not only intellectually highly stimulating, but also, in many ways, a formative stage of my career. When in later years I summoned up remembrance of things past, I realized that one of the more bitter lessons that I also had to learn in Cambridge was a widespread attitude in international academic circles (not only in classical scholarship) that was usually left unsaid, but on one occasion precisely and bluntly put by a colleague in the Classics Faculty: "An idea not conceived in English is probably not worth thinking at all." At the time, the heavy irony was not (quite) lost on me, but the implicit message certainly was—in fact, it took me years to realize and at last resign myself to accepting it as a fact of academic life: "Teutonica sunt, non leguntur" (nor, for that matter, anything in a language other than English)—and even by basically open-minded and well-meaning people who consider themselves serious scholars in a field that has traditionally been, and still is, international and multilingual. This translation is an offer to give them an idea that, to use another famous Shakespearean phrase, there are more things in heaven and earth than are dreamt of in their Anglocentric philosophy—namely, that there is a lively, possibly interesting and important debate out there, of which they may have an inkling; a debate among a select few, whose names they may even have heard of; a debate, alas, that was (in large part) led in idioms as exotic as French, Italian, and even German—a debate not only about the Roman republic and its 'political culture,' but also about fundamental issues of theories and methods; about modern views of, and approaches to, the ancient world and 'classical' civilizations in general; about the contents and aims, concepts and categories as well as, in the final analysis, about the future of ancient history as an academic discipline.

To be fair, the original book did meet with a good deal of interest, and not only in Germany and the German-speaking academic community, but also abroad; there were quite a few colleagues in France and Italy, as well as in America and Britain, who took notice of the ideas proposed in this book, actively participated in the aforementioned debate, and above all published substantial contributions of lasting importance on a number of central concrete topics that could, by the nature of this book, only be mentioned or touched upon here in rather general terms. It has been their interest, initiative, and energy that convinced me that the project of a translation was worthwhile in its own right, and they encouraged me to embark on producing an updated version of the German original. I revised the whole text, rewrote many passages, included additional material and figures, and above all I tried to update the bibliography. The latter may strike some people as (over)extensive. However, on the one hand, this book is about the history of ancient history as a discipline, its topics, issues and interests in the second half of the twentieth century; on the other, it deals with theories and concepts, methods and models from a range of other disciplines, with which our discipline could (and should) enter into a fruitful dialogue, as I already suggested in the preface to the German edition. Both themes obviously require a comprehensive coverage and documentation of modern scholarship. Moreover, I for one still cherish the idiosyncratic and naïve conviction that—when it comes to taking notice of, and acknowledging, other people's ideas and intellectual efforts—ignorance, demonstrative lack of interest, and the kind of arbitrary selectiveness, which seems nowadays fashionable and is sometimes even advocated as a value and a particular privilege or mark of senior status, is not a 'virtue' to be emulated by a scholar. I hope that the updated bibliography, if it does not fully live up to my own exacting standards of comprehensive coverage, at least attests to my sustained interest in other people's work.

More maiorum it is a duty, but for me also and above all a pleasure, gratefully to acknowledge my debts to colleagues and friends on both sides of the pond, their suggestions, intellectual acumen, ideas, and inspiration: Harriet Flower (Princeton), Bob Morstein-Marx (Santa Barbara), Matt Roller (Johns Hopkins) and—last, but not least—Christopher Smith (St. Andrews, now Rome). If, by letter and in personal conversation, Fergus Millar (Oxford) generously and gracefully agreed to disagree, he and I share a passion for the Roman past as well as for the present and future of Western democracy.[1] Paul Cartledge (Cambridge) deserves a special mention—because he believed in what I did when I needed it most. And in this context, it is only fit and proper to name three German colleagues and friends, Egon Flaig (Rostock), Martin Jehne (Dresden) and Tonio Hölscher (Heidelberg)—they as well as the international community of aficionados of Republican Rome will know why.

A very special occasion (and a signal honor for me) was the roundtable discussion especially dedicated to my "reconstruction(s) of a Republic"

---

[1]Cf. also the review of Millar, 2002a and 2002b, by Tim Cornell, in *JRS* 93, 2003, 351–54, especially 353f.

that was organized by the "Istituto italiano per la storia antica" and took place in the congenial ambience of this Institute in Rome in October 2005—it was hosted by its president, Andrea Giardina (Rome), and masterminded by Giuseppe Zecchini (Milan); the other participants—Jean-Michel David (Paris) and Alex Yakobson (Jerusalem)—also formulated constructive criticisms and complementary ideas, which were published in the *Studi storici* (47, 2006, no. 2)[2] and are now implicitly and sometimes explicitly taken up in this revised edition. The project of a French translation (published by Les Éditions Maison)[3] and a stay in Paris as Visiting Professor at the Université Paris I Pantheón-Sorbonne provided both the opportunity to discuss the issues once again with colleagues and students as well as the experience of being encouraged to pursue the project of yet another translation further—thanks (again) to Jean-Michel David, who also provided a thoughtful preface to the French edition,[4] and to Frédéric Hurlet (Nantes), who not only invested time and considerable energy into directing a translation, which can certainly be called brilliant, but also helped me further to clarify many ideas and concepts. Furthermore, I had the opportunity to discuss and develop my ideas on a number of concrete problems and general perspectives,[5] which I deal with in this book, in discussions with audiences in Greifswald, Munich, Münster, Bamberg, Kiel, and Bielefeld, and also in St. Andrews, London and Cambridge, Paris, and finally in Nantes—their questions and criticisms were yet another source of inspiration. I also thank Henry Heitmann-Gordon and Richard Gordon for providing the first English version of a difficult text in a heavily 'Teutonic' academic style; my colleagues and students in Cologne, especially Gunnar Seelentag, Julia Kreische, Carlos Grajales, and Simon Lentzsch, for technical support in the final stages of preparation and production; Jon Munk, for a perfect job as copyeditor; Jill Harris and Ian Malcolm, both of Princeton University Press, for showing the classic virtue of editors, a balanced combination of patience, encouragement, and the occasional reminder.

Once again, I owe more to Elke Stein-Hölkeskamp than is fit for public declaration—may she gracefully accept yet another dedication *carissimae uxori consortique in rebus antiquis eruditissimae.*

Cologne, on the Ides of March 2009   Karl-J. Hölkeskamp

---

[2]David, 2006b; Yakobson, 2006b; Zecchini, 2006; and my own contribution, Hölkeskamp, 2006c.

[3]Hölkeskamp, (2004) 2008.

[4]David, 2008.

[5]Some papers have already been published, a few others are in press: Hölkeskamp, 2006d; (2006) 2007; 2008; 2009a, forthcoming a and b.

PREFACE TO THE GERMAN EDITION

THIS BOOK HAS A HISTORY OF ITS OWN. The text is based on lectures that I gave in Greifswald, Bonn, Trier, Innsbruck, and a number of other places, but also on my introductory and concluding contributions to the section "Trusting the power of the great name. Gentilitial charisma and family tradition in the middle Republic" at the 44th National Conference of the Association of German Historians in Halle on the Saale in September 2002.

Over the years, the reactions of various audiences have clearly shown that the topic has gradually been attracting more and more interest. Until the early 1990s most ancient historians had been under the impression that the Roman republic was a wide but also rather exhaustively tilled field. A decade or so later, however, it seems to be generally accepted that the 'political culture' of the *libera res publica* is currently one of the big topics in ancient history. This alone should justify a preliminary summary of the international debate. The aim of this short book is thus to chart the origins and different levels of this debate, describe the issues and problems raised in it, and point towards the general theoretical and methodological potentiality and concrete perspectives for further work both on the topic as such and on its individual aspects.

While I was working on an essay that was intended to make the structures of the *libera res publica* accessible to a wider, historically interested audience,[1] it became clear to me that a well-documented overview of such a complex subject would be useful and, above all, could contribute to a more differentiated and precise description and clarification of individual positions put forward in the debate. Such a record of current research might also be of interest to historians in neighboring fields. The primary aim of the following text is to invite ancient historians and other classicists as well as specialists from the neighboring areas of history to continue this important and ongoing debate.

I should like to thank the various audiences of my lectures and the contributors and respondents of the section at Halle—namely Hans Beck, Harriet Flower, and Uwe Walter—for their critical questions and suggestions. Moreover, I am grateful to my assistants in Cologne, Frank Bücher and Tanja Itgenshorst, who proofread several versions of the text. I am very much obliged to Lothar Gall and Hartmut Leppin for publishing

---

[1]Hölkeskamp, 2000c.

this booklet in this form and in this series.[2] My deepest gratitude, however, is to Elke Stein-Hölkeskamp—and not only for her support, help, and advice. It is to her that I dedicate this result of my research.

Cologne, May 2003   *Karl-J. Hölkeskamp*

---

[2]The German edition was published in the new series of supplements (*Beihefte*) to the *Historische Zeitschrift* (*HZ*) (as No. 38), edited by Lothar Gall. As member of the editorial committee of the *HZ*, Hartmut Leppin is responsible for contributions in ancient history.

RECONSTRUCTING THE ROMAN REPUBLIC

Chapter 1

FROM 'PROVOCATION' TO 'DISCUSSION'
A PLEA FOR CONTINUATION

THE CURRENT DEBATE on the political culture of the Roman republic began almost twenty years ago and has lost little of its momentum since. For the first time in decades, the focus was not on the countless individual issues but on the really basic questions. The status, identity, functions, and interactions of citizen body and popular assemblies, of Senate and magistrates were problematized and reopened to discussion, thus raising fundamental questions about the very character and structure of the *libera res publica*. Essential issues in this debate are the relative importance and relations of institutions and procedures of deliberation and decision making, the nature of social hierarchies, rank, and reputation, of influence, authority and, last but not least, power and participation in the political life of this Republic, and indeed its whole political culture. There began a search for adequate terms for the peculiar sociopolitical order of the imperial Republic that attempted to clarify the basic meaning of terms like 'constitution,' 'democracy,' and 'sovereignty,' 'process,' 'structure' and 'ritual,' 'city-state' and its character as a 'state' (in whatever sense of this controversial concept), 'aristocracy,' 'meritocracy' and 'oligarchy,' 'élite' and 'ruling' or 'political class.'

This international discussion was triggered by Fergus Millar, who radically questioned a basic consensus, which had—in spite of many differences concerning approaches, perspective, and interpretation—been accepted in the field without serious challenge for almost a century.[1] Up to then, it had been agreed that the social and political order of the *libera res publica* had been aristocratic or even 'oligarchic,' meaning that all institutions and positions of power were controlled by a particular kind of ruling class, which recruited not only magistrates, generals, priests, and senators from its ranks, but also the official representatives of the people, the *tribuni plebis*. Scholars had generally taken for granted that this ruling (or 'political') class—often called an "aristocracy of office" or

---

[1] Millar, 1984; idem, 1986; idem, 1989 (review of Raaflaub [Ed.], 1986, and Hölkeskamp, 1987); idem, 1995a and 1995b (review of *CAH*, ix). These contributions have been reprinted in Millar, 2002a. I will cite from this collection in the following (cf. my review in *SCI* 21, 2002, 308–11; Benoist, 2004, 371ff.).

the "senatorial aristocracy"—had an inner circle, the true *nobilitas*, consisting of those families with a consular tradition and a kind of virtually, though not formally, hereditary claim to the highest magistracy. This nobility also controlled the Senate, because the (higher) magistrates regularly returned into its ranks after their year of office; the Senate was taken to have been the central institutional organ of this aristocracy and, therefore, the actual decision-making and thus, in the full sense, 'ruling' body.

Millar has accused this established "orthodoxy" of a "remarkable distortion" of the true importance of the constitution's central institutions; he even calls it a distorted, if not completely false, view of the entire political order. He criticizes two specific aspects. According to him, the *populus Romanus* itself, "as represented by the various forms of assembly," was "in a formal sense the sovereign body in the Republican constitution"—and "the fact of this sovereignty has to be central to any analysis" of the "Republic as a political system." The Senate, on the other hand, was never a "parliament," let alone a "legislature" of a "representative" government. He believes that the traditional perspective not only plays down the institutionalized participation of the people (which no one in fact has ever doubted), but also dismisses it as merely "formal," "passive," "powerless," and "nominal," even as a "charade, managed from above"—namely, "determined by a self-perpetuating oligarchy."[2] Since Matthias Gelzer's classic book on the *nobilitas*,[3] the idea that Roman citizens, the inhabitants of Rome and Italy, and the whole *imperium Romanum* were linked in a complex system of patron-client relations had been generally accepted without further discussion. This dense network of vertical dependencies, mutual obligations, and duties was thought to include the 'ruling class' as well as all the other groups of citizens, reaching down even to the great mass of *plebs* and provincials. For Millar, it has been this "modern myth" that legitimated—again without further discussion—the conclusion that these complex interrelations secured the oligarchy's control over all votes, processes of legislation and jurisdiction, and, above all, the elections to the highest magistracies. And as a consequence, it was this control that in turn allowed the oligarchy to reproduce itself and ensure its position. These main points are—according to Millar—the basis of the generally accepted "fiction of a collective parliamentary rule of the Senate" and "misleading presuppositions" of a ruling class as a closed shop.[4]

For Millar this leads to a second fundamental question, which he raised in his characteristically provocative way: "Was there a 'governing class,' an 'aristocracy,' or an 'élite'? Was it defined by descent, and if so, in what way?" He does not deny that there were—of course—patricians, who

---

[2] Millar, 2002a, 111, 124, 127, 137, 145, and also idem, 1998, 1, 4ff., 197ff. and passim.
[3] Gelzer, 1912, in idem, 1962, 17–135; new edition 1982.
[4] Millar, 2002a, 137, 145f., 150, cf. 92, 149; idem, 1998, 7ff., 11, 216.

were "descendants of earlier generations of patricians." However, "nothing guaranteed a patrician a public office, a priesthood, or a seat in the Senate." Also there were "some persons in public life," who were called *nobiles*, because one of their ancestors "had held a major public office." But, according to Millar, this term was "social or political, not constitutional": a *nobilis* cannot be compared to—for example—an English peer and his hereditary constitutional rights. Millar denies the existence of such a situation in the Republic: "Even a person who was both a *patricius* and a *nobilis* had to compete for office." In his opinion, the resulting competition took place between individuals who as such (and not as members of a political class with a specific collective identity) promoted themselves in public life. In consequence, Millar flatly denies the existence of the nobility or of any homogeneous patrician-plebeian political élite in general; for him, to put it in a nutshell, neither an aristocracy nor an oligarchy ever existed in Republican Rome.[5]

Only if we abandon these "fictions" and "misconceptions" can we truly understand the *libera res publica*. For Millar, the Republic was not simply a city-state but a true "direct democracy"—much closer to the Athenian democracy than most scholars would have been prepared to admit. This interpretation adds the Roman republic to the "relatively small group of historical examples of political systems" that "might deserve the label 'democracy'" at all—and therefore it is for Millar only fit and proper, and indeed high time, that the Roman people be restored "to their proper place in the history of democratic values."[6] According to Millar, the *populus Romanus* itself was the sovereign true and proper—and not merely in an abstract formal, symbolic, or ideological sense. The assemblies of the people—the *comitia centuriata*, *comitia tributa* and the *concilia plebis*—always had the final word in the political process. This includes not only the election of magistrates, but also matters of foreign policy, decisions about treaties, war and peace, and, most importantly, the whole spectrum of legislative competences, ranging from issues of citizenship, the founding of colonies, and distribution of land to civil and criminal law, legal procedure, and even matters of the constitution.[7]

Millar insists that real day-to-day political issues were not decided behind the closed doors of the *curia* by the Senate and its exclusive inner circle, but were publicly discussed, under the open sky, in the central civic spaces of the city-state Rome, such as the Forum Romanum, *comitium*, and the Campus Martius, and not only before and, in the true sense of

---

[5] Millar, 1998, 4; cf. idem, 2002a, 126f., and 87, 90ff., 95f., 104f., 111, 141.

[6] Ibid., 7, 11, 209, and idem, 2002a, 112, 132ff., 138ff., 148, 150, 158, 163ff.; idem, 2002b, 6.

[7] Millar, 2002a, 112ff., 120ff., 136f., 151ff., 165f.; idem, 1998, 15ff., 92, 209ff., 224; idem, 2002b, 6. Cf. Lintott, 1987, 41ff.

the term, under the eyes of the citizens assembled there, but also among them. Therefore, these public spaces were the essential fields of activity, in the concrete as well as metaphorical sense of the term, for the individual actors playing the different public rôles that this "direct democracy" provided—as our sources for everyday political life show. According to Millar, these actors 'performed' as office holders or candidates going around *in toga candida*—as advocates in civil lawsuits, as prosecutors or defense counsels in political trials, as spokesmen, supporters of, or opponents to, the numerous issues that had to be presented and explained to the people of Rome, and that were often discussed heatedly before the people in formal assembly finally came to a decision. Moreover, Millar calls all these different functions mere facets or aspects of the single, most fundamental public rôle in this system—namely, that of the orator addressing the crowds in the political arenas of Rome. Only orators who were able to convince the assembled citizens of their views could hope for success and higher office.[8]

Even Millar concedes that—in this sense—the political structure of the Republic was a "social system" after all, but only because it was based on human interaction in the most concrete sense. As all political action was at all times determined by the dense and small-scale topography of a 'city-state' and the direct face-to-face communication that resulted from it, political power always remained concentrated upon the space between forum and *comitium*—namely, the *rostra*, the platform from which orators addressed the crowds. What Millar calls the "direct democracy" of the Republic was clearly and obviously defined by this fundamental form of interaction in specific public spaces.[9]

As Millar himself says, his intention in putting forward such deliberately one-sided claims is to force a debate with the supporters of the received "orthodoxy" about their fundamental "preconceptions," which he believes to have remained unchanged for decades: These "assumptions" are alleged to have dominated research on Republican Rome throughout the twentieth century.[10] His implicit opponent in this dialogue turns out to be one of the prominent supporters of an older, indeed truly orthodox variant of the basic consensus—namely, Millar's own teacher Sir Ronald Syme.[11] With a

[8]Millar, 2002a, 141f. and 105, 111f., 143ff.; idem, 1998, 1, 44ff., 217ff., 223ff. and passim.
[9]Millar, 1998, 38ff., 209ff.; idem, 2002a, 91, 101, cf. 117, 171, 179f., 208f.
[10]Ibid., ix. Also cf. Hopkins, 1991, 492, whose view of the "conventional scholarly opinion over the last few decades (misled [. . .] by the elitist preoccupations of leading scholars)" is just as undifferentiated.
[11]This becomes clear in his author's prologue: Millar, 2002a, 12f.

characteristic kind of aristocratic self-confidence, Syme had already formulated the inspiring principle of this orthodoxy in terms of a broad general-
ization in his famous book on the "Roman Revolution," magisterially declaring it a metahistorically valid universal truth: "In all ages, whatever the
form and name of government" or "whatever may be the name and theory
of the constitution," "be it monarchy, republic, or democracy, an oligarchy
lurks behind the façade." Even Robert Michels's well-known 'iron law'—
insisting on the "historical necessity of oligarchy"—could hardly be more
explicit. And for Syme, "oligarchy" (be it "open or concealed") is not "a
figment of political theory, a specious fraud, or a mere term of abuse," but
"something real and tangible"—that is, "very precisely a collection of individuals," whose "shape and character" clearly "stands out, solid and manifest."[12] And that was certainly true for Rome: "In any age of the history
of Republican Rome about twenty or thirty men, drawn from a dozen
dominant families, hold a monopoly of office and power." On the receiving
end, the amorphous and anonymous "other classes" were (at best) "sus-
ceptible to *auctoritas*, taking their tone and tastes from above"—in fact,
the "lower classes" not only "had no voice in government," but Syme even
denied them a "place in history."[13]

As a consequence, political life was not characterized, according to
Syme, "by the ostensible opposition between Senate and People, *optimates* and *populares*, *nobiles* and *novi homines*," let alone "by parties
and programmes of a modern and parliamentary character," but simply
consisted in nothing but "the strife for power, wealth and glory"—a
never-ending struggle that invariably and exclusively took place within
the closed circles of the senatorial aristocracy, "in the heart of the governing oligarchy, in court and cabinet." In the same context, Syme stated in
his typically 'imperious' tone that the whole of Roman history, "Republican or Imperial," is "the history of the governing class"—"an aristocracy unique in duration and predominance." For him, this "oligarchy of
government" and its "composition" always remained the "guiding," indeed "dominant theme of political history, as the binding link between
the Republic and the Empire."[14]

Sir Ronald Syme, Friedrich Münzer, the recognized and (rightly) re-
vered doyen of Republican prosopography,[15] and Matthias Gelzer—who
has been listed among the founders of the consensus mentioned above, in

---

[12]Syme, 1939, vii, 7, 18, 346, cf. 10ff.; also see idem, 1991a, 323ff., and generally Michels,
1989, 369, cf. 351ff. Cf. the trenchant criticism by Ober, 1996, 18ff. Cf. also Galsterer, 1990,
12ff.; Walter, 2002, 137ff.; Hölkeskamp, 2001b, 94f., with additional references.

[13]Syme, 1939, 459, 476.

[14]Syme, 1939, vii, 11, 405; idem, 1986, v, 13, and idem 1991a.

[15]Münzer, 1920 (=1999). Cf. Hölkeskamp, 2001b, 92ff. (on the man and his work), with
further references.

spite of his reservations about an all-too-schematic model[16]—agreed that
the aforementioned "strife for power, wealth and glory," and indeed political conflict in general, took only one concrete form throughout the
whole Roman republic: The formation of "aristocratic parties" or "factions" inside the *nobilitas*, which confronted each other in meetings of
the Senate or even (at least during elections and in criminal trials) in the
assemblies. However, this does not mean that these institutions were anything else but two stages of contest—and eventually even less than that:
at least for the *princeps*, the "senate no less than the assembly of the
sovran people was a cumbrous and unsatisfactory body to deal with."[17]
According to Syme, apparently alluding to a famous saying attributed to
Caesar,[18] "the Roman Commonwealth, *"res publica populi Romani,"*"
was not only just "a name"—the "constitution" of the Republic (as well
as, for different reasons, that of the Principate) was indeed nothing but a
"façade," "a screen and a sham."[19]

As a consequence, the kind of aristocratic 'parties' that Münzer and
Syme envisaged could never influence the ordinary citizen body, let alone
split the people as a whole into political groups. On the contrary, these
'parties' or 'factions' were exclusively alliances of leading families, sealed
and stabilized—often for several generations—by typically "dynastic"
forms of personal relationships—that is, by marriages and adoptions, personal obligations, political friendships and alliances between *nobiles* as
heads of "noble houses," and downright "dynasties," patrician and plebeian. According to another prominent advocate of this approach, Howard Scullard, "an elaborate system of groupings and counter-groupings"
had emerged by the mid-Republic, and it was this "system" that "formed
the real, if unadvertised and unofficial, basis of Roman public life"; John
Briscoe insisted as late as the early 1980s that it was "entirely natural,
indeed inevitable, that such groups should have existed." At last, Roman
Republican 'factionalism' had achieved the status of a metahistorical law
of nature.[20]

As Münzer and Syme explicitly pronounced, the one and only purpose
of these "parties" was to obtain and maintain "power" in the state by
holding the two highest offices, the dual magistracy of the consulship.

---

[16]Gelzer, 1912; idem, 1921, 186ff. Cf. Bleicken et al., 1977; Burckhardt, 1990, 77ff.;
Jehne, 2006, 5f. See below at n. 28 for details. Cf. on Gelzer's work as a "turning-point"
Ridley, 1986, and Simon, 1988.

[17]Syme, 1939, 408.

[18]Suetonius *Divus Iulius* 77, quoting T. Ampius, who recorded Caesar to have said in
public: "nihil esse rem publicam, appellationem modo sine corpore ac specie."

[19]Syme, 1939, 11f., 15, 340.

[20]Scullard, (1935) 1980, 333; Briscoe, 1982, 1076; cf. also idem, 1972 and 1992.

The machinations of the "parties" and the typical "weapons" that their noble leaders held and wielded in order to achieve this one and only end were the true *arcana imperii* of the *nobilitas* throughout the entire Republic, from earliest times to its fall—and even beyond.[21] And as "hardened prosopographers," they were confident that these *arcana*, though "concealed by craft or convention," could and did not "evade detection" by means of their particular method of investigating personal relations.[22]

These assumptions and presuppositions gave rise to a specific concomitant "conception of the nature of Roman politics" that by definition, as it were, excluded the possibility that concrete issues, pragmatic problems, and programmatic differences could be (or ever become) the stuff that 'politics' was made of. Accordingly, 'politics' was understood as a kind of perpetual, unending hustle and bustle among the aforementioned leading figures as heads of individual families and representatives of their respective coalitions, the rise and "rule," "domination" and fall of dynasties and of one "governing party" following another, revolving around the central pivot of the consulate as an end in itself: to quote Syme again, it was the "lust of power" that was the "prime infirmity of the Roman noble."[23]

Long before Millar started the current discussion, however, some scholars had already felt uneasy about this concept of politics, with its implicit preconceptions and downright ideological assumptions in the guise of apparently self-evident axioms—a concept of (and a methodological approach to) the fundamental character of Republican politics that simply took for granted what should have been questioned, analyzed, and put to the test of empirical research in the first place.[24] Already in the 1980s, Chester Starr ironically but accurately observed that "the popularity of chasing down who was whose uncle may at last be waning," referring to fastidious, and increasingly speculative, traditional prosopography. A decade later, Allen Ward (who self-critically remarked that he had himself been one "who sometimes too zealously tracked down uncles—and aunts

[21] Münzer, 1920, 1ff., 133, 317, 427f. (= 1999, 5ff., 127, 291, 362f.) and passim.
[22] Syme, 1939, 10ff., esp. ix and 12; idem, 1991b, 338ff.
[23] Syme, 1939, vii, 18, 22, 23, etc..
[24] See Meier, 1966/1980, 163f., 174f., 187f.; Shatzman, 1974, 197ff.; Astin, 1968, and 1989, 167ff. (who in his earlier work had still advocated, though with caution, "the consideration of 'family-group' factions and of motivation by factional rivalry" as being "indispensable for the understanding of Roman politics." He denied, however, the existence of "monolithic parties" or "coherent factions" in the mid-2nd century: 1967, 80, 95f.; Brunt, 1988, 463ff.). Cf. Ward, 1997, 66ff.; Hölkeskamp, 1987, 44ff., 53ff., and more recently idem, 2001b, 100ff., with details and references.

and cousins too!") declared, perhaps a little over-optimistically,[25] that it had long since been silently agreed that such alliances between aristocratic families and factions based on dynastic relationships had never existed, much less been stable over several generations or even decades.[26]

It is a rather telling paradox that it was Matthias Gelzer—who had been Millar's special target because his work had allegedly contributed to the establishment of the orthodox consensus[27]—who as early as 1950 had begun explicitly to doubt the concept of stable aristocratic 'parties,' factions, or "family groups as constituent factors in Roman politics" and became increasingly sceptical about "the schematic crudeness" of the all-too-simple and mechanical prosopographical method, which Münzer (and some of his followers, including Scullard) employed to reconstruct them.[28] Interestingly enough, a leading American historian of Republican Rome and a master of the prosopographical approach of the next generation, who knew only too well what he was talking about, Erich Gruen, also warned against "dogmatism or slavish adherence to a schema," "abuse" of the method, and problematic "generalizations," insisting on the fragility of "loyalties to family, class, and faction" and generally emphasizing the fluidity of associations, cooperations, and groups and "the rapidity of change, the shifting and slippery nature of political events" in the (late) Republic. Though still convinced that "the prosopographical method, its use as a tool remains indispensable for any understanding of the Roman republic," Gruen apparently did not share the optimism of the "whole new school of prosopographical research investigating marriage alliances, adoptions, *amicitiae*, and *clientelae* in order to reconstruct

[25]Twyman, 1972, not only once again tries to make a case for the existence of a "Claudio-Metellan factio" in the 70s BC, but also takes issue with general criticism of the 'factionalist' approach. His own concept of the "structure of politics," however, simply fails to meet the standards that the debate on the analytical status and value of concepts such as 'factio,' on the potential and limits of prosopography as such, and on the character of (Republican) politics had already established by the early 1970s. The same is true for the (only slightly) modernized restatement of the old orthodoxy by Briscoe, 1992.

[26]Starr, 1987, 41; Ward, 1997, 66f. Cf. also Wiseman (1976) 1987. The best detailed refutation is Brunt, 1988, 443ff.

[27]Millar, 2002a, 145ff., cf. 92, 126; idem, 1998, 7ff., and 2002b, 139.

[28]Gelzer, 1950, and the review of Gelzer, 1962–64, by Ernst Badian, in *JRS* 57, 1967, 216–22, quotation: 218. Scullard's reply (1973, xviii ff.) reveals that this "hardened prosopographer" was on the defensive: on the one hand, he relativized his concepts of "political groups," e.g., xx: "False emphasis may ... arise ... from conceiving such groups as self-conscious corporate personalities," et cetera; on the other, however, he did not address the fundamental issue, raised already in the severely critical review by Alfred Heuss, 1956a, whether (or not) Roman politics and political culture should be explained in terms of "factionalist" patterns or parallelograms at all. Cf. also Hölkeskamp, 2001b, 96f., for further evidence; Gwyn Morgan, 2006, 174f.

the groups that dominated Roman politics."[29] The same is true for the American doyen of Republican prosopography, T. Robert S. Broughton. It is certainly true that he was convinced that "a prosopographical approach *of some sort*" (explicitly to be "used with due caution and a comprehensive view") was "necessary for a description of the Roman governing class from the early period of the Republic through its fall" (and beyond):[30] especially for, as it were, the 'microhistorical' reconstruction of individual careers and aristocratic profiles as well as for the 'macrohistorical' analysis of general patterns of office holding, criteria of ranking and social status, the composition, definition, and identity of social groups such as the senatorial aristocracy and the *equites*, prosopography has been, and remains, "an extremely powerful tool and technique."[31] However, Broughton as well as Gruen were also well aware of the limits (and dangers) of a one-sided reliance on the method: The "evidence that prosopography provides" may in some instances give "aid, but only partial aid, in dealing with other important questions" that have indeed remained central and will therefore be raised again and again in later chapters, such as the "reasons for the acceptance by all classes of so aristocratic a government for so long" and "the reasons for Roman expansion."[32]

But Millar seems to have had no time (and perhaps no sense) for such nuances and the peculiar irony implied.[33] Speaking generally, the "implicit dialogue, or argument" that he wanted to conduct with what he took "to be the ruling presuppositions about Roman society and politics

[29]Gruen, 1968, 1ff., quotations: 25, 2, 3, 4, 7, cf. also idem, 1974, 47ff., 105 etc. (and in the second edition: 1995, xi f.).

[30]Broughton, 1972, 260f. (my italics, K.-J. H.).

[31]Barnes, 2007b, 93. The classic discussions of the "payoffs and pitfalls" of "prosopography" remain Stone, 1971; Carney, 1973; Eck, 1993 (and the comment by Barnes, 2007b, 86ff.), as well as already Nicolet, 1970, and Barnes, 2007b, 82ff. (for the Roman republic in particular). Cf. on the history of prosopography as a "methodology" Galsterer, 1990, 5ff., and Barnes, 2007a, with further references. Cf. on modern concepts of the method and its potential Eck, 1993, and the other contributions in idem (Ed.) 1993; idem, 1974, republished in an updated and augmented Italian translation in idem, 1996, 27–83, and his other contributions in this volume. See also Näf, 2001, 1074f., with further references; Eck, 2002 and 2003; Magdalino, 2003, and the other contributions in Cameron (Ed.), 2003; Keats-Rohan, 2007, and the other relevant contributions in eadem (Ed.), 2007. Cf. on the prosopographical approach to a full-scale analysis of the Republican *equites* Nicolet, 1966, 147ff.

[32]Broughton, 1972, 260f. Cf. already Momigliano, 1940, 77f.

[33]Unfortunately this also applies to John North, who calls the traditional orthodoxy "frozen waste theory of Roman politics" and believes it to be the established model (1990a, 6f.; idem, 1990b, 277f.), and to Peter Wiseman, who holds "the sheer inertia of the Gelzer model" responsible for the persistence of an alleged "prevalent orthodoxy" (2002a, 309, cf. 305ff.). Already Harris characterizes this as an "artificial target" and calls North's perception "curiously insular" in idem, 1990, 291; Hölkeskamp, 1993, 15 and 17.

that have characterized historical writing" in the twentieth century has stopped short of a true debate. An "ongoing dialogue" between Millar (and his followers), on the one hand, and his critics as well as the most important advocates of a 'revisionist' school of thought who had long since embarked on a systematic deconstruction of the traditional orthodoxy, on the other, has regrettably not taken place at all. He has explicitly refused to "argue directly and continuously with any of the major interpretations" (mentioning, however, the 'elitist' variants proposed by Christian Meier and Erich Gruen in passing). He has not been prepared to be involved in a debate that he himself had demanded, nor has he responded, at least up to the present moment, to the differentiated and detailed critical responses to his publications.[34]

The following chapters have three intentions. First, I will attempt to record and review these responses[35]—this seems necessary as they are being increasingly simplified, misrepresented, sweepingly dismissed out of hand, or even simply ignored by scholars who seem to subscribe to a radical revisionism à la Millar.[36] At the same time, rather crude versions of Millar's views—"partial, superficial, and inadequate" though their author himself, in a classic *captatio benevolentiae*, has characterized them[37]—seem now themselves to be growing (or even solidifying) into a new orthodoxy. His books and articles have been characterized (not quite unjustly) as the "most significant contributions to recent debates about the character of Roman politics," revolving around the central topics of "the practice of popular participation and indeed sovereignty"(!) in the

[34]Millar, 1998, ix, 4. His selective and somewhat opinionated comments on "some contemporary approaches" here and elsewhere (e.g. Millar, 1998, ix f. on Pina Polo, 1996 etc.; idem, 2002b, 135ff.) do not respond to the debate itself.

[35]Cf. Burckhardt, 1990, 89ff.; Jehne, 1995a, 1ff.; Gabba, 1997, 266ff.; Ward, 1997, 68f.; Hölkeskamp, 1993, 14ff.; recently idem, 2000a. Cf. also the (from different points of view, somewhat critical) reviews of Millar, 1998: Keith Bradley, in *Phoenix* 53, 1999, 140–47; Roberta Stewart, in *AHR* 104, 1999, 1359–60; Garrett G. Fagan in *EMC* 18, 1999, 437–41; Anton Powell, in *CR* 50, 2000, 516–18; Andrew J. E. Bell, in *JRS* 90, 2000, 220–21; Erich S. Gruen, in *CPh* 95, 2000, 236–40; Michael C. Alexander, in *AJPh* 121, 2000, 162–65; Wilfried Nippel, in *Gnomon* 73, 2001, 232–36, and the rather more positive appraisals by T. Peter Wiseman, "Democracy *alla romana*," in *JRA* 12, 1999, 537–40; Geoffrey S. Sumi, in *CJ* 95, 1999–2000, 197–99, and the balanced assessments of Millar 2002a by Timothy J. Cornell, in *JRS* 93, 2003, 351–54; Craige B. Champion, in *IJCT* 11.1, 2004–5, 114–17, and Frédéric Hurlet, in *Latomus* 64, 2005, 1021–24. Detailed discussions of Millar's argument (again from different perspectives) also include Yakobson, 1999, 10f., 231f.; Mouritsen, 2001, 2ff.; North, 2002, 1ff., and recently Benoist, 2004, 376ff.; Ward, 2004; Morstein-Marx, 2004, 6ff.; Marcone, 2005, 89ff.; Gwyn Morgan, 2006; Jehne, 2006, 14ff.; Hölkeskamp, 2006d, 360f., 363 and passim, with additional references.

[36]For example by Jeremy Paterson in his review of Yakobson, 1999, in *JRS* 92, 2002, 229f., who simply dismisses all critics of Millar as representatives of the old orthodoxy.

[37]Millar, 1998, ix.

shape of "voting in the assemblies," the general "importance of the assemblies themselves," and, last but not least, "the closely connected theme of the composition and rôle of the Roman 'élite.'" This concept, its complex meaning(s) and applicability are not discussed, but crudely denounced as "a misleading characterization of a somewhat fluid body, rather than the rigid aristocracy controlling political events that is imagined in traditional works"—which are (unsurprisingly) not even mentioned, let alone taken seriously and examined in detail.[38] Millar himself, who wanted to provide nothing but "a one-sided contribution" to a future and (in his view) "more satisfactory" comprehensive "analysis of the late Republic as a political system," can not really be content with such a development.[39]

Secondly, these different views, their preconceptions and problems, concepts and categories must be presented—especially those opinions that Millar merely skims over and leaves aside as orthodox. A careful examination will show that some of these authors had anticipated some of his central ideas, and that Millar's radical criticism of the old orthodoxy might not have been possible without the probing questions and innovative views formulated and tested already since the 1960s. Finally, I will attempt to develop some new theoretical, methodological, and empirical approaches to further research on the political culture of the Roman republic.

[38]Dench, 2005, 105f., who seems to be well aware that "the study of politics has been reinvented as the study of political culture" and then (again unsurprisingly) declares (364 and ibidem n. 7) that "Athenian political culture ... has been the subject of intense scholarly activity in recent years; the subject of Roman political culture has been somewhat quieter" [sic!]. Cf. Laurence, 1994, 62: "This debate has demonstrated [!, K.-J. H.] that the Roman citizen was actively involved in voting, and made conscious decisions about which candidate he should vote for at elections, and whether to vote for or against a bill at the meetings of the comitia." Cf. also May, 2002a, 56, and Purcell, 1994, 645, who seem to base themselves on Millar: The latter grants the populus Romanus "an important practical and theoretical standing" in "what could be regarded as a spectacular example of a mixed constitution." In his (otherwise thoughtful and balanced) survey of Millar's work, Guy Rogers (2002, xiv)—obviously "accepting that Polybius was right" and modern scholars were wrong—emphasizes "Millar's restoration of the citizen body to its rightful place within the constitutional structure of the res publica" (!, K.-J. H.). Cf. Paul Lewis, in the New York Times, July 24, 1999.

[39]Millar, 1998, ix, 4. Cf. the important new book by Bleckmann, 2002: his accuracy and diligence force the author himself to concede (though somewhat unwillingly) that it seems to be impossible to ignore the current debate (227ff. and 11ff.).

Chapter 2

'REALITY' VERSUS 'SYSTEM'

CONVENTIONAL CONCEPTUALIZATIONS
OF A 'CONSTITUTION'

MILLAR'S CONCEPTION of the Republic as a "direct democracy" on the "strictly and purely formal" basis of a "constitution" soon met with criticisms of different sorts. In the first place, scholars attacked his terminology as such, especially the very idea of a Republican "constitution," which he regarded as having a determinate and relatively firm "structure," even as a static "system." He went so far as to describe it as a complex "(constitutional) machinery" of institutions, formal rules, and procedures.[1] Apparently without any theoretical 'second thoughts' or methodological reservations, Millar seems to be drawing on a conceptual framework based on ideal types and oversystematization, and thus remains firmly committed to a perspective focused on a traditional brand of Roman law and its legal and constitutional history, whose categories used to be taken by its nineteenth-century protagonists as metahistorically valid.[2] Millar thus simply ignores an increasingly intensive debate on the highly problematical reconstruction of Republican 'public law' in the tradition of the famous Theodor Mommsen—this debate on the "Staatsrecht," its dogmatic presuppositions and concomitant approaches, has in fact been ongoing ever since this magisterial monument of classical scholarship was published (1887–1888).[3] In

---

[1]Millar, 1998, 15, 99, 208ff.; idem, 2002a, 99, 165, 172. Cf. the critique by Jehne, 1995a, 8; Hölkeskamp, 2000a, 211ff. How problematical Millar's concept of 'constitution' really is can be understood by considering the complex history of the concept and its implications: see Mohnhaupt, Heinz and Grimm, Dieter, "Verfassung" in *GGr* 6, 1990, 831–99.

[2]Rainer, 1997, recently showed that this approach is still being promoted, if only in a conservative German school of Roman law: he talks about the "system of the Roman Republican constitution," the "realisation of which could only be achieved by employing a legal terminology and systematic approach" (9); cf. also idem, 2006, 13ff. See the review by Wilhelm Simshäuser, in *TRG* 67, 1999, 129–35 on the subject. Ulrich Manthe also treats the Roman law as "law that contains the rules of legal relations between individuals of the same rank, without differentiating between different types of society." Manthe calls this "ein Recht der reinen Vernunft": i.e., a "law of pure reason" (!): idem (Ed.), 2003, 12f. Cf. Keller, 2005, 175f. on this approach.

the final analysis, it is precisely the by-now-controversial Mommsenian tradition from which stems Millar's somewhat simplistic and superficially conventional conception of the Roman Republican constitution as a 'system' based on 'constitutional law'—that is, as an autonomous area, independent of, and indeed isolated from, social structures and cultural conditions, with specific laws and rules, terms and concepts of its own. Even though such systematic and dogmatic doctrines of *Staatslehre*—a typically German legal concept, only inadequately translated as '(science of) constitutional law'—and the equivalent (or even identical) 'science' of *Staatsrechtslehre* ('public law') are long since outdated and nowadays only rarely encountered,[4] constitutional history is in fact still—and not only in the field concerned with Roman law—understood to be the history of institutions, in the strict or 'legal' sense of the concept (magistracy, senate, popular assemblies), their procedures formalized through statutory law or at least legally binding conventions and the concomitant "system" of equally structured interactions.[5]

It may seem paradoxical, but it is just such an outdated idea of the Republican 'constitution' that seems to inspire Millar's apparently modern and deliberately radical revision of our understanding of the political order of the *libera res publica*. His conception of the sovereignty of the Roman people, manifested in the right to elect the magistrates and tribunes and above all to legislate in the *comitia* and *concilia plebis*, respectively, is clearly—though he never admits as much—indebted to Mommsen's theory of the citizen body as being institutionalized in the popular assemblies, and thus and therefore being the legal holder of sovereign authority in the state.[6] Only against this dogmatic backdrop could Millar insist upon his "strictly and purely formal" concept of constitution and introduce his (as a matter of course, equally formal) notion of democracy. This reliance on the peculiarly old-fashioned and outdated epistemological

---

[3]Cf. the fundamental study by Bleicken, 1975, 16ff. (and the review by Meier, 1978a); cf. Heuss, 1956, 44ff.; Kunkel, 1955, and idem, 1972, 1984; Flaig, 1997; Hölkeskamp, 1997, 93ff. and more recently idem, 2005b (especially on Mommsen's concept of the Senate); Lintott, 2005 (on the magistracy); Jehne, 2005 (on the assemblies) and the detailed survey of the debate by Nippel, 2005, all with further references.

[4]This characterization is found in Bleicken, 1975, 31; cf. Heuss, 1956, 56f.; Kunkel, 1984, 379f. Rainer (1997, 3f., and idem, 2006, 13ff.) is merely an exception; cf. the review of Rainer, 2006, by Frédéric Hurlet, in *Latomus* 67, 2008, 1090–93.

[5]Cf. Bleicken, 1996, now in: idem, 1998, 526–50, especially 537ff., 549 (on Kunkel/Wittmann, 1995).

[6]Mommsen, 1887–1888, 3/2, 1030 and especially 3/1, 127ff., 300ff. and on the same subject Bleicken, 1975, 28ff.; Hölkeskamp, 1997, 107; Behne, 2002, 124ff., with references. Cf. on the problematic concept of "sovereignty" in this context Meier, 1966/1980, 117f.; Flaig, 1993b, 423ff.; idem, 1997, 321ff.; Jehne, 2005, 134ff.

presupposition that institutions and formalized procedures were autonomous entities *sui generis* makes his attack upon the alleged orthodoxy itself
look regressive—a kind of relapse behind more modern and sophisticated
approaches, methods, and models.[7] This becomes even clearer if one takes
a closer look at the most important stages in the long and complex discussion about the Republican 'constitution,' its theoretical conceptualization
and the best methods and concepts to describe it. Therefore, the background presented above seems to justify a more detailed excursus into the
recent history of this discussion, in the hope of sparing the field further so-
called new discoveries.[8] In order to clarify the current stage of the discussion and then to map out new perspectives, it will be necessary to reconstruct in detail the central aspects of the recent (and still ongoing) debate
about the above-mentioned theories, models, methods, and concepts, their
applicability and explanatory potential, which should enable us to arrive at
a more exact description and in-depth analysis of the Republican political
order, and indeed of ancient political culture in general.

It was the increasing unease about traditional constitutional history—
especially its one-sided fixation upon "formalized units of organisation,"[9]
rules, and procedures, and the underlying abstract, metahistorical, and
normative concept of the 'state' and *Staatlichkeit* ('statehood')—that
provided a strong impulse and major inspiration for the first serious and
sustained attempt at developing a more differentiated holistic picture of
Roman Republican politics and its 'order.' Christian Meier's now classic
book "*Res publica amissa*," first published in 1966, sported the decep-
tively conventional subtitle, "a study of the constitution and history of
the Roman republic."[10] Indeed Meier did initially employ a terminology
that seemed to take the traditional concept of a 'constitution' as its point
of departure. In the course of his argument, however, he contrasted it

[7]Cf. also Jehne, 2005, 159f.

[8]Describing the Roman republic as a (sort of) 'democracy' is not a new idea either—cf.
Guarino, 1979, which Millar, 2002a, 140 merely mentions. Cf. Bleicken, 1972, 11 with
footnote 8 (= idem, 1998, 190); Claude Nicolet, in idem (Ed.), 1983b, 77f. with footnotes
1f.; Jehne, 1995a, 1f. and footnotes 4 and 7; Pani, 1997, 140ff. Also see Heuss, 1963, 183.
Münzer—despite being the doyen of an arch-oligarchic orthodoxy—already used the term
"democratic constitution," which however did "not provide the equality of all citizens"
(1920, 427 = 1999, 362); cf. Wieacker, 1961, 28f. and most recently Marcone, 2002, 39ff.
and 2005, 89ff.; Ward, 2004, 106ff.; Polverini, 2005, 92ff.

[9]A term coined by Martin Jehne in idem, 1995a, 8.

[10]The new edition contains a preface and an important introduction (14-57) with theoretical and methodological considerations, which I will be referring to later. An exact examination of the book's direct and indirect influence, which the author himself probably
does not acknowledge to its full extent, might be worthwhile, especially because it is obviously often not mentioned in bibliographies: see for example Beard and Crawford, 1985,
and the notes in Crawford, 1992. The bibliography in Wiseman (Ed.), 1985, 70 just mentions Peter Brunt's review article (cf. n. 13).

with the new concept of an "organic constitution"—as he insisted, a merely descriptive and by no means "romantic" term, which he preferred to the "purely negative expression" 'unwritten constitution.'[11] According to Meier, the opposite of an "unwritten constitution" is not a "written" constitution but a "foundational" constitution: that is, a rationally planned and organized framework of institutions established by a single and conscious act of foundation. As opposed to such a "foundational" constitution, the "organic" constitution was capable of functioning with a minimal set of institutionalized structures because it was pragmatically developed and worked in practical politics, without much institutionalization or formalization. As a consequence, the 'state' and its typical functions did not have to be "objectified," resulting in the relatively low degree of "political formalization in institutions and regular procedures," even in the late Republic. As a matter of course, it was this low degree of (institutionalization of) 'statehood' that in turn inevitably implied "a relatively high degree of imbalance" or even "lack of technical perfection."[12] In coining this terminology, Meier found himself forced to accept that he tended to define the Republican political system by its deficits and deviations from some abstract normative ideal of a 'state' and its 'constitution.' However, he tried to balance this: although he did not (yet) embark on a theoretically based and systematic development of a new analytical framework of his own, he tried to contrast his general conceptualization with his empirical reconstruction of what he labeled "constitutional reality" or "political grammar."[13]

Meier was not primarily concerned with what was even then a widely accepted fact—namely, that the state institutions, magistracies, Senate, and popular assembly were embedded in their concrete social, political, and cultural contexts, possibly in the form of a partially autonomous subsystem. Meier described this "wonderful and wondrous" order as a

[11]This term, which was certainly intended to express the unease I mentioned above, was still commonly used at this time; see, e.g., von Lübtow, 1955, 310; Meyer, 1964, 253; Kunkel, 1972, 17. Cf. Brunt, 1988, 13, 296f.

[12]The terms in inverted commas are directly translated (where possible) or indirectly gleaned from Meier, 1966/1980, 56 with footnote 177, 57, and also pp. 3, 14, 49, 59; cf. 4, 50, 58, 61f., 159 and 328 (see the index s.v. "Verfassung"); cf. also Meier, 1984a, 63f.

[13]Meier was not only aware of the problem (idem, 1966/1980, 5), but later put forward a number of ideas about categories and concepts in various publications on theoretical problems of (ancient) history. However, he never chose to develop them systematically or test them empirically. Cf. idem, 1966/1980, XXff., XXXIIff.; idem, 1976, 39ff., 46ff.; idem, 1978b, especially 34ff. Cf. Rilinger, 1982, 288ff.; Schneider, 1998, 24ff., 45ff. Some reviewers have acknowledged the importance of the book (in spite of all criticism of Meier's general approach, empirical results and concrete use and understanding of terminology): The most trenchant discussion is by Jochen Bleicken in a detailed review in *ZRG RA* 85, 1968, 451–61 (= idem, 1998, 778–88); cf. also the reviews by Jean Béranger, in *REL* 45, 1967, 590–94; Chester Starr, in *AJPh* 89, 1968, 480–83; Peter A. Brunt, in *JRS* 58, 1968, 229–32 (more critical); Wilhelm Hoffmann, in *GGA* 221, 1969, 63–70.

particular, and peculiar, symbiosis of "state" and "society," combining a strong orientation toward the "state"—an exceptional focus upon "power," politics, and war, rule and empire—with a high level of an asymmetrical kind of interpenetration and interchange between society and the state's "institutions, powers and procedures," which were subordinated to, indeed turned into, functions of a traditional society and its hierarchical order.[14] In retrospect, this conceptual pattern may seem unsatisfactory and imprecise: for example, the obvious ambivalence of the term 'state' and, as Meier himself admits, the problem of an ideal-type construction of a dichotomy between state and society. His misleading expression "unity of state and society" was really only to mean that to Republican Rome (as to premodern societies in general) the differentiation between these two concepts (and between the different forms of collective organization that they stand for) was still unknown because it only emerged in (early) modern history.[15] Nowadays, the entire line of argument seems questionable because it suggests that the strict and narrow understanding of the 'state,' which is derived from typical modern European structures, is the only possible and legitimate one. I will be coming back to this point in a different context.

But Meier is to be given credit for seeing more than just a dangerous structural weakness in these constitutional deficits.[16] He recognized that certain peculiarities of this state were actually strengths and that they in fact provided the basis of its remarkable and fascinating stability, flexibility, and ability to adapt to dynamically changing conditions over the course of several centuries—and that it is this fact that stands in need of explanation. This extraordinary combination of features and factors, however, may have depended on certain conditions that were not necessarily part of the rudimentary system itself. This provisional diagnosis had to lead to the next step—namely, to identify these peculiarities, as well as the preconditions that made them possible and the factors that underlay them and determined their further development, in greater detail, and above all in a more precise conceptual framework. Only then would it become possible to propose an explanation for the disappearance of the stabilizing factors and, in a further step, for the subsequent crisis of the Republic, which resulted in its fall.

The approach outlined above has been generally accepted in the field—and this is also true for those scholars who deal with Republican constitutional history as part of the study of Roman law, as Franz Wieacker

[14]Meier, 1966/1980, 45f., 50, 156; cf. idem, 1978a, 384ff.
[15]Meier, 1966/1980, XXIIf., 13 and footnotes 40f. (with reference to Brunner, 1959).
[16]Cf. already Wieacker, 1961, 27f.; Heuss, 1963, 183f.; idem, 1976, 37f.

wanted it to be understood in his very good up-to-date handbook of Roman legal and constitutional history.[17] For him, a modern "survey of the classical Roman state" can only approximate the actual system and its complexity. One can only describe it as a kind of store, or perhaps conglomerate, of "institutions and formalized rules of political action" that, as a whole, were "perceived and practically applied as a legally binding framework" and only occasionally "endorsed, reformed or developed by laws": that is, by statutory law.[18] However, we must avoid interpreting this peculiar constitution as a "permanent status quo or stable framework" of institutions and formal procedures, rules, and regulations, as it were, at a standstill. Rather, we should learn to conceive it as a "function of a continual political process" that could only be properly understood by taking the complex fabric of political and social relations and the specific dynamics of the formation and change of social groups into account. The embeddedness of the Republican constitution in Roman society, its complexity and its character as a process have been emphasized in many other modern surveys: this view seems to have attained the status of an orthodoxy.[19]

Wieacker goes on to list several fundamental features of this process. He stresses the importance of a "firm basis" of (in the strict modern sense, "non-" or "extra-legal") "moral rules for political action," which were "not themselves part of the system of public law" proper (*ius publicum*) but were nevertheless recognized as "a socially binding standard" or code of behavior in public life, and even—to a certain extent—applied in "legal" matters and by courts as though they were laws. According to Wieacker, these moral standards and rules of behavior revolved around key concepts like *auctoritas*, *dignitas*, *gratia*, and *honos*. The most important concept was of course *mos maiorum*.[20] The literal translation of this term—ancestral custom—is (at best) rather vague. Its range of reference and meanings was almost unlimited and indeed, as it were, defied limitation: any modern attempt to narrow it down must fail to grasp its true constitutive importance. This notional stock of time-honored principles,

[17]Wieacker, 1988. Remarkably enough, this has received hardly any attention in reviews.

[18]So Wieacker says in his fitting description in idem, 1988, 345 and 353. He explicitly refers to Meier, 1966/1980. Cf. also Wolfgang Kunkel in idem/Wittmann, 1995, 15, 52, 321. Grziwotz, 1985, provides more material, but no new concepts. Cf. now Nippel, 2009.

[19]Cf. Brennan, 2004. Modern surveys include Bleicken, 1995, 12ff.; Astin, 1989, 163ff.; Cloud, 1994, 491ff.; Lintott, 1999, 1ff. (on which cf. Jerzy Linderski, in *AJPh* 122 (2001): 589–92); North, 2006. Cf. also Keller, 2005, 177ff.

[20]Wieacker, 1988, 353f., 374ff., 502ff.; cf. idem, 1961, 28, 31, 58. Consequently, *lex*, *ius*, and *mos maiorum*, "legal order" and "social order," should not really be treated as opposites (neither conceptually nor heuristically)—cf. Meier, 1978a, 383ff. (on Bleicken, 1975). Cf. also Gehrke, 1993, 218 with footnote 17 (on the 'Friedrich Vittinghoff school'); Keller, 2005, 178ff.

traditional models, and rules of appropriate conduct, of time-tested policies, regulations, and well-established practices not only prescribed social
behavior in 'private' life, but also regulated all criminal and 'public' law,
the state religion as well as the military system, the ways and means of running politics at home and abroad. Last but not least, *mos maiorum* also
included what one might call the "constitutional conventions."[21]

This aspect is particularly important in the present context. All magistrates had to comply with *mos maiorum* throughout their whole term of
office—from the very beginning of their careers. The 'right' of standing
for office, the election procedures themselves, and the range of rituals ac-
companying the magistrates' year from taking up to leaving office were
based on received rules enshrined in *mos maiorum*, as well as the general
principles for the administration of a province, ranging from the delega-
tion of tasks to the transfer of authority to the next (pro)consul.[22] Above
all, the complex network of the responsibilities, rights, and competences
of the Senate was also based exclusively on *mos maiorum*, not on positive
normative law—it was just due to this fact that the range of powers of
this formally advisory body was practically unlimited and its collective
auctoritas almost absolute. Finally, the (partly) competing and even (at
least potentially and occasionally actually) colliding competences of the
individual institutions were also regulated by *mos maiorum*, just as it controlled the day-to-day procedures and interactions of magistrates, Senate,
and popular assemblies.[23] At last, it was therefore in fact *mos maiorum*
that made the Roman republic's peculiar "capacity for self-regulation"
possible,[24] which really constituted the functional equivalent of a differentiated system of statutory law and formal procedural regulations by
guaranteeing the practical working of the political process.

All this is indisputable. As far as the received rules for popular assemblies and law-courts are concerned,[25] the most striking feature of the
Republican political system is the omnipresence of institutionalized hier-

---

[21]Meier, 1966/1980, 54, 57, with reference to Max Weber's definition of the concept
(Weber, 1976, 17f., 187ff. etc.). Cf. Kunkel, 1972, 17; Eder, 1996, 446ff. and now Nippel,
2009.

[22]Cf. for details, sources, and references Kunkel/Wittmann 1995. Cf. Stewart, 1998, for
the process of institutionalizing the magistracies; Bunse 1998; Brennan 2000.

[23]Cf. von Lübtow, 1955, 310ff. and the fundamental studies by Kunkel, 1971, 377ff.,
Bleicken, 1975, 354f., 364f. (cf. Meier, 1978a, 383ff.). Also see Hölkeskamp, 1996, 316f.,
with further references. Grziwotz, 1985, 222ff., 252ff., 263ff. fails to convince his reader of
his concept of differentiating between *exempla*, *instituta*, and *mores*.

[24]Meier, 1966/1980, 50, with reference to Heuss, 1976, 37.

[25]The relevant evidence is (in the full sense of the concept, systematically) collected in
Mommsen, 1887, 3/1, 369ff. Cf. Taylor, 1966; Staveley, 1972, 121ff.; Meyer, 1964, 190ff.;
Nicolet, 1980, 207ff.; Wieacker, 1988, 388ff.; Laser, 1997, 45ff. and recently Lintott, 1999,
43ff.; Jehne, 2006, 17ff.; North, 2006, 260ff.

archies that were not hidden from view, but rather openly in place and patently at work. All popular assemblies—the *comitia centuriata, comitia tributa*, as well as the assemblies (*concilia*) of the *plebs*—were divided up into voting units with one vote each. The centuriate assembly was organized on the basis of census classes and *centuriae* (notionally groups of one hundred citizens)—the majority of the 193 *centuriae* as voting units was reserved to the uppermost classes. The latter two forms of assembly were subdivided by the rural and urban territorial districts (thirty-one *tribus rusticae* and four *tribus urbanae*), in which Roman citizens were (formally) registered according to residence. After a complicated reform of the *comitia centuriata* in the middle of the third century BC, these two criteria were combined—the controversial details and problems are not of interest in this context. It is only necessary once again to emphasize the basic fact that the citizens of Rome never enjoyed either a direct or an equal right to vote. To a very high degree, the value of an individual citizen's vote depended on his social status, not only formally, but also in the actual practice of voting.

Moreover, the popular assemblies did not meet on a regular basis: that is, for example, according to a fixed annual calendar of sessions. There were no formally prescribed rules for meetings—except for the iron principle that they had to be called and formally opened by a magistrate, who invariably also held the chair and was in absolute control of the procedure and the agenda. This fundamental rule applied not only to the highest officeholders with *imperium*, the consuls and praetors, who presided over the *comitia centuriata* (and the *comitia tributa*), but also to the representatives of the plebs, the *tribuni plebis*, who presided over the *concilia plebis*. Only the magistrates and tribunes were entitled to propose new laws and decrees—the assemblies were limited to accepting or rejecting them. At this final stage of the formal procedure, there were no more debates: *privati*, let alone ordinary citizens, did not have the right to submit proposals of their own or modifications of magisterial or tribunician motions in these formal (or any other previous informal) assemblies—and as far as we know, this was never considered even as a theoretical possibility, let alone a concrete issue on the political agenda.

The right to accept or reject candidates running for office was also a prerogative of the presiding magistrate of the electing assembly—candidates who had not been formally admitted and registered could not be elected. The results of an election had to be solemnly proclaimed by the magistrates—it was only this declaration that gave them formal validity. This involved *mutatis mutandis* that in the case of an unwelcome or otherwise 'unfortunate' outcome, the magistrate had the right simply to refuse to perform this *renuntiatio*—and by his authority as presiding magistrate, he could then order the whole electoral procedure to be repeated.

Finally, the magistrate alone was allowed to close a meeting that he had called and presided over, even if no (proclaimed and valid) results had been achieved.

Of course all of this is widely known—even Millar does not deny the basic facts and at least occasionally refers to them—but only ro relativize, or altogether dismiss, their relevance for his case.[26] Even this brief summary of a specific, if central aspect of *mos maiorum*, however, makes a reconstruction of the Republic that focuses on the popular assemblies and chooses to represent them as formal institutions with well-defined competences seem rather questionable, especially if it then proceeds to treat them as virtually autonomous bodies of decision making of great practical significance in a kind of abstract isolation from other institutions and their respective rôle. The problems inherent in such a perspective, which must be characterized as one-sided in multiple respects, become even clearer if we consider Millar's claim to be able to find analogies to the democracy of classical Athens, and especially to the central functions of the *ekklesia* within the complex institutional framework of its constitution. In fact the differences are striking—a direct comparison with the formal rules for summoning and running a meeting, as well as those governing the successive stages of open public debate and decision making, make the particular rôle of the popular assemblies in the hierarchical structure of the Roman republic stand out even more sharply. For, unlike the Romans, every individual Athenian citizen had the right to speak out in the *ekklesia* and cast his vote—which was counted according to the egalitarian principle of 'one man–one vote.' As a collective body of deliberation and decision making, the Athenian assembly met at regular intervals—apparently no less than forty times per year. Sessions were presided over by a chairman who was appointed by lot and did not have any significant power, certainly not over the agenda. The *ekklesia* was not only entirely independent of holders of executive office, but exercised a very strict control over *strategoi*, archons, and all the other functionaries. To put it in a nutshell, the Athenian assembly, if any at all, was truly sovereign.[27]

At Rome, moreover, there was not even an attempt to increase the importance of the assemblies by introducing changes of procedure: The ancient hierarchical and corporative structures of the *comitia*, and the traditional 'competences' of the magistrates remained untouched by leg-

[26]See, e.g., Millar, 1998, 16ff., 203f.; idem, 2002a, 94, and 2002b, 18ff., 144, 178ff.

[27]See Bleicken, 1994, 161ff., 265ff., 306ff., and most recently Welwei, 1999, 107ff. On the general issue of comparing the two 'types' see Eder, 1991, 169ff.; Marcone, 2002; Ward, 2004, 106ff. Among important recent interpretations of Athenian democracy, Ober, 1989, is one of the most influential; cf. also the essays in idem, 1996, and now Cartledge, 2009.

islative reforms throughout the whole Republican era.[28] On the contrary, it appears to have been yet another principle enshrined in the *mos maiorum* itself that the fundamental structure of the institutional system as such was not to become an issue of positive law and formal decision making, or even a matter of controversial political debate.[29]

In fact we should go yet another step further: it was very exceptional for popular assemblies to create normative public law at all, that is, by passing legislation touching on (the core of) *ius publicum*—at least so far as the middle Republic is concerned.[30] Institutions, rules, and procedures only became subject to legislation in the course of the second century BC, when these sensitive topics gradually became disputable and the range of (regularly rather controversial) issues submitted to assembly decisions widened.[31] For example, the so-called *leges tabellariae* were passed to introduce secret ballot successively in electoral, judiciary, and legislative assemblies.[32] There was also a series of attempts to ban certain forms and practices of campaigning and (self-)advertising in the run-up to important elections (*leges de ambitu*),[33] which was naturally another very sensitive issue in a highly competitive system. *Mutatis mutandis* one can probably draw the same conclusions as have been drawn from the similarly sensitive issue of gradually formalizing the hierarchy of magistracies in so-called *leges annales*: it was a growing disregard or disrespect for, and an increasingly wide-spread abuse of, the rules of the *mos maiorum* that seems to have overstrained the considerable flexibility and adaptability of these rules and brought about an erosion of its traditional

[28]Laws concerned with time limits and other rules for the promulgation of new laws (*leges Aelia et Fufia*; *lex Caecilia Didia*; *lex Clodia*) are always addressed to the magistrates and deal with their prerogatives. The same is true for regulations of intercession against new proposals (cf. Rotondi, *LPPR*, and Elster, 2003, for sources and further references).

[29]Cf. Meier, 1966/1980, 52f., 119ff. See also North, 1990b, 284; idem, 1990a, 14f., who refers to Finley, 1983, 70ff., 84ff.

[30]Cf. Kunkel, 1971, 368ff.; Meier, 1966/1980, 121; Bleicken, 1978, 148ff. (= idem, 1998, 286ff.). I do not think that this contention is invalidated by the most detailed recent study of Republican 'public law,' patterns of lawmaking, and individual laws (Williamson, 2005—cf. the detailed critical evaluation of her approach and results by Elizabeth A. Meyer, in *BMCR* 2005.09.68).

[31]Meier, 1966/1980, 128, cf. 121, and now Nippel, 2009.

[32]The exact contents and the aims of these laws (cf. Rotondi, *LPPR*, and Elster, 2003, for the evidence and modern studies) are still controversial: cf. Gruen, 1991, 255ff.; Jehne, 1993; Yakobson, 1999, 126ff., with further references; idem, 2006a, 388ff.; Williamson, 2005, 306ff.

[33]Once again, the content and intention of these laws (cf. Rotondi, *LPPR*, and Elster, 2003, for sources and references) have been controversially debated: cf. Fascione, 1984 (with the review by K.-J. Hölkeskamp, in *ZRG RA* 104 [1987]: 791–96); Lintott, 1990; Gruen, 1991, 257ff.; Jehne, 1995b; Nadig, 1997 (with full documentation for individual laws); Riggsby, 1999, 21ff.; Yakobson, 1999, 25f., 32f., 75f. etc., with additional references; Schuller, 2000; Williamson, 2005, Index, s.v. "crimes," *ambitus*.

binding force. This development in turn ultimately led to procedures, regulations, and rules of all sorts being prescribed (and thus preserved, renewed, and/or enforced) by statutory law, resulting of course in a decrease of flexibility.[34]

The increasing importance of the popular assemblies as legislative bodies thus indicates not only a reduction of flexibility, but also a deterioration and eventual disintegration of the traditional consensus within the ruling class rather than an increase in 'democratic' freedom—*pace* Fergus Millar, who insists on the prime importance of legislation and the legislative functions of the popular assemblies, especially the *comitia tributa*.[35] The tendency to objectify social rules and turn them into normative laws and the (often unsuccessful) attempts at prescribing norms and sanctions appear to be means of compensating for a decline in consensus about the traditional store of regulative rules and mechanisms. They also indicate a gradually dwindling capacity to find a balance between (potentially and acutely) colliding conventions, on the one hand, and to pacify and channel concrete conflicts, for example between senior magistrates, the Senate, and tribunes of the *plebs*, on the other. The entire process is to be seen rather as a symptom of torpor and crisis,[36] and it can certainly not be taken as proof of the alleged smooth working or the unbroken vitality of this type of 'democracy.' Even in crisis, no member of the Roman political class—not even a professed *popularis*—ever questioned or debated the organization of the *comitia* or the powerful position of the presiding magistrates even in theory.

[34]Cf. Bleicken, 1975, 175ff. and now the fundamental study by Beck, 2005a, 51ff.
[35]E.g. Millar, 1998, 204, and passim; idem, 2002a, 94, and see the references in n. 26.
[36]Meier, 1966/1980, 62f., cf. 119f.; Bleicken, 1975, 399ff. etc.; Lintott, 1999, 63f.; Eder, 1996, 455ff. The most recent view is presented in Martin, 2002, 170f.

Chapter 3

FROM 'SYSTEM' TO 'STRUCTURE'
NEW QUESTIONS ABOUT THE SOCIAL
FRAMEWORK OF POLITICS

IT WILL BE EVIDENT even from these general statements that such constitutional conventions of the kind mentioned in the previous chapter are not only of interest because they make up the specific formal framework of the typical Roman Republican political landscape—it should be clear by now that this bird's-eye view calls for new questions and approaches. So far, however, the peculiar forms of delayed and restricted institutionalization and the areas and limits of political action and participation *in politicis* that they defined have merely been outlined and not exhaustively analyzed or explained. It is precisely this task that the traditional approach focused on 'constitutional' history has obviously failed to tackle, since it is by definition, which is at least partly self-imposed, too limited to be able adequately to answer the following fundamental questions about relations and restrictions, proportions, and relative importance of formal and substantial, symbolic and practical, political participation.

The interdependencies between politics and policies, political decision making and implementation, on the one hand, and their social, cultural, and, as it were, collective mental underpinnings, on the other, have long since become the main focus of interest in current research. In view of their (at least, partly) shared sources of theoretical inspiration, their methodological starting points, and their use and understanding of terminology, and due to the lack of a more precise concept, we might provisionally summarize the different approaches under the label 'structural history' as a kind of conceptual common denominator.[1] I will be coming back to this point shortly. Confronted with conventional reconstructions of the Roman republic, which were fixed on the 'constitution' and formal 'constitutional' law, on the one hand, and presupposed an iron axiom of Republican politics being fragmented into 'parties' or 'factions' struggling for the 'constitutional' positions of 'power,' on the other, the first step of deconstruction obviously had to be to examine these (apparent) interdependencies more closely—and this step was radical and fundamental

[1] Meier, 1976, 51.

enough since the whole set of assumptions underlying the traditional picture of Roman Republican politics had never been made explicit, let alone
systematically demonstrated: Their validity had simply been taken for
granted. Consequently, Christian Meier called for a general theory of
political parties in pre-modern societies—he preferred to speak of *Parteiungen* ('groupings' as a kind of generic term) instead of *Partei* or *Parteien*
('party' or 'parties') because the latter concepts were under suspicion not
only of being contaminated with modern connotations of parliamentary
politics, but also of presupposing a particular form or structure of 'parties,' 'party politics,' and the process of political decision making in general. Meier demanded a radically new approach with the intention, as it
were, of going back to the basics and working on the subject from scratch,
in the full sense of the term: that is, by systematically avoiding any axi-
omatic presuppositions of the kind just mentioned (as far as I can see, he
first mentioned this program in 1976). He insisted that we are simply not
entitled to take for granted that the political landscape of the Roman (or,
for that matter, any other pre-modern) Republic was regularly split into
'parties' or, to put it more precisely, into some principally unchanging
pattern or basic tableau of 'parties' or '(aristocratic) factions,' which
functioned according to given mechanisms of 'power politics.' As a consequence, the institutional, social, and cultural framework of political life
cannot be taken as a given either. And as a further consequence, a plausible general theory of the (formation of) political groupings would have
to address not only the process of group formation, but also form and
structure of the group(ing)s themselves, the specific requirements, conditions and (de- or re-)stabilizing factors as well as their possible change
over time, their emergence, modification, and disappearance. Another
key topic included in this approach would have to be the variety—or rather,
the possible range of variations of group(ing) formation in a given sociopolitical order and during a given period. Only on such a sound methodological basis would it eventually become possible to clarify the hitherto
unresolved problems of the specific areas and boundaries of politics and
'the political,' as well as the range and reach of political decision making in
a pre-modern (Republican) society. Such a theory would have to address
three central aspects of political action and its specific interdependencies:
namely, in Meier's own terms, the "constellation" of the (institutional as
well as social) "centers of decision making"; the "distribution" of (political
as well as social) power; and finally the actual "content" of politics, policies, and 'the political'—that is, the concrete issues that could be put on the
political agenda of these "centers" under the given conditions.[2]

[2]Meier, 1976, 39ff.; idem, 1966/1980, XXXIIff.; idem, 1984a, 45ff., and idem, 1996,
260ff.; Hölkeskamp, 1987, 14ff.; idem, 1998, and 2001b, with further references. Cf. on
'politics,' the (character of) the 'political,' and related problems of terminology now Cartledge, 2009, 11ff.

I will begin with the first aspect: namely, the actual character and constellation of deliberative and executive, elective and legislative institutions as well as the social groups represented in (or dominating) them, which obviously involves a broad range of related concrete (sub-)questions and approaches. What is more, these approaches necessarily have to go beyond the mere construction of a simple chart that sets out a formal, normative, and therefore static structure of decision-making bodies and procedures. What is called for is a precise and detailed analysis of the institutional context of the political process that not only includes a fresh look at the exact number of such bodies, their functions and functioning, and their relative importance—an aspect that is obviously inseparably interconnected with the relative social power of the personnel or social group present in any one body. Furthermore, it is indispensable to take into account the interrelations of these institutions, the institutionalized hierarchies and forms of interaction between them, along with the extent and areas of their rights of decision making, the complementarity and/or overlapping of these rights and functions, as well as the resulting inherent potential for conflict between individual "centers."

In the case of the Roman Republican 'constitution,' this last aspect in particular has always received a lot of attention—already in antiquity, some observers noted it.[3] It was Polybius, whom Millar frequently exploits for his arguments against the alleged established elitist 'orthodoxy,' who focused his famous excursus on the 'composite' or 'mixed constitution' on the particular complex complementarity (or perhaps muddle) of the 'rights' and functions of magistrates, the Senate, and the people in assembly (as well as the tribunes of the *plebs*)—significantly enough and *pace* Millar, only to point out its basically aristocratic character.[4] From a modern perspective focused on 'constitutional history,' a complex mixture of this kind is taken to be the typical feature of the peculiar Republican constellation of political institutions, which—because of its apparently irrational and counterproductive potential for conflict—calls for analysis and explanation. This fundamental problem becomes evident from the unusual relationship between the consulate, with its full or absolute executive power (*imperium* and *auspicia*), and the tribunes of the *plebs*, with their time-honored right to intercede and veto magisterial orders and other political decisions. At least in principle and within the sacred perimeter of the *urbs Roma*, the tribunes were able to prohibit or annul any official action by any magistrate, since their 'negative' rights were not, and could not be, formally subject to any limit—as were, again in principle, the

[3]Cf. Meier, 1960/1980, xxxvi.
[4]Polybius 6, 11–18 and especially 51, 6–8; 23, 14, 1–2. Cf. Nippel, 1980, 149ff.; Nicolet, 1980, 208ff.; idem, 1983a, 16ff.; Lintott, 1999, 16ff., 214ff., and recently Welwei, 2002, 25ff.; Polverini, 2005.

power and executive privileges of the consuls.[5] The practical use and concrete application of these formal rights, however, was limited by a number of social traditions, conventions, and rules that derived from time-tested precedents and well-established informal procedures concerning the 'correct' (that is, 'adequate' and flexible) or 'incorrect' (that is, 'inadequate' and uncompromising) use of such rights. Such 'customs' or 'conventions,' which naturally belonged to the very core of the *mos maiorum* and were therefore taken to be untouchable, and indeed self-evident, guaranteed that such power was only used within certain limits—at least as a rule and for a long period of time.

Conflicts could and did of course arise between magistrates and the *tribuni plebis*—and for that matter between any other organs with potentially conflicting competences—at any moment and for all kinds of reasons, even more or less trivial ones. This was a natural consequence of the, in Meier's terms, "technical imperfection" and "imbalance" that had been produced in the long process of the gradual emergence of the conglomerate of institutions that was the Republican 'constitution.' At the same time, it was this situation that made the development of a center of decision making with generally accepted superior authority possible as well as necessary, if not inevitable—that is, an institution that magistrates and also tribunes could appeal to in case of such conflicts and that could act as a kind of arbiter and defuse these conflicts: namely, the Senate. Down to the late Republic, this function of the Senate remained in principle uncontroversial—and that is yet another reason why formal regulations of its powers and scope of 'competence' were not only not needed, but indeed undesirable: normative rules, defined limits, and their inherent inflexibility would have diminished the general authority of the Senate as a body and as guardian of the constitutional conventions as a whole and therefore obstructed its function as the institution to turn to for decisions and pragmatic solutions.

In other words, the power of the Senate was really based on the fact that it did not have any formally defined or precisely circumscribed responsibilities and was therefore not restricted to a specific set of concrete political topics or areas of 'competence.' It was the very lack of positively defined 'rights' that was the real reason for its immense authority. That is why the Senate could and did have a say in all important political, strategic, and administrative decisions. It served as the institutional forum of debate on all matters of foreign policy; it received embassies from foreign

---

[5] Meier, 1966/1980, 157f., cf. 124 etc.; idem, 1968, 86ff. Cf. also Bleicken, 1968, 87ff., 150ff.; idem, 1981a, 87ff. (= idem, 1998, 484ff.); cf. Roland Wittmann, in Kunkel et al., 1995, 554–664, who (not altogether successfully) tries to fulfil Bleicken's program of a "functional analysis of this institution." Cf. Hölkeskamp, 1987, 140ff., 243f., 257f.; Badian, 1996, 187ff., and recently Lintott, 1999, 121ff. etc..

powers and sent out Roman embassies abroad, consisting of (senior) members of the Senate itself; it discussed the terms of treaties, declarations of war, and conditions for peace as well as the organization of provinces. But the Senate also dealt with quite minor issues, for example conflicts between Greek city-states over specific territorial claims. Another major—and sensitive—power of the Senate was the assignment of *provinciae* (in the general as well as concrete meaning of this complex concept)[6] to consuls, praetors, and pro-magistrates, a power that in the course of time had to be subjected to certain rules. In times of military crisis, however, the rôle of the Senate in the creation of extraordinary commands and the granting of such *imperia* to suitable individuals remained unchallenged, at least until the late Republic. Finally, the Senate traditionally had the right to decide about the honors to be awarded to victorious holders of *imperium auspiciaque*—it authorized triumphs proper, 'small triumphs' (*ovationes*), and the solemn ceremonies of thanksgiving to the gods in case of an important success on the battlefield (*supplicationes*). Additionally it had to give its approval to the consecration of new temples, often vowed and commissioned by successful generals, the erection of other public buildings, honorific statues, victory and other memorial monuments, which enhanced the prestige of their founders and donors.

It was therefore a complex conglomerate of complementary rights and interconnected responsibilities that made the Senate the "central organ of Roman Republican government."[7] At the same time, these competences combined, and the authority derived from them, caused the high magistrates (who were nominally very powerful) to be turned into a kind of executive instrument of the Senate. Nobody has characterized this (only seemingly) paradoxical situation so well as Theodor Mommsen in his *Staatsrecht*,[8] in spite of the fact that it went completely against the grain for him to admit that the Senate "simply ruled over Rome and through Rome over the world" by just fulfiling its functions and using its "pre-eminent and effective as well as undefined and unrestricted position of power" ("ebenso eminente und effective wie unbestimmte und formell unfundirte Machtstellung").[9] At the same time, however, there was another basis of

---

[6] Cf. now Richardson, 2008.

[7] Meier, 1966/1980, 50; cf. Kunkel, 1955, 14ff., especially 18 and 20, where he observes (long before Millar!) that the Senate was not a "legislative body." Cf. also Astin, 1989, 165f.

[8] In this context, it is worth mentioning that it was Mommsen who declared that the Senate was "less a parliament" than a "governing body" (1888, 3/2, 1035).

[9] Mommsen, 1887–1888, 3/2, especially 1022–36 (quotations: 1033 and 1022); cf. Hölkeskamp, 1997, 104ff., and idem, 2005b, 95ff., on Mommsen's self-confessed "extraordinary difficulties" in trying to fit the "description of the Senate's sphere of influence" into his "system" of a *Staatsrecht* because this institution was not really a *Rechtssubject* ('subject'

this "position of power"—the equally informal rôle of the Senate as the institutional center of the privileged social group from which the magistrates, generals, and priests were recruited. We have to bear in mind that all (senior) magistrates were also senators—or rather, they were, and during their careers always remained, senators in the first place, as they served in 'magisterial' functions of administration, jurisdiction, and military command only for strictly limited periods of time. Former quaestors and tribunes of the *plebs* entered the Senate after their term of office, and the aediles, as well as all magistrates with *imperium* such as praetors and consuls, had anyway already been senators before their magistracy: They regularly returned to its ranks at a higher level once their year of office had ended. For although the Senate might have appeared to an outsider as a homogeneous "council of kings"—that was the aphoristic description attributed to the Greek Kineas, who was an Epicurean philosopher and eloquent ambassador on behalf of King Pyrrhus; Kineas was said to have been very familiar with the more exclusive circles of Roman society around 270 BC (although in that case one might have thought that he would have known better)[10]—in truth this 'council' was just as hierarchical as all other Roman institutions, the aristocratic political class itself, and the *populus Romanus* as a whole. I will be coming back to this point again in due course.

Let us move 'bottom-up' and begin with the lower magistrates on completion of their office. They had to remain in the Senate (and in the respective rank or 'class' in the internal hierarchy, which their previous office conveyed) for at least two years before they could apply for the next and higher magistracy in the *cursus honorum*. From this initial stage of their careers onward, they were destined to spend the better part of their political lives in the Senate—given that even the particularly prominent and successful *nobilis*, who managed to become consul (perhaps more than just once) and who got himself appointed to an extraordinary command, actually spent only some five or six years in (senior) office or in command with *imperium*.[11] This dual identity of (senior) magistrates as

---

or institution in an 'abstract,' that is, strictly legal sense of the concept). According to Mommsen's general 'system(at)ic' approach, the Senate therefore lacked "every corporative right" (idem, 1888, 3/2, 1034 and 1025f.).

[10]Plutarch, *Pyrrhos* 19, 6; cf. Appian, *Samnitica* 10, 1f.; Florus 1, 13, 20 etc..

[11]The careers of the most prominent generals during the (Second and Third) Samnite Wars and, above all, the Second Punic War were at least extraordinary, if not already irregular in a general sense of the concept: Q. Fabius Maximus Rullianus, consul I 322, II 310, III 308, IV 297 (and *imperium pro consule* 296), V 295, censor 304 etc.; P. Decius Mus, consul I 312, II 308, III 297 (and *imperium pro consule* 296), IV 295, censor 304 etc.—cf. Hölkeskamp 1987, 126ff.; Q. Fabius Maximus Verrucosus, consul I 233, II 228; dictator 217, consul III (suffectus) 215, IV 214, V 209, censor 230 etc.; M. Claudius Marcellus, praetor I ca. 224, consul I 222, praetor II 216, consul II (suffectus and *pro cos.*) 215,

senators—or vice-versa—meant that they always thought and usually acted like senators not only when dealing with everyday problems but also in more complex or controversial matters. It also meant that they respected the consensus about the rules and limits of official behavior, and were aware of their rights and the appropriate ways of exercising them—all of which was encoded in the *mos maiorum*. One of the basic rules of this code of behavior was to exercise moderation and reason in cases of conflicts with other members of the ruling class (in or out of office), and to submit to the Senate's decisions in such cases because it was the only institution in the system that was always at hand and capable of solving such conflicts. This system proved its worth in many difficult and highly sensitive situations: for example, when it came to clashes of personal interests, aspirations, and ambitions between high-ranking individuals. It also provided the necessary minimum degree of objective judgment needed when it came to the distribution of, appointment to, and/or extension of important, prestigious, and profitable commands—the objects of such individual ambitions. These examples illustrate another very important function of the Senate: the 'administration' of the *mos maiorum*, its maintenance and authoritative interpretation, the implementation and pragmatic application of the rules, principles, and norms encoded in it to concrete problems as well as, last but not least, their adaptation to changing conditions.

The power of the Senate thus resulted from a combination of its political and strategic functions and its 'human resource management,' its important rôle as an arbiter of acute conflicts, and finally its (hardly tangible, but generally accepted) collective authority as guardian of the Roman system of values and norms. On the other hand, it was the only decision-making center that was at all capable of combining and fulfilling all these

---

III 214 (and *imperium pro consule* 213–211), IV 210 (and *imperium pro consule* 209), V 208, and P. Cornelius Scipio (Africanus), *imperium pro consule* 210–206 (Spain), consul I 205, *imperium pro consule* 204–201 (Africa), censor 199, consul II 194 etc.—cf. Beck 2005a, 136ff., 269ff., 302ff., 328ff. In the last century of the Republic, the careers of a series of prominent figures must be considered as 'irregular'—or rather, contrary to the rules—in every respect: The well-known (or perhaps notorious) examples are C. Marius, consul I 107 (and *imperium pro consule* 106–105), II 104, III 103, IV 102, V 101, VI 100, VII 86; L. Cornelius Sulla, consul I 88 (and *imperium pro consule* 87–84 and in Italy 83–81), *dictator legibus scribundis et rei publicae constituendae* 82–79, consul II 80; Cn. Pompeius ('Magnus'), *imperium pro praetore* 83–79 (Italy, Sicily and Africa successively), and 77 (against Lepidus), *pro consule* 77–71 (Spain), consul I 70, *imperium pro consule* (against the pirates and Mithridates) 67–61, consul II 55, *imperium pro consule* 54–49 (Spain), consul III 52, *imperium pro consule* 49–48 (against Caesar), and C. Iulius Caesar himself, consul I 59, *imperium pro consule* 58–49 (Cisalpine and Transalpine Gaul, Illyricum), dictator I 49, consul II 48, dictator II 48–47, consul III 46, dictator III 46–45, consul IV 45, dictator IV 45–44, consul V 44 and dictator *perpetuo*. Cf. Broughton, 1951–52, 2, Index of Careers.

different, and even divergent, requirements because it assembled all (former) magistrates, priests, commanders, and patrons of peoples, cities, and
colonies and could therefore draw upon their experience and knowledge.[12] This resulted in a permanent accumulation and exclusive concentration of expertise and experience in this institution—over the four or
five generations from the establishment of Roman hegemony in Italy
through the Punic Wars and the expansion to the Greek East, virtually all
the political, diplomatic, military, administrative, legal, and religious skill
and knowledge available to the emerging imperial Republic was collected
and stored in the Senate, and it was the Senate alone that was in a position to put it to good use under the rapidly changing conditions.

By discussing the rôle and functions of the Senate, we have already
touched on the second group of factors in Meier's theory of the formation of political groupings, mentioned above. The question of access to,
and presence and influence in, the most important loci of decision making,[13] the rules, opportunities, and restrictions determining them, leads
directly to another question that takes us beyond the level of formal institutions and procedures, for it also concerns the status of individual
actors in the political process as well as the definition, social identity, and
(degree of) exclusiveness of different groups and classes involved. These
actors possess (or lose) or successfully try (or fail) to gain access to the
different 'decision-making centers' and are thereby present (or absent) in
these institutions and can (or cannot) thus take part in the political process of deliberation and decision making. In other words, this is the range
of factors that Meier has subsumed under the sweeping and therefore
rather vague category of "the distribution and relations of power."[14]

[12]Cf. Hölkeskamp, 1987, 184ff., 217, 250; idem, 1990, 449ff.; idem, 1993, 33ff.; idem,
2005b, 125ff. with further references. On the extraordinary *auctoritas senatus* see Meier,
1966/1980, 48ff.; idem, 1984b; Bleicken, 1975, 294ff., 304ff.; idem, 1995, 208ff.; Nicolet,
1979, 357ff.; Lintott, 1999, 86ff.; Martin, 2002, 169; North, 2006, 266ff. Cf. also Cornell,
2000, on the "emancipation of the Senate" in the wake of the *lex Ovinia*, with references.
A systematic and detailed modern analysis of the Senate and its functions remains a desideratum, as the substantial (and still useful) work by Willems, 1878–1885, is outdated in
many ways. Bonnefond-Coudry, 1989, concentrates upon the rules and procedures of the
decision-making process; this also applies to the (rather opinionated) treatment of "rank
and participation" by Ryan, 1998.
[13]Cf. Meier, 1976, 41, and Harris, 1990, 293, who formulates similar questions from a
different point of view.
[14]Meier, 1966/1980, XXXVIf.; idem, 1976, 41. In the debate about a new 'political history' after the 'cultural turn' the very concept of 'power' as well as its general character and
the fundaments, the concrete functioning and relations of 'power' have gradually moved

However, it is not only necessary to take account of individuals, social groups, classes, and 'castes'—that means, in more precise terms, of their respective social and legal status and its degree of formalization and exclusiveness, on which their rôle and legitimacy as holders of power was based in a given pre-modern society. Moreover, a close look at the basic structures is essential: The primary objective of an inquiry must be, on the one hand, to determine those fundamental factors that constitute 'power' and, on the other, to define what 'power' actually meant in this society, how it manifested itself, became visible and tangible, and in which ways and by which means it was actually wielded. Only then can we begin to deal with the fundamental problem of the character and structure of 'power' as such, the interrelation between social, economic, and political dimensions of power, and, last but not least, the sensitive questions of access to, and management or handling of, such 'power' in this society. Once we have understood these different aspects and the specific ways in which they are interconnected and interact, we might eventually also be able to understand the character of élites as 'political classes' as well as the processes of consolidating and restricting, closing and opening up of such social groups 'in power.' Lastly, we might then be able—beyond a mere prosopographical description of the rise and fall of powerful individuals—to identify continuities and changes in the social identity of individual and collective agents and carriers of 'power.'

In the past two decades, there have been various attempts, from different points of departure, to make out layers or manifestations of 'power' in the Roman republic and beyond and to establish their bases and structures, distribution, and interrelation,[15] yet the full program that Meier had mapped out, if only in rather general terms, has never been worked through step by step, as mentioned above. Some basic facts are well known: The social structure of Rome was always characterized by a distinct, and indeed steep, stratification into classes, based on enormous differences in wealth, income, and status. This is generally acknowledged, although it may be debatable whether the differences in power resulting from the social and economic inequalities might not have been extraordinarily or disproportionately large, even by comparison with other pre-modern

---

into the focus of interest, cf. generally Julliard, 1974, 243; Pedersen, 2002, 41f., 46; Landwehr, 2003, 110ff. and passim; Stollberg-Rilinger, 2005, 15ff.; Goppold, 2007, 24ff., and also, in the more concrete context of early modern history, Braddick et al., 2001.

[15]The comprehensive and comparative analysis of 'power'and its construction in historical societies by Mann, 1986, (especially 1ff. on theory and terminology; 250ff. on the Roman territorial state) is inspiring, but cannot replace an exact analysis of the specific form(s) of 'power' in the Roman republic; cf. the review by Greg Woolf, in *JRS* 77, 1987, 193. Cf. also on the interrelation of 'culture,' 'identity,' and 'power' Miles, 2000; Huskinson, 2000; and the other relevant contributions in Huskinson (ed.) 2000.

societies. At any rate, Roman society was certainly not only characterized by a well-developed and pervasive dominance by the members of the upper classes in general, but also by a specific, particularly strong position of power held by an inner circle of these classes, based on the accumulation of economic affluence, social ascendancy, and the continuous exercise of the political, military, and religious rôles of prominence, formal or informal. In other words, the members of this political class all belong to a wider, but generally homogeneous, privileged class of great land-owners, which commanded a substantial, and indeed increasing, share of the most basic and necessary resource of all pre-industrial societies—but on top of that, from the third century BC onward, members of the political class had privileged access to the unprecedented profits from the greatest empire hitherto seen, at least in the world of Mediterranean city-states.[16]

The social and economic difference between the land-owning class, on the one hand, and the peasants, tenants, and landless proletarians, as well as day-laborers, craftsmen, and small merchants, on the other, was mirrored in the equally pervasive hierarchies inscribed in the sociopolitical system: as members of the political class, senators regularly moved into, and out of, formal positions of power—namely, magistracies, military commands, or priesthoods, thereby changing between different rôles of prominence.[17] Due to the internal hierarchies based on the *cursus honorum*, this process permanently produced differences of *political* rank (as well as reproduced the hierarchy itself), a problem that I will return to in later chapters. What needs to be emphasized in this context is the fact that these differences did not affect the principle of basic *social* equality between members of the privileged ('senatorial') class. At the same time, all senators—no matter whether of junior or senior rank, as quaestor or consul, military tribune or general—were always superior to all the other social strata of the *populus Romanus* collectively, as well as to the man in the Roman street individually—as ordinary citizen and rank-and-file in the legions. These facts of life were even more true for the conquered population in the provinces, who simply had to submit to the unlimited power of Roman might and obey governors, magistrates, or military commanders.

[16]The basic works on this subject still are Brunt, 1971, and, for details, Shatzman, 1975. Garnsey and Saller, 1987, though focusing on the empire, provide a broad range of insights into Roman "economy, society and culture" in general. Cf. also, e.g., Hopkins, 1978, 49ff.; Finley, (1973) 1999, and idem, 1983, 1ff.; Runciman, 1983, 164ff.; Alan E. Astin, in *CAH* 8, 174–88; Claude Nicolet, in *CAH* 9, 599–643, and idem, 1979, 185ff.; David, 2000a, 68ff., 90ff.; Flaig, 2003b, 40ff. with further references (in the notes, 263).

[17]Cf. now Beck, 2008a and 2009, for a systematic description of the accumulation of different, but complementary and mutually re-enforcing rôles of prominence as constitutive for aristocratic status.

These hierarchical structures and the omnipresence of hierarchy as a self-evident principle remained fundamental throughout Roman Republican history (and beyond), the manifold changes of social, political, and institutional conditions notwithstanding.[18] The same is true of the basic social unit, the family—indeed, it is the most distinctive feature of the Roman *familia* that it was based on a combination of hierarchy and power, authority and obedience, which in a way mirrored that of Roman society as a whole. Even though the *familia* was constructed in law and conceptualized in ideology as a kind of autonomous or extrasocietal microcosm under the absolute authority of the *pater familias*, it was also a normative ideal, model, and reflection of the social order of the entire external world.[19] In fact, Roman society was interwoven with a great variety of horizontal as well as vertical—that is, hierarchical and 'asymmetrical'—relationships between individuals, small and large groups, leading families and entire political units such as cities. The vertical relations were invariably characterized by degrees of difference in wealth, influence, rank, and prestige. They are often described rather vaguely as close and dense, based on mutual trust, or a little less vaguely as a system or network(s) of patronage, patron-client relations,[20] which certainly emphasizes the reciprocity and a resulting morally (if not legally) binding force of such relations.[21] At the same time, however, just because of the large economic, social, and political differences between client and patron, they were also essentially, and indeed by definition, relations saturated with the palpable power of social superiority. This is made clear by the concept that underlay the complex network of mutual obligations between *patronus* and *cliens*— namely, *fides*. This is a very typical Roman value concept that can only be

---

[18]Cf. Meier, 1966/1980; Beard/Crawford, 1985, 40ff., and finally the brilliant short survey by David, 2000a, 19ff., 30ff. See Kelly, 1966; Kolb, 1977, 240ff.; Runciman, 1983; Richardson, 1991; Jehne, 2000a, 169f.; Martin, 2002, 156ff. The fundamental publications by Géza Alföldy and Friedrich Vittinghoff are still very important for the conceptualization and variety of hierarchies, even though they were primarily concerned with the Roman Empire: Alföldy, 1976, 42ff.; idem, 1986a, 69ff.; Vittinghoff, 1990, 172ff., 205; idem, 1994. Cf. on their work Rilinger, 1985; Winterling, 2001, 99ff., and Eich, 2005, 20ff., 48ff.

[19]Cf. Rilinger, 1985, 310ff.; Martin, 1997, 2ff.; idem, 2002, 158ff. on the *familia* and its 'linear hierarchical' order. Cf. also Garnsey and Saller, 1987, 107ff.; Dupont, 1992, 103ff.; Gardner, 1993; Saller, 1994, 72, 102; Lacey, 1986, 121ff.; Thomas, 1996, and recently Hölkeskamp, 2004b, and Robert, 2008, 207ff.

[20]Meier, 1966/1980, 24ff. Cf. Gelzer, 1912, 68ff., and idem, 1920, 164f., 167, as well as, more recently, the important contributions in Wallace-Hadrill (Ed.), 1989b (with different approaches and perspectives), and David, 1992; 1997 and 2009; Dupont, 1992, 18ff.; Deniaux, 1993, and now eadem, 2006, with further references, to which add Nippel, 2004, and Eich, 2005, 69ff.

[21]See David, 1992, 196ff., and Cosi, 2002, 7ff. on the relevant concepts like *necessitudo/ necessitudines*, etc.

very roughly translated as 'trust and faith,' 'confidence,' and 'reliability' because in modern usage these terms tend to minimize, or even obscure, the hierarchical difference between the individuals involved that the Latin word strongly suggested: The superiority of the person 'owning' *fides*, proving or even dispensing it in his actions, on the one hand, and the inferiority of the person appealing to, or even 'entering into,' the *fides* of the former, on the other, is indelibly inscribed in the concept.[22]

Certain social groups and their individual members were automatically considered to be in a position of inferiority that made them clients by definition closely bound to their patrons in many ways: for example, slaves after manumission (and even their descendants) had always to remain in a close relationship of subordination, deference, and obedience to their former masters and their families—and it is certainly not coincident that freedmen regularly adopted their *nomen gentile*. In the middle Republic, a similar relationship is to be found between the population of conquered cities, territories, and nations, on the one hand, and the commanders of Roman armies, on the other: a holder of *imperium* in command, who had first vanquished them in the field, then accepted them into his *fides* by the formal act of *deditio*,[23] and eventually initiated their incorporation into the empire, automatically becoming their patron. This traditional practice favored the emergence of extensive 'international' patron-client relations between members of the politico-military governing class of Rome, on the one hand, and leading representatives of regional and local élites in Italy and the provinces, as well as 'client-kings' of (nominally) independent border states, on the other, which formed the fundamental structural framework of Roman control over the rapidly expanding empire. As the degree of institutionalized power exercised by the 'central administration' during the whole period of the Republic remained low and its activities intermittent and restricted in range, and as imperial rule, at least on the level of cities and regions, had to be based on the oligarchic self-administration by such élites, senatorial patrons functioned as representatives, agents, or intermediaries of Roman presence and 'power'—and because of their detailed knowledge of local conditions, their networks of influence and authority with prominent key

[22]Cf. Hölkeskamp, 2000b. See Freyburger, 1986, on the basic concept of *fides*; cf. on the "language and ideology of the patronage" Saller, 1982, 7ff., and David, 1992, 49ff.
[23]Cf. Hölkeskamp, 2000b, 237ff., with further references. Cf. especially Dahlheim, 1968, 5ff.; Freyburger, 1986, 7ff.; Nörr, 1989, and the review article by Dahlheim, 1993; Eilers, 2002, 19ff. A contrasting comparison with the "negotiated and meticulously staged ritual" of *deditio* to defuse conflicts in the Middle Ages might be interesting—cf. Althoff, 1997, 99ff.; idem, 2003, 53ff., 143ff.; Garnier, 2008, on the medieval performative "culture of imploring submission."

figures, this indispensable rôle also enabled them to intervene if need be, especially in situations of crisis or political tension.[24]

Such relationships of dependence and (asymmetrical) obligation were not only established by being freed by one's master or by formally entering into it by *deditio*, but in fact also informally, through any kind of service rendered by a person of socially superior standing to another person of lesser status. Such 'services' included any concrete act of protection, aid, and assistance, such as representation in court, as well as occasional (more or less generous) gifts or other forms of tangible 'benefits.' Although these relationships were by no means invariably and equally firm and binding, they were definitely considered to be a real and reliable commitment and might even be hereditary. According to the codex of values deeply ingrained in this society, such *beneficia* automatically created a claim to gratitude and tangible repayment. In the case of ordinary citizens and veterans, who might not have too much to offer in terms of tangible *officia*, this 'return' often consisted of various acknowledged, and even ritualized, forms of open demonstration of loyalty, which was of considerable symbolic value for senatorial patrons or former commanders. The sheer number of 'friends' and clients who—after they had respectfully 'saluted' their patron at the early morning reception in the *atrium* of his residence (*salutatio*)—escorted him as a kind of retinue on his way to the forum was effectively taken as a visible indicator of a senator's rank and influence.[25] In the late Republic, the veterans, as particularly loyal clients of their former commanders, occasionally intervened in political life in more palpable, sometimes indeed very physical, ways.

Furthermore, on the general level of "*histoire des mentalités*," one can show that the social relationships between the Roman upper and lower classes were generally conceptualized and ideologized as an asymmetrical network based on *fides* and permeated all personal relations between individuals and groups. The traditional belief that Romulus—the mythical founder of the *urbs Roma* and of many fundamental institutions that were to make her great—had divided the entire 'ordinary' folk, the *plebs*, into *clientelae* and, as it were, allotted them to the members of his newly created Senate clearly shows, if anything, the deeply ingrained ideology

[24]The basic work remains Badian, 1958. Cf. recently David, 1996, 48ff., 99ff., 127ff. and also Meier, 1966/1980, 35ff., 42ff.; Rich, 1989; Braund, 1984, 1988a; 1988b and 1989; Eilers, 2002, 84ff., 109ff.; Coşkun, 2005 (with bibliography), and the other relevant contributions in idem et al. (Eds.), 2005. Cf. now, on the special relations with Italian local and regional élites, Lomas, 1993 and 2004; Patterson, 2006b. Cf. also Quaß, 1984; Rawson, 1973 and 1977 (= eadem, 1991, 102ff. and 227ff.); Eich, 2005, 71ff. etc.

[25]Cf. Deniaux, 1997.

of reciprocity of collective paternalistic care, on the one hand, and, in return, of dutiful loyalty, deference, and obedience, on the other.[26]

But even if we acknowledge the omnipresence of such relationships of dependence, with their varying degrees of intensity, stability, and binding force, we do not necessarily have to draw the same conclusions as the founders of the 'old orthodoxy'—conclusions that Millar (quite wrongly) considers still to be an uncritically accepted dogma. The basic (however implicit) assumption underlying the reconstructions of 'factional' politics proposed by Münzer, Scullard, and others was that large groups of clients were important factors in the battle for power within the senatorial aristocracy precisely because they were not only fixed and stable, but also and above all essentially passive, easily manipulable, and that they could therefore, whenever their respective patron pleased, be more or less mechanically mobilized and arbitrarily utilized to influence votes in general and especially the elections to the positions of power in the state.[27] In fact, it was long before Millar that this idea, its general presuppositions and implications, had been criticized, once again, by Christian Meier,[28] albeit without much argumentation, and also by Jochen Bleicken, who proposed a kind of minimalist model of a relatively loose and volatile "political clientèle."[29] Finally, it was Peter Brunt who—in a detailed analysis of *clientela* as a social phenomenon—radically disposed of this basic axiom of the 'old orthodoxy' once and for all: he showed that the traditional 'political reading' of the phenomenon is simply wrong.[30]

However, this does not necessarily mean that patronage and personal relations of all kinds were of no importance whatever in politics in general and in elections in particular, as Millar has implied.[31] Again, he has failed to register Meier's much earlier attempt at analyzing the structure and (relative) importance of the *Bindungswesen* ('system' or 'network of social bonds') within the complex sociopolitical order of the middle and late Republic. Meier had already taken a step beyond the relatively simple and conventional model that envisaged a development in three phases. Although he also postulated the existence of an early phase with a kind of "primal, rigid and comprehensive form of *clientela*," characterized by

[26]Cicero, *De Republica* 2, 16; Dionysius Halicarnassensis, *Antiquitates Romanae* 2, 9, 2f.; Plutarch, *Romulus* 13, 7ff. Cf. also Brunt, 1988, 400ff.; Drummond, 1989a, 89ff. and the important contribution by Wallace-Hadrill, 1989a, 71f., 84f.; Martin, 2002, 161ff.
[27]Cf. especially Gelzer, 1912, 102, 134f.
[28]Meier, 1966/1980, 38ff., especially 40 and 175.
[29]Bleicken, 1981b, 245ff. (= idem, 1998, 475ff.); idem, 1972, 66ff. (= idem, 1998, 244ff.).
[30]Brunt, 1988, 382ff. However, he (like Millar and North) fails to present Meier's and Bleicken's differentiated positions accurately (i.e., 385). Cf. Wallace-Hadrill, 1989a, 68ff., and David, 1997 (with the comments by Ungern-Sternberg, 1997) on the different positions in the debate.
[31]Millar, 1998, 7ff.; idem, 2002a, 124f., 137f., 145f.

precise forms and strict rules concerning the 'rights' and mutual duties of patrons and clients,[32] he believed that already since the fifth century BC these "relatively compact *clientelae*" as "power bases" of the patrician *gentes* had already begun to dwindle in importance and finally disintegrate. Not only is the basis for this hypothesis in the extant (invariably much later) sources rather fragile, however, but also the form, functions, and indeed the very existence of these early *clientelae* are certainly debatable.[33]

Meier's argument that another form of *clientela* emerged in the fourth century BC, constituting the second phase in the development of the *Bindungswesen*, seems much better grounded. He claims that this form was not just a weakened variant of the original system, brought about in a linear development by the reduced dependency of the clients, but that it was a novel form of a patron-client 'system' with entirely different qualities. It was created by Roman expansion throughout Italy and the unprecedented increase in sheer numbers of Roman citizens brought about in the process, on the one hand, and the new and different kind of *clientelae* that ambitious and powerful plebeian families started to build up by means of the political representation of the interests of the *plebs*, on the other. Both developments, and above all their contingent combination and mutual re-enforcement, were bound to have a marked effect on the very character of the *Bindungswesen*. According to Meier, this process continued throughout the fourth century and brought about a third stage of this development at the turn of the century—namely, a variety of different types and degrees of loose and relatively informal personal relationships, some of which were based upon gratitude or some kind of direct personal contact.[34] The networks of personal relationships, duties, and mutual obligations—the horizontal ones of *amicitia* between senators as well as the vertical ones between them and ordinary citizens or local dignitaries in Italy and the provinces—had increased in scale, number, and density at a pace that paralleled the dynamic speed of imperial expansion. As a result, every member of the senatorial aristocracy necessarily had multiple and far-reaching connections of ever-increasing complexity—'vertical' and 'horizontal,' formal and informal, direct, close, and occasionally intimate, as well as loose, more indirect, and even impersonal contacts, which were only established through the mediation of other (senatorial) patrons, prominent local figures outside Rome, or other 'agents' of lower social rank.

The omnipresence of such relationships forming a variegated network of interrelations necessarily resulted in what Meier calls a "plurality" of commitments and obligations, which regularly tended to conflict with, or

[32]Meier, 1966/1980, 24ff., 174f.; cf. Gelzer, 1920, 158ff.

[33]Cf. the references in n. 20, as well as Laser, 1997, 110ff., and most recently Welwei, 2001, and Smith, 2006, 168ff.

[34]Meier, 1966/1980, 30, cf. 15ff.; David, 1997, 208ff.; Nippel, 2004, 139ff.

at least neutralize, one another, and it was this consequence that was evidently the main concern of Meier, who himself was referring to Gelzer. Meier was certainly right to insist that this situation in turn made the permanent concentration of influence, or the creation of *clientelae* in the sense of large, stable, and easily deployable groups of followers entirely impossible—in fact, not even a regular, consistent, and (therefore) identifiable 'family policy' inside the large and often widely ramified *gentes* could be feasible.[35] Although loyalties, connections, and commitments could and did influence concrete decisions of all kinds—especially elections to a certain extent and above all under particular circumstances—they always had to be revived and renewed, recombined and reorchestrated in order to be put into effect in a specific occasion, which required a lot of time, energy, attention, and personal canvassing. However, even if these laboriously created networks of influence could be brought to bear in a given situation, they were precarious, ephemeral, and regularly short-lived. Above all, they were always only one of a broad variety of different factors that influenced elections: a candidate for a high magistracy profited most from personal qualities such as brilliant oratory, prowess on the battlefield—preferably proven by (recent) heroic deeds and/or memories of magnificent games—and a great name and its attendant 'symbolic capital' generated by a long family tradition. I will be coming back to this again in a later chapter.[36]

It was again Meier who pointed out further ramifications of the "plurality" of connections and relationships. He drew the conclusion that the multiplicity of commitments inevitably resulted in a pronounced fragmentation or 'divisibility' of interests (*Vereinzelung der Interessen*) and a high degree of 'separability,' or even 'fissility,' of policies, politics, and political issues (*Teilbarkeit der Politik*). As a consequence, it is not only unsurprising but indeed to be expected that it turned out to be impossible to prove a (regular and decisive) influence of large stable groups—let alone coherent "parties with substantial power and durability"—either on the outcome of elections or, for that matter, in any other concrete field of day-to-day politics.[37]

Moreover, Meier went still another step further and pinpointed, and radically questioned, yet another basic assumption of the traditional orthodoxy that had never been made explicit, let alone put to the test of empirical application: The idea that these 'parties' or 'family factions' were not in any way bound to specific political issues and never commit-

[35]Meier, 1966/1980, 15, 163 (with reference to Gelzer's review of Scullard, 1973, 203f.); 176f.

[36]Meier, 1966/1980, 8; 175f. etc.; Morstein-Marx 1998, 283ff., and chapter 8 on the concept of 'symbolic capital.'

[37]Meier, 1966/1980, 40, 163ff., 189f., cf. also 17ff., 89, 174f., 182f.

ted themselves to concrete political goals (he speaks of a specific *Gegenstandsunabhängigkeit der Parteiungen*, a term that is intranslatable). This assumption in turn necessarily entails the presupposition that these 'parties' must have held the same convictions and shared the same orientations in the whole range of Republican policies, that they followed the same lines and co-operated in all areas of politics—in other words, all politically active senators must always have found themselves aligned according to one and the same 'party line' and therefore regularly ended up in the same coalitions, regardless of the actual issue. This is of course highly questionable, not only on the grounds of general considerations. Indeed it can actually be disproved empirically. In looking more closely at actual cases, one sees that it was on the contrary a specific issue, concrete decision, or vested interest of some sort operating in a concrete situation that triggered the formation of a particular 'political grouping'—in Meier's terms, in Roman Republican politics 'groupings' were in general and regularly *gegenstandsabhängig*.[38] It was the very 'divisibility' of interests and 'fissility' of politics and policies mentioned above, and the resulting kaleidoscope of different pressures and interests, obligations and commitments that necessarily forced every individual senator permanently to take up a stance according to the demands of his personal network, to realign himself and readjust his position accordingly. He might well find himself siding with certain senatorial 'friends' in one matter and with other *amici* in another controversy, in which he might even strongly disagree with the former, and all that possibly even at the very same time.[39] On a general level, this necessarily led to a continuous shifting of coalitions, constellations, and, for that matter, lines of confrontation. Political 'groups' and entire patterns of 'group formation' were therefore wholly dependent on current political issues and dissensions, producing a large variety of political groupings, the only common denominator of which was their being highly volatile and ephemeral, as there was at any given time a broad range of concrete problems on the agenda of Roman day-to-day politics.

It is the very character of these concrete issues—or, in Meier's terms, the actual "contents of politics" in a given pre-modern sociopolitical system—with which the third level of Meier's theory of 'formation of political groupings' is concerned. These contents consisted of those topics that could be put on the agenda in this society: that is, that could be made

[38] Meier, 1966/1980, xxxii; xxxviii, 163, cf. 40f., 174ff., 182ff.
[39] Cf. also Shatzman, 1974, 220 and passim.

objects of politics and policies. Only then could they be explicitly addressed, become the foci of open debate, and only then could they eventually be dealt with in, and, above all, within, the decision-making institutions. We must then ask which problems and matters could at all, in Meier's terms, be "politicized" within the given structural framework of the sociopolitical "distribution of power."

In fact, these general considerations lead to two further important questions. The first one is whether or not (and how much of) the political order itself could become an object of politics and institutionalized decision making—or, more abstractly, it is the "degree of fundamentality" that needs attention. The extreme variant—or theoretical possibility—would have been that it was (or, under certain circumstances, became) possible in a given sociopolitical system to put the whole framework itself on the agenda. The pragmatically and historically more probable variant would be that only single aspects—for example, certain institutions or rules—could become a matter of debate and even reform, whereas the system itself was beyond any form of criticism. A third possibility would then be that the range of 'politicizable' issues was radically restricted so that political controversy was in fact limited to everyday topics, interests of individuals, and minor administrative problems.

The other question goes even further and is especially important with regard to the debate about Roman Republican political culture. Once we have identified and defined the actual topics possible in its political game, we can ask what could *not* be raised for political debate—in other words, what could not become the stuff that politics were made of under the constraints on the range of 'politicizable' issues in a given sociopolitical system. Once again, the range of theoretical possibilities is broad: There might be conflicts of interests, collisions of principles, or other structural problems, which (at least from a modern point of view) may all seem to be obvious enough or even evidently urgent, and which could simply not be addressed in open political discussion, let alone effectively solved by political decision making. A plausible conclusion would be that the political capacity of the system, its spectrum of tolerance of 'politicization' of sensitive issues, and, as a consequence, its potential for genuine political solutions, were inadequate and did therefore not allow it to tackle such controversial topics by, and in, the institutional centers of decision making.[40]

On the other hand, an analysis of the limits and restrictions on the range of topics that could be politically addressed in a given society may reveal its very fundaments of accepted institutions, social conditions, rules, norms, principles, values, and moral orientations, which did and could

---

[40]Cf. Meier, 1978b, 41, 53; idem, 1960/1980, xxxi, XLII ff.; Hölkeskamp, 1987, 15f.

not become objects of political debate precisely because they remained absolutely undisputed or were even part of a deeply rooted collective consensus. Ideally and theoretically, therefore, such an analysis would allow a reliable determination of the (degree of) homogeneity, coherence, and stability of the society, group, or class in question. This degree is especially high if heated and open debates take place on a large number of politically addressable topics, while the shared basis of rules, norms, and values remains untouched. Of course, the inverse is true too: The more the basis itself becomes a matter of controversy and the more the universal consensus about this basis erodes as a result, the more strain is put upon the stability and functionality of the political system as such.

These different conditions and degrees of 'politicizability' have been concretely, and indeed paradigmatically, exemplified by the decisive stages of development of the Roman republic. On the one hand, there is the end of the so-called 'struggle of the orders.' This struggle between the archaic aristocracy of patricians, and the socially heterogeneous '*plebs*,' under the leadership of its upper crust of ambitious families, the consolidation of the resulting new patricio-plebeian 'political class' and the development of the *nobilitas* as its inner circle in the fourth and early third centuries BC, was a process in the course of which certain political issues that had previously been highly controversial simply disappeared—for example, the leading plebeians' demand for equal access to the higher political, military, and religious positions of power. At the same time, other issues lost much of their pressing political relevance—for example, as a consequence (or side-effect) of Roman expansion in Italy, the problem of the land hunger of the plebeian peasants. The process that resulted in the end of the 'struggle of the orders' actually benefited from a pragmatic and increasingly successful application of a growing set of rules, norms, and principles that had previously been controversial and then became part of a consensus. It was in the process of resolving conflicts, and sometimes only after painfully bitter struggles, that such new rules were first created by way of compromise and then merged into a common basis accepted by both groups, which thus (at least in some respects) grew almost by itself—classic examples are the set of rules about the access of plebeians to curule office and priesthoods, as well as those relating to the (regular and irregular) iteration of the consulship.[41]

[41]Cf. Hölkeskamp, 1987, 192ff. etc.; idem, 1993; idem, 1988, 271ff.; Cornell, 1989, 334ff., 391ff.; idem, 1995, 340ff., 369ff. Cf. on the development of the "struggle of the orders": Drummond, 1989b, 172f., and the relevant contributions in: Raaflaub (Ed.), 1986b, and the review by K.-J. Hölkeskamp, in *Gnomon* 61, 1989, 304–18. Cf. also the surveys by Ward, 1997, 58ff.; Oakley, 2004, and recently Forsythe 2005, 157ff., 268ff., 324ff.; Sordi, 2005 (somewhat impressionistic and highly selective), and Raaflaub, 2006, 139ff.

On the other hand, there is the 'crisis of the Republic,' which can be described as a series of specific conflicts about a range of disputed issues such as the distribution of public land, the accommodation of veterans, and long-term extraordinary military commands with alarmingly extensive powers:[42] conflicts that put the political capacity of the system and its potential for genuine political solutions to the test. These disputes brought about multiple violations of the rules and norms, thereby eroding their validity and binding force as well as, as a result, the fundamental consensus about these rules as such. This process of disintegration was not only pushed forward by famous (or notorious) *popularis* politicians from the Gracchi brothers onward, who imitated their method of deliberately circumventing the Senate by submitting highly controversial legislation directly to the popular assembly, thus automatically coming up against the resistance of the majority of their peers. In the long run, the 'optimate' strategies of counteracting *popularis* initiatives of one kind or another turned out to be no less detrimental to a consensus that was, after all, also part and parcel of the legitimacy of the sociopolitical régime of the senatorial class as such.[43] Thus, disputes over concrete issues as well as the respective tactics and strategies to deal with them not only simply fueled the crisis, but turned it into a kind of dynamic, self-evolving process—Christian Meier has coined the term "autonomous process."[44] By the end of this process, it had become virtually impossible to address any urgent political problem according to the received principles and procedures of political decision making: The more urgent (and therefore sensitive) an issue was, the more was it prone immediately and automatically to result in sharp, fundamental, and increasingly violent controversies and paralyzing standoffs that could no longer be resolved in the traditional centers of decision making, but only by resorting to violence: that is, according to recent studies, to new variants of quasi-institutional organization and mobilization of popular support outside (and in opposition to) the traditional élite-controlled institutions and procedures, including various forms of ritualized violence against persons and/or symbols.[45] This is,

[42]Recent surveys of dates and facts include Ungern-Sternberg, 2004; Konrad, 2006, and Tatum, 2006.

[43]Cf. for details of *popularis* politics Martin, 1965; Meier, 1965, and (1966) 1980, 116ff.; 127f.; 144ff.; cf. also David, 1980; Mackie, 1992, and more recently Ferrary, 1997 (with the comments by K.-J. Hölkeskamp, in Bruhns et al. (Eds.), 1997, 232–35), with bibliography; Roddaz, 2005 (on the notions of *popularis* politics, 'popularity' and 'populism'). Cf. Thommen, 1989, and David, 1993 (on the tribunate of the *plebs* in the late Republic); Burckhardt, 1988 (on 'optimate' strategies), and Ungern-Sternberg, 1998 (on the system's loss of legitimacy).

[44]This is the core of Meier's results (i.e., 1966/1980, 128ff.); also see idem, 1978b, 34ff.; idem, 1976, 47ff.; Martin, 1965.

[45]Cf. on the range of ritualized and other forms of political violence in the late Republic Vanderbroeck, 1987, and especially Nippel, 1988a, 54ff., 71ff., 108ff., and idem, 1995, 47ff.

however, not more than a theory, or perhaps only a suggestion and a position, which is by no means uncontroversial. In fact, the debate on the causes of the decline and fall of the Republic and, presently and more concretely, on the relative importance of structures, deficits inscribed in the sociopolitical framework of the Republic, and *longue-durée* factors in general, on the one hand, and of 'contingency,' 'events,' and mere 'accidents,' on the other, is certainly not over (and probably will never be closed).[46] It is a debate that by now certainly deserves a book in its own right.

---

[46]Cf. the view proposed by Erich Gruen, who (*contra* Meier and others) denied the relevance of "underlying causes" and rejected "abstract explanations": "civil war caused the fall of the Republic—not vice versa" (1974, 504, cf. 4f.; 498ff.)—see the reviews, e.g., Crawford, 1976; David R. Shackleton-Bailey, in *AJPh* 96, 1975, 436–43. Interestingly, however, some German scholars have proposed similar views of the causes and final stages of the 'decline and fall,' e.g., Welwei, 1996, and (more radically) Girardet, 1996. Cf. also, e.g., Bleicken, 1995a; Deininger, 1998, and among recent surveys of the present state of the debate Morstein-Marx et al., 2006; Jehne, 2006, 8f., and now idem, 2009; Hölkeskamp, 2009b, with further references. Cf. also the other contributions in Hölkeskamp et al. (Eds.), 2009, especially the interesting and innovative study by Walter, 2009, on the complex relation of 'structures' and 'contingency' in this process.

Chapter 4

FROM 'STRUCTURES' TO 'CONCEPTS'

PROBLEMS OF (SELF-)CONCEPTUALIZATION
OF AN ALIEN SOCIETY

Q UITE A FEW of the fundamental problems mentioned in the previous chapter—for example, the questions revolving around the character, basis, and extent of the particular Roman kind of social consensus about the political order and the causes and determining factors that brought about the gradual erosion of binding rules—had long since been raised in the discussion of the political culture of the Republic. Indeed, some of these questions had already been asked even, as it were, *avant la lettre*: that is, before a new research interest in the Republican political culture, in the specific sense of this term (to be discussed in chapter 5), was explicitly formulated by ancient historians. Once again it was a number of concrete, pragmatic questions that prompted the discussion, and once again they originally had rather general conventional assumptions as starting points. To begin with, these questions were no longer (or rather, no longer exclusively) focused on the immediate causes of the fall of the Republic and its various stages from the mid-second century BC onward. The more interesting question was now why this 'polity' had not perished long before the crisis actually became acute, given that it was confronted with the new, and indeed unprecedented, reality of a Mediterranean-wide empire: after all, it was a fact that the *res publica* with its old (or old-fashioned) aristocratic constitution geared to the needs of a small city-state could not only conquer the whole of Italy and then dynamically expand in the Western and Eastern Mediterranean, but also manage to keep the vast territories that came under its sway in rapid succession under control. Further, this fact was no longer taken to be self-evident, but on the contrary now stood in need of explanation. In other words, how was it possible that the *res publica* functioned so well for such a long time without significantly changing its structures and character?[1]

Meier (as well as other scholars) attempted to explain this peculiar longevity by assuming an extraordinarily stable and tenacious social con-

---

[1]Meier, 1966/1980, XV, 3, cf. 4, 301ff. and passim.

sensus, the core of which was never politically questioned (or rather, could not be 'politicized,' in the sense explained in chapter 3), but remained uncontroversial, even in times of severe crisis, and was conjured up or appealed to in the face of increasing difficulties. According to this view, this consensus was the basis of an extraordinary feeling of unity, uniformity, and solidarity within the Republican ruling class that remained strangely unaffected by the usual, omnipresent, and indeed increasingly intensive aristocratic rivalries about rank and prestige. Once again, it was Meier who tried to capture the core of this consensus by coining concepts such as 'state-orientation' (without allowing himself, at least not in this context, to be drawn into the discussion about the actual identity or character of this 'state' or the applicability of this concept).[2] He meant by this that the senatorial aristocracy deeply and unreservedly identified with the Roman 'state' and constantly strove to increase the "power and grandeur of the *res publica*." This particular sort of state-orientation also functioned as the ideological core of an aristocratic ethos, which in turn constituted a "collective morality" that was valid and binding for the whole of Roman society and indeed deeply inscribed in its collective mental fabric. It was this "collective ethos" and its uncontroversial validity that engendered a "new kind of political will" that could freely dispose of "all talents, achievements and aptitudes of the people." For Meier, this explains the "readiness," indeed willingness, of the people at large to obey the aristocratic régime as a matter of course and comply with its omnipresent hierarchies and command-structures. In his opinion, aristocracy and *plebs* were tied together in a "basically monistic society" based upon this "collective morality."[3]

Because of its rather general nature, its terminological inaccuracy, and its inherent static and idealistic view of collective mental dispositions, such an interpretation and its conceptual framework were not (and of course could not be) final.[4] More than thirty years ago, however, these questions, concepts, and considerations did clear the way for a more precise analysis of individual aspects and for a revision of the overall picture. This wave of innovation was furthered by a general opening-up and reorientation of the whole field of ancient history: at last, for the first time in the recent study of ancient history (not only in Germany), notice was taken of debates that were taking place in neighboring fields

[2] See chapter 5, below.

[3] Meier, 1966/1980, 47f., 52f., 57, 59f., cf. generally 32f., 45ff.

[4] Cf. now Flaig, 2003a, 13ff. on the extraordinary degree or particular "Gehorsamstiefe" ('depth of obedience') of the Roman *plebs*.

about new topics, questions, and aims, about concepts and categories, and about problems of methodology and theory. These new intellectual challenges and stimuli were (at first slowly, and sometimes reluctantly) being accepted and applied to topics specific to the history of the classical world.[5]

One of the first of these new developments was the emergence of a new brand of *Begriffsgeschichte*: that is, a modern, comprehensive history of key sociopolitical concepts and their semantics, which was embedded in both modern social history and *histoire de mentalité* and based on a broad, explicit, methodological, and theoretical foundation. In Germany (and, to a certain extent, even in other European academic cultures), it was the publication of the first monumental lexicon of core sociopolitical concepts and the respective history of their specific meanings, the *Geschichtliche Grundbegriffe. Historisches Lexikon zur politisch-sozialen Sprache in Deutschland (GGr)*, in eight volumes, that triggered a general discussion of this foundation.[6] The debate about the program, theoretical basis, and methodological approach of this collection was later, after an intense discussion about 'historical semantics,' extended to include the history of sociopolitical 'discourse(s)' itself.[7] The entries on individual central items of the political and social terminology—the "conceptual world"[8] of ancient Greece and Rome—were intended to explore the potential of historical semantics for a historical examination of past societies and their mentalities in a systematic, comprehensive, and methodologically controlled way. This produced several attempts at a differentiated reconstruction of ancient concepts of freedom, which developed very differently and in specific ways in the political and social contexts of

---

[5]Cf. the relatively positive account by Gehrke, 1993, and idem, 1995, 160ff. Nippel, 1988, 300ff. was less optimistic.

[6]Christian Meier, who was co-editor together with Werner Conze and Reinhart Koselleck, contributed a large number of pieces on "nobility and aristocracy" and "democracy" in antiquity (*GGr* 1, 1972, 2–11, 821–35). The other contributors from the field of classics and ancient history—Jochen Bleicken, Jochen Martin, Fritz Gschnitzer, Peter Spahn, and the Latinist Viktor Pöschl—certainly participated in the debate on the general program. Cf. Gehrke, 1993, 217f.; Raaflaub (1985) 2004, 5ff.

[7]The stages and aspects of this discussion cannot be expounded in detail here. Cf. the fundamental introductions by Daniel, 2001, 345ff., and Landwehr, 2008, 31ff. and passim. The following selection of contributions is admittedly idiosyncratic: Koselleck, 1979, 107ff., 211ff. and the collection of seminal articles in idem, 2006; Busse, 1987, 50ff., 302ff. and passim; Richter, 1995, 32ff. and passim; Lottes, 1996, 32ff.; Reichardt, 1998, and the contributions in Bödeker (Ed.), 2002; Reingard Eßer, in Eibach et al. (Eds.) 2002, 281–92, with further references (321ff.); Schorn-Schütte, 2006, 73ff.

[8]Term translated from "politisch-soziale Begriffswelt" that was developed by Meier, 1977, which has been revised and republished in idem, 1980, and (in English translation) in idem, 1990.

archaic and classical Greece,[9] on the one hand, and Republican Rome,[10] on the other.

From the early stages of the debate onward, the primary intention was not to study the history of isolated words or to develop a lexical definition of individual items, even though such frequently used words as *eleutheria* and *libertas* can certainly be seen as "linguistic codes" or "ciphers" for "habitualized ideas," [11] and might therefore be eligible for an interpretation along the lines of a history of mentalities. Though the debate about the methods and categories, possibilities and limits of the new conceptual history,[12] of 'historical semantics,' of 'discourse-analysis,' and its different variants and their status in a modern social (or perhaps societal) history, had only just begun at that time, the main focus was not—in Reinhart Koselleck's terminology—on the "semasiological" or "onomasiological" approach to individual concepts: that is, on the analysis of their meanings and semantic fields, their uses in texts of various genres and periods, or to their meanings in the context of other semantic fields. Rather, as Koselleck emphasized, the main focus was always on the "tension between the term and its corresponding entity"—the political, social, and ideological phenomenon behind the word: on the shifts of meaning, on the one hand, and (the changes of) these "entities" and contexts, on the other.[13]

The idea therefore was to take the whole range of contexts of a past 'life-world' into account,[14] for it is in this environment that the terms in question were coined, charged with meaning(s), and used, sometimes in

[9]Cf. Raaflaub, (1985) 2004.

[10]Cf. Bleicken, 1962, 1972, and 1976, 1–20 (= idem, 1998, 1:156–61; 2:663–682), as well as Lind, 1986, 81ff.; Brunt, 1988, 281ff. (both lacking theoretical reflection); Mouritsen, 2001, 9ff. with further references. Cf. for a comparative approach Raaflaub, 1984, 529ff. and most recently idem, 2003, 55ff.

[11]Terms are translated from Reichardt, 1998, 24.

[12]Already in the mid-1970s, Paul Veyne described the general approach and concrete operations of "conceptual history" vis-à-vis Rome and Roman culture in his inimitable way (1976, 25): "Les Romains parlent de la grandeur de Rome, de la coutume des ancêtres, de la sagesse du Sénat; l'historien traduit cela dans le métalangage transhistorique des sciences politiques; il décrypte le texte et y retrouve des invariants: impérialisme ou isolationnisme, couverture idéologique, domination de classe. Il ne partage pas le langage érroné des Romains: il nous explique les Romains en parlant la langue de la vérité scientifique, en mettant au jour les mécanismes et les réalités de l'histoire romaine et en la rendant ainsi intelligible."

[13]Cf. Koselleck, 1979, 114ff., 121, 123; idem, 1986, and the other relevant chapters in idem, 2006. The very first article in *GGr* is a particularly interesting example of this "tension," especially in the present context: Conze and Meier, 1972, on "aristocracy" and related concepts, their contents and change of meanings from Antiquity to the nineteenth century.

[14]This is a rather clumsy translation of the term *Lebenswelt*, which is well known from social theory and philosophy (Edmund Husserl, Alfred Schuetz, etc.).

controversial discourse. To this end, a "social history of the communicative environment" is required that would need to take into account the general framework of the specific communicative situations, the media and institutional channels of communication, as well as the range of locations and occasions for communication. Moreover, such a comprehensive approach would also have to include the social rôles and profiles, the knowledge of contexts, situations, and concomitant options of taking action, as well as the experience and expectations of all participants of such communicative acts—addressors and addressees, speakers and listeners, authors and readers alike. Ideally, such a complex and extensive conceptual history can help to uncover mentalities, and thus become part of a comprehensive history of cognitive and semantic structures of a past society, by providing access to its ethical, affective, and cognitive dispositions, as well as to its complete repertoire of specific imaginative, perceptual, cognitive, and analytic possibilities and modalities.[15] This approach shares some basic elements of theory and method with the modern concept of a "symbol-oriented social history," which also seeks, according to Ute Daniel, to take account of the "evaluative and interpretative activity of historical subjects," who need to make sense of their 'life-world'and "create meaning" for the phenomena of this world, "as a constitutive element of every social world."[16] It also shares some perspectives (and general assumptions) with a history of mentality that focuses on how "a social reality becomes tangible, thinkable, and 'readable': that is, explainable and interpretable "in different times and locations."[17]

Such programs and plans are a new challenge for the field of ancient history, and not merely because of the fragmentary nature of our sources. This challenge has been recognized by now and taken up.[18] In the following chapters, specific questions and issues will be dealt with in detail. At first, however, a closer look at the roots and further development of this reorientation seems to be appropriate. As noted above, even before the theoretical claims and general methodological principles mapped out

[15]Cf. Reichardt, 1998, 24 and 12, with reference to Koselleck as well as Lottes, 1996, 42f. Cf. Raulff (Ed.), 1987 (and his preface, especially 9f.); Dressel, 1996, 263ff.; Burke, 1997, 162ff.; Sellin, 1985 and 1987; Daniel, 1997, 200ff.; eadem, 2001, 221ff. Cf. on "communicating culture, identity, and power" in the Roman Empire: Miles, 2000.

[16]Daniel, 1994, 60; cf. eadem, 1993, 71ff., 92ff.; eadem, 2001, 7ff. Cf. Sieder, 1994, 460ff.; van Dülmen, 1995, 412ff., 420ff. The debate is still current: cf., for example, Mergel and Welskopp, 1997a; Medick, 2001.

[17]Chartier, 1992, 11f., 17, 21f. on "representations" and "methods" as ways of obtaining "social and terminological configurations."

[18]Cf. Rebenich, 2005, 42ff.

above had been set out explicitly, there had been a sort of vague hope of uncovering this peculiar Roman mentality by way of a historical analysis of individual key concepts of the Roman sociopolitical language. The underlying, fairly ambitious goal has been maintained since, and the method has taken center-stage when it came to more systematic attempts at exploring, in detail as well as in depth, the peculiar "collective morality" of the Republican *populus Romanus*. The key to accomplishing this aim was an analysis, based on the new methods of 'conceptual history,' of those specific values that formed what might be called the collective ethos, conceived as an interrelated network of terms and 'moral' concepts. As a matter of course, the initial focus was on those concepts of value that had already been addressed by the traditional, narrow, philological, and theoretically quite unsophisticated method of 'single-word lexicography.' The approach had strong roots in a particular German 'school,' which (at least, partly) had a rather problematic ideological and political hidden agenda revolving around a peculiar ideal of 'Romanness' and its 'value(s).'[19] The core terms were the classic, 'typically Roman virtues' of courage and constant effort, selfless and self-denying attention to duty, unwavering equanimity, unfaltering endurance and pertinacity— especially in times of war, in the face of danger, and under adverse circumstances (*virtus, fortitudo, constantia*).[20] Other terms of interest denote personal qualities such as reliability with regard to all kinds of social commitments (*fides* and *gratia*), which in turn were inseparably linked, and partly synonymous, with the allegedly Roman principle of strict observance of the iron rules of reciprocity: that is, the personal duty to honor obligations incurred by returning favors (*beneficia/officia*).[21] Another central 'virtue' (pertaining to senior senators in particular) was a sort of pragmatic wisdom based on practical experience in all fields of administration, politics, and war and showing itself above all in pragmatic and coolly calculated deliberation in political debates (*sapientia*). But the scope of this terminology—in the literal sense of the word—also included those terms relating to the unwritten code of appropriate behavior, dignified appearance, and bearing and habitus, especially in those political and social situations that were visible in public (*gravitas*). Finally, one could add the specific repertoire of concepts that describe rewards

[19]Cf. the important studies by Schmidt, 2005, and Rebenich, 2005.

[20]Comprehensive studies of Roman 'value concepts' as a system, of individual '*virtutes*,' and their inseparable interconnection include Hellegouarc'h, 1963; Eisenhut, 1973; Moussy, 1966; Lind, 1972, 1979, 1986, 1989,1992, and 1994; Drexler, 1988; Moore, 1989; Miles, 1995; Thome, 2000, and recently Gärtner, 2000; Köves-Zulauf, 2000, and also Schneider, 1998, 48f.; Mutschler, 2003, and now Badel, 2005, 39ff.; McDonnell, 2006a; Morgan, 2007; Robert, 2008, and Pignatelli, 2008.

[21]Cf. Lendon, 1997, 63ff.

and 'prizes' for relevant achievements and personal success (once again, in politics and war): reputation and fame (*fama* and *existimatio*); glory (*gloria*); esteem, rank, and influence (*dignitas* and *auctoritas*); and especially 'honor' and public distinction that were bestowed by the higher magistracies on the individual incumbents (*honos* and individual *honores*).

Admittedly, we do not yet have detailed studies of all these individually important terms, which meet the whole spectrum of exacting methodological standards discussed in the modern 'historiography of concepts' and 'discourse.' Some general perspectives have become apparent, however, that are beginning to mold this repertoire of individual terms and their respective range of specific meanings and complex connotations into an interrelated system.[22] The fundamental feature of this, as it were, 'world of Roman household words' is the fact that they all denote, or somehow refer to, different facets of acceptable or even desirable public (or, more precisely, publicly visible) social and political behavior of individuals in general and of prominent—that is, again publicly visible—persons of rank in particular. Accordingly, Viktor Pöschl called these concepts 'terms of relation,' referring to the close, enduring, and reliable 'links' between individuals, social groups, classes, and generations.[23] More concretely, they conceptualize various aspects of such a 'partnership' and the assumptions it is based on, such as acknowledging the reciprocity of *officia* and *beneficia*, mentioned above, and fulfiling the resulting obligations under all circumstances—and this specific kind of reciprocity of course includes the necessity of rewarding success in politics and war by 'honor' in the shape of both *honos* as well as tangible *honores*.[24] Another important aspect—or rather, the other side of the very same coin—is the extraordinary effectiveness and disciplinary potency that were inherent in the conceptions and standards of prestige, status, and honor (but also of the fear of losing it and the resulting 'shame') because the underlying 'values'

[22]Cf. now Rosenstein, 2006, who not only describes "aristocratic values" as a system, but also emphasizes their embeddedness in a web of interconnected media and messages. Cf. already Earl, 1967; Groß, 1983; Hölkeskamp, 1987, 207ff., 248ff.; idem, 1993, 29f.; idem, 2000b, passim; Classen, 1988 (= idem, 1998, 243ff.); idem, 2000; Pani, 1997, 43ff. Cf. Haltenhoff, 2000, 16ff.; idem 2005, and the relevant contributions in the edited volumes Braun et al. (Eds.), 2000; Linke et al. (Eds.), 2000b; Haltenhoff et al. (Eds.), 2003, and idem et al. (Eds.), 2005 (which also elucidate the literary and other contexts in which 'value concepts' were used, affirmed, [re-]defined or otherwise implicitly or explicitly discussed). See also Lendon, 1997, 30ff., 272ff.; Roller, 2001, 20ff.; Morgan, 2007 (on the Roman Empire); Stemmler, 2001, 221f. Barton, 2001, 34ff. provides a somewhat opinionated approach (which is nevertheless worth discussing) as she attempts to present "the most complex understanding of the spiritual and emotional life of the ancient Romans" (xi) and repeatedly refers to the absolute social integration of the bearers of these emotions (or, accordingly, their exclusion as a form of punishment): cf. my review in *Klio* 86, 2004, 485–87.

[23]Pöschl, 1980, 189ff.; cf. now the detailed study by Cosi, 2002.

[24]Cf. Hölkeskamp, 1987, 216; idem, 2000b, 231f., and now Lentano, 2005.

and ideas were not only beyond dispute, but indeed internalized on both the individual and collective levels.

Another peculiarity of this system of values is that the individual concepts of value always imply (directly or indirectly, explicitly or tacitly) that virtually all forms of 'partnership' and reciprocity are based on some degree of inequality—in more precise terms, that they are invariably affected by a more or less marked disparity in power and in the concomitant respective ability of the 'partners' involved to 'honor' obligations by fulfilling duties and claims. This in turn creates a hierarchical distance between the strong and the weak, superior and inferior, those giving and those receiving orders—a point that goes far beyond terms like *imperium*, *honos*, *dignitas*, and *auctoritas*, which explicitly signal hierarchical differences in political power, social standing, and influence.[25] Using the terminology of the modern theoretical debate mentioned above, one might then say that the omnipresent asymmetry of social relationships is inherent (or 'inscribed') in the discourse about their reciprocity.

These terms, which one might also call 'cognitive concepts' designed to construct and affirm (social, ethical, et cetera) 'meaning' in this society,[26] not only dominate the language or 'rhetoric' (in every sense of the word) of politics, of argument in the Senate, and agitation in the Forum Romanum, as well as of legal dispute, as we can see from sources such as Cicero's speeches.[27] The corresponding terminology also permeates all other forms and levels of social, religious, and literary discourse (at least as far as it can be reconstructed), ranging from catch-phrases, formulae, and metaphors to trite phrases, hackneyed sayings, and empty clichés. It is this omnipresence that seems to legitimate a sophisticated strategy of penetrating the fundamental levels of the Roman 'collective mentality'—namely, by interpreting these terms as the intersection or 'interface' between the surface of political rhetoric and explicit ideology, on the one hand, and those deeper structures and layers, on the other, that contain the values, indisputable and unquestionable convictions, 'cognitive concepts,' and prejudices that make up what Meier once called "collective morality." Recent research has been trying to apply this approach in order to describe this special consensus in as differentiated a manner as possible and to examine the specific degree or depth of its being inscribed in society, which was an aim of Meier's original 'theory of formation of

---

[25]Cf. on these concepts Awerbruch, 1981; Richardson, 1991, and now idem, 2008. Cf. on individual concepts also Lind, 1979, 22ff., 29ff., 38ff.; Pöschl, 1989; Rilinger, 1991, 81ff.; Hölkeskamp, 2000b, 232ff.; Pignatelli, 2008, 21ff., 29ff., 83ff., etc.

[26]Cf. Rüsen and Hölkeskamp, 2003, 1ff.

[27]In fact, these are the texts that Millar uses for his reconstruction of the Republic's political culture. He chooses, however, systematically to ignore the conceptual historical approach and the results that were mentioned above. Cf. Hölkeskamp, 1995, 38ff.

political groupings,' mentioned above, and which conceptualized it as the "collective morality" of a "monistic society." This seems to be the general direction that, for example, recent research on *mos maiorum* is moving in, at least so far as the conceptualization and concrete content, terms, and other forms of this complex mass of values and rules are concerned.[28]

However, the extraordinarily pronounced and extensive degree of effectiveness and binding force of the aforementioned collective morality is not explained by this concept of 'monism' as such. Neither the universal acceptance and indisputable validity of these moral concepts, nor their concrete conversion into a code of behavior, and corresponding practical sociopolitical applications, can simply be taken for granted. Above all, it is the peculiar 'degree of obedience' of the *populus Romanus* and, to put it in Egon Flaig's terms, its unusual "depth" or profundity of obedience,[29] that ought not be presupposed or taken as given—be it with a certain amount of amazement or, as indicated above, with a conservative nostalgic awe. This central feature of Roman culture and society has to be acknowledged as a significant problem that needs to be tackled by any worthwhile social and cultural historical analysis of the Roman republic.

[28]Cf. for details and bibliography chapter 2, at nn. 20ff., as well as Lind, 1979, 48ff., and recently Blösel, 2000, 25ff.; Haltenhoff, 2005, 101ff.; Keller, 2005.

[29]Flaig, 1993a, 194; idem, 1994, 20ff.; idem, 1995a, 105, and recently idem, 2003b, 13ff.; Goltz, 2000, 243f.

Chapter 5

FROM 'CONCEPTS' TO 'POLITICAL CULTURE'
THE BENEFITS OF THEORY

IF WE ARE TO put these new approaches to good 'practical'—that is, histori(ographi)cal—use in the future, we need to integrate the detailed deciphering of the collective moral 'code,' as well as the 'theory of formation of political groupings,' expounded above,[1] into a more comprehensive description of the political culture of the Roman republic as a complex multidimensional system.[2] One might even formulate the ambitious ultimate aim of this project in the classic Geertzian terms: we have to learn how to read this 'culture' of the *populus Romanus* and (not only) its ruling class as "an ensemble of texts, themselves ensembles," which are inseparably interconnected by referring to, and affirming, each other or inescapably "suspended in webs of significance" and "an historically transmitted pattern of meanings embodied in symbols, a system of inherited conceptions expressed in symbolic forms by means of which men communicate, perpetuate, and develop their knowledge about and attitudes toward life."[3] Obviously, therefore, our attention is no longer focused on actual politics, such as the decisions and actions of magistrates,

---

[1] Cf. chapter 3, above.

[2] Cf. on 'political culture' as a concept (originally borrowed from political science—cf. now Fuchs, 2007, with references) and a central topic in modern research, as well as its meaning, 'career,' and present status in modern history and historiography, Rohe, 1990; Lipp, 1996; Schwelling, 2001; Pedersen, 2002, 42, 56; Mergel, 2002 and 2004 (especially on the impact of the 'cultural turn' on modern concepts of 'politics,' 'policy,' and also 'political history'); Landwehr, 2003; Frevert, 2005, and already eadem, in Eibach et al. (Eds.), 2002, 152–64; Schlögl, 2005, 115ff. and idem, 2008; Blänkner, 2005, 71ff., and now the survey by Schorn-Schütte, 2006, 85ff.; cf. also for the application of concepts, etc., to pre- and early modern societies and polities Freist, 2005; Stollberg-Rilinger, 2005; Hölkeskamp, 2009a, all with further references. The aim must be an integrative open approach, which does not create a new opposition between the history of 'structure' and the history of 'events' (see chapter 9, below)—as Bleckmann, 2002, 16 (with footnote 1) seems to imply. On the contrary, it is necessary to overcome the conventional compartmentalization of analytical levels, approaches, and aims. Bleckmann himself overlooked this in his introductory account of the current development: "The thematic examination of single aspects, such as the *clientelae*, the senatorial self-representation, the importance of wealth *or* (!) 'political culture,' must be flanked by descriptions of specific stages in the development of this leading aristocratic class (the *nobilitas*)." (idem, 2002, 9 [my italics, K.-J. H.]).

[3] Geertz, 1973, 452, 5 and 89, respectively (quotations).

commanders, and the Senate, or speculations on alleged policies, trends, and tendencies within the political class; nor can we just look at the social framework and/or the 'subsystem' of the political institutions and formal procedures of decision making in an isolated way. What becomes the center of our interest now is not easy to characterize—it is the question that was only implicitly raised (and not directly addressed, let alone positively answered) by the by now well-known 'theory of formation of political groupings': what was *not* (and could not be) politically addressed, explicitly debated, and put on the agenda of decision making? Is there anything—and if yes, what—that remains implicit in the discourse of politics, but must nevertheless be considered a fundamental part of the system (and its basis of legitimacy)? Does this apply, for example, to the collective mental 'horizon' of Romans and their lost world of concepts, 'meanings,' and ingrained views? We are talking not merely of a system of moral concepts and their corresponding terms, or of a number of generally accepted convictions about the conventions and customs of a political order, but also of an entire range of images of reality, a system of 'making sense' of: that is, perceiving, interpreting, and evaluating one's immediate environment, as well as the world at large—what one might call in a different context 'nomological knowledge.' Such knowledge has a normative or 'prescriptive' side, comprising attitudes to, expectations and standards of, right (and wrong) behavior in a given situation. At the same time, it is also necessarily, and indeed by definition, related to 'real life,' providing practical or applied knowledge, patterns or 'templates,' remedies, concepts, and even clichés for perceiving and processing reality and dealing with everyday problems.[4] This deeply rooted knowledge is pre-theoretical and unreflected, and that makes it very hard to grasp, describe, and assess for badly documented periods.

The important point of departure for our further enquiries is that this level of collective ethical and cognitive disposition always, in every society and political culture, strongly influences, determines, or even controls the public view of politics, policies, and 'politicizability' of topics (and its limits, which can be expected to vary considerably in different cultures and therefore needs to be looked at). What we have called 'nomological knowledge' of a given society also invariably conditions the socially accepted general requirements for obtaining and holding positions of political leadership and power and the rules of recruiting the acceptable actual holders of these positions, as well as the hopes and expectations that the society at large places in these figures, in their abilities and potentialities, individually as well as collectively: that is, in their class as a whole, its rôle and functions. Moreover, it is a kind (or part) of 'nomo-

[4]Cf. Hölkeskamp, 2002, 132ff., 139; idem, 2003, 89f., with further references.

logical knowledge' that determined the fulfilment of such expectations by political leaders, the usual rôles and patterns of behavior, the (re-)construction of their public 'personae,' their individual and collective self-image and self-understanding, as well as the means and media of presenting and profiling themselves: that is, it applies to the complex 'dramaturgy' of political action and public appearance in general. It thus affects all media, forms, and levels of social interaction and communication, once again individually as well as collectively, inside the political class itself: between *nobiles*, 'ordinary' senators, patrons, as well as between this class and the 'man in the Roman street,' the *populus Romanus* or the *plebs* at large.[5]

As we have seen, to put it in yet another way, a 'political culture' has by definition more than just one side: There is the 'technical' or rational side of politics, as it were, its 'surface,' concrete agenda, explicit content and matter—and there is an 'expressive,' 'ceremonial,' and a corresponding cognitive side: it has symbolic, affective, and aesthetic dimensions that together underwrite, permanently reproduce, and renew the legitimacy of the political system on the 'surface' and ensure its acceptance by assuring its 'meaning' and sense.[6] It also confirms affiliations, generates compliance, grounds, and maintains a collective identity of a group—and this is a fundamental function of political culture, understood as a 'language of legitimation.' This language comprises, on the one hand, "a *vocabulary* of images, metaphors, rituals, assumptions, and performances" through which "political negotiations are conducted," as well as, on the other hand, "a *grammar*, a set of conventions, governing the appropriate use of this vocabulary,"[7] a definition that seems to tie in quite nicely with Christian Meier's concept of a 'grammar' of Roman Republican politics.[8] In this sense, political culture "constitutes the discursive environment in which power is legitimated";[9] furthermore, this 'language' is instrumental not only in *representing* power, but also in stabilizing and even *generating* it.[10] That is why a broad range of symbolic forms of communication has always to be part of it, too, regardless of culture, period, and

---

[5]Cf. O'Neill, 2003, on what he describes as a "widespread popular culture of discussion, deeply embedded in a popular culture and everyday life" (162 and 163).

[6]Cf. Rüsen and Hölkeskamp, 2003, on the German "*Sinn*" and "*Sinnkonzept*" (which denote 'meaning' rather than 'sense' and its conceptualization) as a category in Cultural Studies. Martin, 1997, should also be mentioned in this context because of his interesting anthropological and comparative reflections. Also see Flaig, 2003b, 9ff.

[7]Braddick, 2005, 69 (quotations—my italics, K.-J. H.); cf. Muir, 2004, 231ff. and passim.

[8]Cf. chapter 2, at n. 13.

[9]Braddick, 2005, 69.

[10]Stollberg-Rilinger, 2001b, 12ff., and eadem, 2005, 13ff.; cf. Muir, 2004, 245, cf. 226 and passim; Freist, 2005, 26ff.; Goppold, 2007, 22ff.

society:[11] performances, games, and other variants of theatrical spectacles, festivals, and ceremonies, such as processions and other civic rituals of all kinds—which in this context, to be sure, also include genuinely 'political' forms and formal procedures of decision making. It has long been acknowledged that symbolic and ceremonial (or "expressive") functions and forms of rituals, on the one hand, and the "technical" (or "instrumental") functions of open-ended procedures, on the other, that aim at decision making and/or formal enactment of decisions, cannot be compartmentalized in specific types of ('rational') procedures (versus 'ceremony,' 'ritual,' or even 'performance'). Nor can these alleged types be neatly assigned to particular stages of historical development, let alone to a unilinear process of 'rationalization': it is by no means only and alone in pre-modern cultures that, on the one hand, genuine 'political' processes and apparently 'rational' procedures also have symbolic, ceremonial, and ritual dimensions and that, on the other hand, pageantry, ceremonies, rituals, and a whole range of other public performances and 'performative' practices are more important and play a kind of special rôle *sui generis* in the "language of legitimation" that makes up the complex 'dramaturgy' of politics and power.[12] Both are also true in modern societies and political cultures, in an illimitable variety of complementary or mixed forms.

In different ways and on different levels, procedures, ceremonies, and civic rituals all serve the regular reproduction and affirmation of the "indigenous civic identity and ideology," as Edward Muir calls it, an identity based on a broad consensus about social norms and values.[13] Such rituals

[11]Cf. on the concept of 'symbolic communication' Althoff, 1999; Stollberg-Rilinger, 2000 and 2004; Schlögl, 2005 and 2008; Schorn-Schütte, 2006, 104ff., and Krischer, 2006, 21ff. Cf. also Hunt, 1984, 19ff., 52ff. and passim, on the specific "rhetoric of revolution" and "symbolic forms of political practice" developed during the French Revolution.

[12]Cf. the inspiring survey by Stollberg-Rilinger, 2001b (who has coined the terms quoted: "*symbolisch-zeremonielle*" / "*-expressive*" and "*technisch-instrumentelle Funktionen*" of procedures of decision making in pre-modern societies); see Sikora, 2001, on the explanatory potential that lies in conceptualization of procedure(s) from the point of view of systems theory. Cf. also Stollberg-Rilinger, 2000; 2004; 2005, and now, in book-length, eadem, 2008; Hölkeskamp, 2006d, 363f. with further references, to which add Schlögl, 2004, 34ff., and idem, 2008, 191ff.; Krischer, 2006, 17ff.; Weller, 2006, 14ff. Goppold, 2007, 30ff; Rexroth 2009, 75ff. See on processions as 'civic rituals' Löther, 1999, 6ff., 330ff. Cf. on the category of 'performance,' 'performative practices,' et cetera (and on the 'performative turn' in Cultural Studies generally) Martschukat et al., 2003; Fischer-Lichte, 2003, and Bachmann-Medick, 2006, 104ff.

[13]Muir, 1981, 5 and passim on this concept; cf. Trexler, 1973 and 1994 (with the discussion of his approach by Schwerhoff, 1994, and Löther, 1999, 8ff.), as well as generally Edelman, 1964; Dittmer, 1977; Muir, 1997, 1ff., 229ff. and passim, with extensive bibliographies with commentary. Cf. also the introductions of Wilentz (Ed.), 1985, and Cannadine et al. (Eds.), 1992, as well as Bergmann et al., 1999a, and Visceglia, 2002, 177, all with

make these abstract values and the 'civic identity' as such visible and, in a way, tangible by 'staging' and putting them on 'public' display (in the full sense of the term) and thereby confirm and renew their validity and the universal consensus.[14] At the same time, according to Muir, the repertoire of rituals and ceremonies provides a "medium of discourse"—or, to put it in other words, an important part of the 'vocabulary' of any language of symbolic communication—between the participating classes or social groups.[15] This is especially true of a political culture such as the Roman that has been appropriately named a "civilisation of spectacles."[16] In the specific sense of the concepts 'spectacle,' 'ritual,' and 'ceremony' underlying this reconstruction of a political culture, the whole gamut of ritualized interaction—social gestures and 'performative' practices, postures, and manners, the range of forums and modes of communication between high and low, senators and citizens, patrons and clients, magistrates and assemblies, commanders and soldiers, tribunes and *plebs*—is part and parcel of the same field of social action.[17]

One of the most complex and interesting civic rituals is the truly 'spectacular' *pompa triumphalis*,[18] the procession in which a consul or other holder of *imperium* as victorious commander-in-chief returns to the city

---

further references; cf. also the other contributions in Bergmann/Kondoleon (Eds.), 1999b. Nippel, 1988, 315ff. expresses some doubts about the significance of these categories of 'symbolic anthropology.'

[14]The fundamental importance of a 'consensus'—if only in the shape of a "fiction" or "façade"—is also emphasized by Stollberg-Rilinger, 2001b, 22f.; eadem, 2004, 519f.; eadem, 2005, 20. Cf. also Löther, 1999, 333ff. on the "integrative function" of civic rituals.

[15]Muir, 1981, 5. Cf. Cannadine/Price (Eds.), 1992; Althoff, 1997, 229ff. and passim; idem, 1999, and 2003; Stollberg-Rilinger, 2000; 2004; and 2005, all with further bibliography; Casini, 1996, 109ff. and passim, and recently the contributions in Howe (Ed.), 2007, and Stollberg-Rilinger et al. (Eds.), 2008. Cf. the classic works on festivals as an integral part of the political culture of revolutionary France: Ozouf, 1976, and also Hunt, 1984.

[16]Cf. on this concept Dupont, 1985, 19ff. Cf. also Parker, 1999, 163ff.; Feldherr, 1998, 10ff.; Beacham, 1999; Flower, 2004a; Bell, 2004; Sumi, 2005; Benoist, 2005; Hervé Inglebert, in idem (Ed.), 2005, 397ff.; Linke, 2006.

[17]Cf., e.g., Hopkins, 1991, 484ff., 492ff.; David, 1980 and 1992; Flaig, 1993a; 1995a; idem, 1998, 49ff.; idem, 2003b, passim; Purcell, 1994, 680ff.; Hölkeskamp, 1995; 2006c; 2006 (2007); 2008; Bell, 1997 and 2004; Laser, 1997, 31ff., 89ff.; Gruen, 1996, 220ff.; Jehne, 2000b, 207ff.

[18]Cf. the fundamental study by Itgenshorst, 2005 (and eadem, 2006, on the controversial question of "Hellenization"); Hölscher, 2001, 194ff.; Hölkeskamp, 2001a, 108ff.; 2006a; 2006c, 339ff.; 2006 (2007) and idem, 2008, 97ff. and passim with further references; Sumi, 2005, 29ff.; Bastien, 2007. The most recent discussions of the character (and value) of the *Fasti Triumphales* are Itgenshorst, 2004, and Bastien, 2007, 41ff. Important earlier descriptions and

at the head of his army and moves through all the central public areas of
the rich politico-sacral topography of the *urbs Roma*: from the Campus
Martius with the *circus Flaminius* through the *porta triumphalis* on the
old sacral boundary of the city to the Forum Boarium and through the
Circus Maximus, round the Palatine to the beginning of the *Sacra Via*,
through the Forum Romanum and finally up to the Capitol and the monumental temple of Jupiter Optimus Maximus.[19]

This time-honored traditional procession,[20] with its lavish deployment
of symbolic elements such as the commander's robe, the display of the
booty, prominent prisoners in person and/or *in effigie*, the soldiers march-
ing in columns, praising their *imperator* and mocking him, is a complex
web of signs and messages. Its significance is by no means confined to the
representation of a single military success somewhere on (or rather beyond) the frontiers of the *Imperium Romanum*. The ritual of the *trium-
phus* is truly itself 'an ensemble of texts' about Rome and its empire, its
past and present, the myth and history, as well as about the underlying
Roman notions of power and glory. It is also a 'medium of discourse' (in
the sense of the concept mentioned above) about the complex and sensitive
relation between a consul and commander, his peers in the political class
and rivals in the Senate, and the thousands of ordinary Romans also involved in the ritual in a variety of rôles: as 'civic' spectators being both
'scenery' and the addressees of the message of power and glory; as legionaries being part, and indeed 'co-actors,' of the procession; and as members
of a citizen body that in assembly had elected the victorious consul and was
going to elect future consuls as commanders and potential *triumphatores*.
Or, to describe this central civic rôle and its specific coalescence of facets as
a post-modern kind of pun on a famous dictum attributed to William
Shakespeare: if, as in this "spectacle," legionaries and citizens were "*actors*
and *spectators*, too"—they should be characterized as '*(spect)a(c)tors*.'[21]

interpretations include Nicolet, 1980, 352ff.; Marshall, 1984, 123ff.; Rüpke, 1990, 223ff.;
Favro, 1994, 151ff.; Brilliant, 1999; Holliday, 2002, 22ff. An innovative contribution to
the discussion about the highly complex and ambivalent character of the ritual is—in spite
of his somewhat extravagant conclusions—Flaig, 2003a; idem, 2003b, 32ff. This is also
true of Beard, 2007 (cf. the review by K.-J. Hölkeskamp in *Gnomon*, forthcoming). Interesting material for comparisons across cultures and epochs (with extensive bibliography) is
provided by Wisch/Munshower (Eds.), 1990; Wilentz (Ed.), 1985; Casini, 1996, 185ff.;
Visceglia, 2002, 53ff., 191ff. and passim.

[19]Cf. on the triumphal route especially Favro, 1999, 205ff.; Bastien, 2000; Hölscher,
2001, 194ff.; Benoist, 2005, 245ff.; Hölkeskamp (2006) 2007, 62ff., and idem, 2008,
101ff.; Martini, 2008; Pittenger, 2008; and Schipporeit, 2008.

[20]The origins of this ritual are still highly controversial: cf. recently Rüpke, 2006, and the
severely critical response by Versnel, 2006, both with further references; Bastien, 2007, 121ff.

[21]"Little, or much, of what we see, we do/We're all both *actors* and *spectators* too":
quoted after Ernest Schanzer, "Hercules and his Load." In *The Review of English Studies*
19, 1968, 51–53 (quotation: 51).

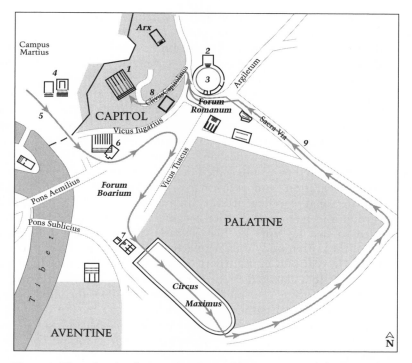

Figure 1. The urban landscape of mid-Republican Rome and the route of the triumph (1: Temple of Iuppiter Optimus Maximus; 2: *Curia*; 3: *Comitium*; 4: Temple of Bellona, Goddess of war; 5: *circus Flaminius*; 6: Temple of Fortuna and Mater Matuta – possibly location of the *porta triumphalis*; 7: shrines of Hercules; 8: *fornix Scipionis*: arch of P. Cornelius Scipio; 9: *fornix Fabianus*: arch of the Fabii, both monuments on the triumphal route) (Hölkeskamp, 2006a, 262: fig. 29, © C.H. Beck oHG, Munich [graphic: Cartomedia]).

At the same time, for all its rich and meaningful complexity, the *pompa triumphalis* was also just one text in a Geertzian 'ensemble' in which the range of other *pompae* constituted texts in their own right: There were ritual processions during games at the Circus Maximus (*pompa circensis*) or as parts of numerous religious festivals,[22] and there was the similarly spectacular *pompa funebris*, the symbolic meanings and messages of which were equally rich and complex and deserve a more detailed analysis in a later context.[23] But these 'spectacles' were by no means the only

---

[22]Cf. Wissowa, 1912, 449f., as well as the overview by Franz Bömer, "Pompa, B. Rom," in *RE* 21/2, 1952, 1974ff.; Scullard, 1981, provides a comprehensive calendar of the Roman festival year; Stambaugh, 1988, 221ff.; Bernstein, 1998; Beacham, 1999; Fless, 2004; Beck, 2005b, and recently Hölkeskamp, 2008.

[23]Cf. chapter 8, below.

important civic rituals—the many 'ordinary' religious ceremonies before acts of state, meetings of the Senate, and popular assemblies were always more than just routine business. They, together with the complicated rituals and rules of these assemblies themselves, were all symbolically meaningful aspects or 'texts' of an 'ensemble.'[24]

This set of rules governed every stage of assembly procedures—from the formal call to convene by the presiding magistrate to the following ritualized succession of steps of the voting or electing process to the equally formal magisterial acts of solemnly declaring the results and dismissing the assembly. The underlying discourse of this 'web' of significant acts was geared to an intensified demonstration and affirmation of affiliation, integration, and performative participation: The 'membership' and personal standing of every individual citizen in a particular status-group and territorial district became visible and palpable as he proceeded to cast his vote in 'his' *centuria* or *tribus*—the individual member of the citizen body thus regularly experienced personal participation, year in year out, in the affairs of the *populus Romanus*. In other words, to refer to a classic definition, Cicero's famous formula that the *res publica* was nothing else but the *res* of the *populus*—the latter being not just any accidental gathering of human beings, but an assembly based on *iuris consensus* and *utilitatis communio*—became somehow real.[25] At the same time, the abstract identity, character, and concrete functions of the different status groups as constituent entities of the *res publica* as a whole were put, as it were, on open show on these occasions: in the *comitia centuriata*, the hierarchical order of the *populus Romanus*, based on wealth and rank, was literally put on stage at regular intervals and in ritual forms, when the assembly was convened and ordered to proceed according to classes and *centuriae*. In the *comitia tributa* and the *concilia plebis*, it was the (formal) equality of all citizens inscribed in the corresponding *tribus*-lists that was ritually made visible. The different voting procedures in the various forms of popular assembly allowed these egalitarian structures to be directly experienced by the voting citizens: as opposed to the procedure in the *comitia centuriata*, there was no firm (hierarchical) order of voting in the assemblies based on the *tribus*, but a new one for every meeting, which was determined by yet another ritual—namely, by drawing lots. So vertical and horizontal, hierarchical and egalitarian structures of affiliation complemented and overlapped each other, thereby creating a very dense integrative network that incorporated every single Roman citizen, every social group and every 'order' and 'status,' as Martin Jehne has recently

[24]Cf. also Sumi, 2005, 16ff., and Hölscher, 2006, 37ff.
[25]Cicero, *De Republica* 1, 39.

shown.[26] This 'web' assigned all citizens, from senior senator to poor peasant, a specific place in the social grid and also supplied them with clearly defined relationships, not only with their peers in their respective group, but also with members of superior and inferior classes. Institutionalized integration and civic identity, social hierarchy and subordination stabilized and confirmed each other in this network.

The inventory of the symbolic or 'expressive' side of this political culture includes many other 'ensembles' of media and subsystems of signs that communicate and reproduce the basic values and orientations mentioned above and literally make the self-image and the collective identity of a political unit like the *libera res publica* visible: The increasingly dense and impressive urban 'text' made up of monuments of different kinds, temples and other public buildings, memorials, statues and images and their specific themes, topoi, meanings, and messages. As this 'text' was to be 'read' and its discourse understood not only by the Roman citizens living in the city, or coming there on the occasions mentioned above, but also by foreigners and visitors, friend and foe, it had to be, in the literal sense of the concept, publicly accessible and 'encoded' in an accepted and acceptable 'language.'[27]

The monumental urban 'text' included a substantial number of temples and shrines for deities that were in fact nothing but deified values (for example, *Concordia*, *Salus rei publicae*, *Libertas*, *Honos et Virtus*, *Fides*, and *Pietas*),[28] as well as a spate of memorial monuments for wars and victories, financed from booty, and paintings shown in triumphs and put up at temples, all of which were heavily laden with a (rather obvious) symbolism.[29] Moreover, the Forum Romanum, Capitol, and other central civic

[26]Jehne, 2001 and now generally idem, 2006, 17ff. Cf. Nicolet, 1980, 383ff.; Dupont, 1992, 287 and passim. Purcell, 1994, 645 introduced the term "registeredness" for this phenomenon: "a system of recording, docketing and assessing the precise place, in a hierarchy of means and status, of all citizens." Cf. David, 2000a, 22f.

[27]Hölscher, 1978, 315ff. provides the fundamental analysis of the subject. Cf. idem, 1980, 265ff.; 1984; 1990, 73ff.; 2001; 2003b and 2006. Cf. also Hölkeskamp, 1993, 26ff.; idem, 1996, 305ff., and idem, 2001a and 2006b, as well as the publications by Filippo Coarelli, which are now to be found in idem, 1996; Richardson, 1991, 390ff. and 392ff. ("The Impact of Empire"); Wallace-Hadrill, 1990; Gruen, 1992, 84ff., 131ff. and passim; idem, 1996, 217ff. and passim; Lahusen, 1999, 199ff., and most recently Holliday, 2002, passim (with the review by Hölkeskamp, 2005a); Mutschler, 2003, 376ff. Cf. on the view of the city's 'urbanity' and topography in Roman literature, see Edwards, 1996; Jaeger, 1997; Feldherr, 1998; Vasaly, 1993.

[28]Cf. Fears, 1981b, 827ff., and now Spannagel, 2000, 237ff.

[29]See Sehlmeyer, 1999; idem, 2000, 271ff.; Frischer, 1982–1983, 51ff.; Holliday, 2002, 80ff. and passim; Edwards, 2003a, 44ff.

spaces were replete with uncountable honorific statues with their formu-
laic inscriptions.[30] There were many other images of different sorts, invariably visualizing *exempla virtutis* in one way or another,[31] that were
also part of this 'inventory.' The numerous monuments for successes on
the battlefield were always also representations of the basic values revolving around *virtus* and 'honor' (in the double meaning of the Latin *honos/
honor*), which were taken to have been gloriously reaffirmed by such
truly memorable victories. Lastly, the very same values were also central
themes of the inscriptions in another, less public context; the well-known
inscriptions in the tomb of the Scipios on the Via Appia, which will interest us again in other contexts, invariably refer to the deceased person's
'exemplary' degree of *virtus, pietas, sapientia,* and *fortitudo.*[32]

An early and truly representative example of the forcefully suggestive,
and indeed unmistakable, 'language' of public monuments was erected
at a conspicuously prominent place, the Forum Romanum, in the immediate vicinity of Comitium and Rostra. It was to commemorate the
stunning victory over the Carthaginian fleet off Mylae in northern Sicily
in the first Punic war in 260 BC, at the same time honoring the consul
C. Duilius, who had commanded the victorious Roman fleet. Already the
very form of the monument—a *columna rostrata*, a column decorated
with the rams of warships—was an unmistakable, and indeed deliberately 'telling,' allusion to its underlying motivation. The inscription,
which was probably attached to the base of the column, recorded not
only the event itself, but also the number of enemy ships lost or captured,
and the amount of booty, in detail, and it did not fail to mention that the
victorious commander had been honored with a "naval triumph" (*trium-
phus navalis*)—incidentally, the very first of its kind.[33]

The particular Roman strategies of visualization and symbolic 'encoding' of values and standards of ideal behavior in a specific kind of imagery
can be observed in entirely different 'registers' of Roman culture: for example, in the down-to-earth medium that the man in the street had in every-

[30]Cf. Eck, 1999, 31ff.; Alföldy, 2001, 11ff. with more references; recent contributions
include Corbier, 1987, 27ff.; Robert, 1998, 73ff.; Witzmann, 2000, 55ff., and McDonnell,
2006b.

[31]Cf. Koortbojian, 2002, 33ff.

[32]*CIL* I2 2, 6ff. = VI 1284–1294 = *ILS* Nr. 1 ff. = *ILLRP* 309ff. Cf. Kruschwitz, 2002,
33f., 86f.; Coarelli, 1972, 36ff. (= idem, 1996, 179ff.); Flower, 1996, 160ff.; Pani, 1997,
44ff. See chapters 6 and 8, below.

[33]Pliny, *Naturalis historia* 34, 20; Quintilian, *Institutio oratoria* 1, 7, 12 and the evidence
in *Inscr.It.*, Vol. 13/1, 548. See Laura Chioffi, "Columna rostrata C. Duilii," in *LTUR* 1,
1993, 309; Sehlmeyer, 1999, 117ff.; Bleckmann, 2002, 116f. deals with the inscription
(*CIL* I² 25 = VI 1300 = *ILLRP* 319) in detail and concludes that "it is in fact only a—however, probably reliable—later copy of the 3rd-century *titulus* on the column of Duilius"
(125); cf. now Kondratieff, 2004. Cf. on his 'image' in the literary tradition Gendre et al.,
2001, 132 ff.

Figure 2. *Columna rostrata* with a statue of IMP(ERATOR) CAESAR (= Octavian), naked except for cloak over left shoulder, holding sword and spear, on a *denarius* (29–27 BC), commemorating a much later, but equally momentous naval victory (courtesy of Numismatik Lanz).

day use—namely, the coinage of the Republic and its telling imagery—as well as in the highly developed and increasingly sophisticated art of portrait.[34] These world(s) of images and messages, forms and substance, covert and overt meanings were everywhere and always entwined in complex ways. The new 'cultural history' mentioned above has made us more aware of the fact that central concepts—such as the 'typically Roman' concepts of value that have been touched on in several contexts—are generally not encoded just in the political and social language of a society, but also in all those socially and mentally 'inscribed' forms of manifestation or texts that enable a society or a social group to locate itself in, and at the same time to reproduce, its own 'web of significance' by cultivating traditions and collective identity and finding its own specific strategies of self-perception and self-reassurance.[35]

In the concrete case of Roman political culture, this fundamental insight, and the methodological approach based on it, is particularly suitable for unravelling the typical ambiguity of this multidimensional imagery, its meanings and messages. On the one hand, the 'ensembles' of visual 'texts' emphasize and confirm the general binding force of a collective morality and the validity of its key concepts for the people and their

[34] Cf. Hölscher, 1980; 1982 and 1984; Classen, 1986, 257ff. (= idem, 1993, 39ff.), and Giuliani, 1986, 197ff.; Flaig, 1993a, 208f.; Gruen, 1992, 152ff.; idem, 1996, 218ff.; Lahusen, 1999, 201ff., and Tanner, 2000.

[35] Cf. Kaschuba, 1995, 87. Cf. the references in chapter 4, nn. 14ff., above.

political class. It was on this fundament that Roman superiority, power, rule, and imperial grandeur was firmly based. This ideology or "theology of victory" was continuously, indeed patently, being confirmed by the successful military expansion of the Empire.[36] In turn, glorious victories on the battlefields and imperial expansion as a result—or rather, reward—were considered to be the best evidence that Rome and the Romans' rule were divinely sanctioned, morally justified, and historically legitimate. Obviously, it was this ideology that could best serve as the basis of the peculiar homogeneous identity of the entire *populus Romanus* and its 'monistic society,' comprising all Roman citizens.

At the same time, however, the political class claimed that the imperial glory of the *urbs Roma* and the extent of her empire were due solely to the political class: its qualities of leadership in war, proven in many battles; its wisdom and discipline in peace; and its superior *virtus* and unparalleled *sapientia*. It was therefore self-evident that the Roman position in the world could only be preserved and improved by maintaining this leadership. This self-confident and 'natural' claim to leadership corresponded to the structural asymmetry of all social relationships in Rome herself, which was institutionalized in the form of what Meier calls the remarkable "preservation of the oligarchic element."[37] The pervasive hierarchical difference between senators and citizens, magistrates and assemblies, the holders of *imperium auspiciaque* and the soldiers in the legions, was itself an essential part of the collective identity of the *populus Romanus*. The ritual of the triumph mentioned above—for all its ambiguity—invariably focused on a holder of *imperium* (in the sense of 'power of command'), putting the sociopolitical hierarchies between all active and passive participants, actors, 'co-actors,' and '(spect)a(c)tors' on the stage of the *urbs*, as well as, at the same time, making them appear as a *conditio sine qua non* for 'imperial' glory and grandeur.[38]

The strict hierarchical order of command and obedience, of authority and reverence, of superiority and acceptance can also be traced in the awe-inspiring religious aura that surrounded symbols of power, like the official attire, the *sella curulis*, the lictors and *fasces*,[39] which higher magistrates and commanders assumed in public, in the city, or in the field. This order was likewise conveyed by the lordly, and often domineering, behavior that holders of *imperium* regularly displayed in public—frequently as a demonstration of unfettered power, and by no means only

---

[36]Cf. Fears, 1981a; Valvo, 2005, 76ff. and passim, and now Richardson, 2008.

[37]Meier, 1966/1980, 48. This aspect is systematically ignored by Millar.

[38]Cf. now Hölscher, 2006, 34ff.

[39]Cf. Gladigow, 1972, 295–314; Kolb, 1977; Marshall, 1984; Schäfer, 1989; Goltz, 2000, 240f. with additional evidence; and Scholz, 2005.

when they were discharging their official duties.[40] After all, the monuments, impressive buildings, and honorific statues on their bases were
also 'manifestations' or 'visualizations' of superiority based on merit and
achievement in positions of power. The monuments indirectly, but unmis-
takably, served to affirm those very hierarchies that the collective claim of
the ruling class to authority, *dignitas*, and 'noble' rank required and that
had to be permanently renewed at the same time. The monuments in
stone—not only the honorific ones, such as statues, arches, and extravagant tombs, but also the temples and public buildings founded by consuls
and commanders and financed from booty—played an especially decisive
part in this culture: that is, the "intense monumentalization of the Republican city," which had already begun at the turn of the fourth century
and ended with truly 'monumental' projects like the *Forum Iulium*, produced "a kind of city in the sky," as Ann Kuttner has aptly characterized
the resulting urban 'ensemble,' in which the whole spectrum of monuments literally and visually "gave high place to the highly placed."[41] And
Géza Alföldy has pointed out that the function of such monuments
(which the civic rituals could not fulfil) was to "*permanently* validate the
differences in rank, stimulate future generations to maintain these rules
and manners and thereby cement this social hierarchy *for the future*." As
Werner Eck put it, the primary objective of individual members of the
élite was of course to "stabilize their own position and thereby escape
death and oblivion—*and also equality*." That is precisely why members
of the Roman ruling class were extremely interested in, and indeed preoc-
cupied with, "creating *memoria*."[42] This function of monuments and
'monumentalization' as a kind of cultural practice must have been of
great importance in a society that lived on, and in, the glorious history of
the *populus Romanus* and its empire, and was imbued with the belief in
an open-ended future of continued grandeur and dominance. I shall come
back to this characteristic in due course.

Since the 1980s, these aspects of the 'expressive' side of Republican
political culture have been the subject of an intensive, and by no means
finished, debate, which was initiated from two different directions—originally independently of each other, and later on in a kind of fruitful dialogue. On the one hand, the theoretical impulse, the methods, and the interpretation of the relevant literary and monumental evidence were initially

[40]Cf. Hölkeskamp, forthcoming b, with references.
[41]Kuttner, 2004, 320, 318, cf. 312, 318ff. passim; cf. also Hölscher, 2006, and (for the
'imperial city') Hope, 2000a.
[42]Alföldy, 2001, 38, and Eck, 1999, 31 (my italics, K.-J. H.). Cf. also Flower, 2006a,
51ff., who demonstrates in detail that "oblivion" and "disgrace" in the shape of various
"(punitive) memory sanctions" were particularly damaging for social standing and symbolic capital in this culture.

supplied by Tonio Hölscher, Paul Zanker, and their new 'schools' of Classical Archaeology, which have succeeded in teaching historians to understand the forms and genres of 'representative' or 'state' art, its multiple media and themes—in Zanker's famous phrase, the peculiar "power of images"[43]—as constituent parts of the imperial plot. We now understand better how to interpret this 'language' as a semantic system (or, once again, a Geertzian "ensemble of texts, themselves ensembles") generated by specific social and cultural contexts.[44]

On the other hand, in the course of the lively general discussion on the closely related concepts of 'collective,' 'social,' or 'cultural memory' and their significance for the understanding of (pre-)modern mentalities, which was mainly initiated by Jan and Aleida Assmann,[45] the problem of contents, themes, and functions of *memoria* in the culture of the Middle and Late Roman republic appeared in a new light. The creation of a specific, and perhaps in many ways even unique, collective identity and of a broad moral and ideological consensus by means of a wide range of 'texts' (again in the Geertzian sense), forms, and media can be precisely and compehensively described by using this new conceptual framework.[46] This 'ensemble' can now be read and explained as a complex cultural strategy that served to (re-)construct the glorious past of the *populus Romanus* (and its leadership) as a series, or continuous and consistent sequence, of preliminary stages and historically necessary steps toward the imperial grandeur of the present. The remarkable omnipresence of the multidimensional, and often quite ambiguous, *exempla maiorum*— which were designed to 'exemplify' (in a specific sense of the word) and

[43]Zanker, 1987 (and the reviews by Géza Alföldy, in *Gnomon* 61, 1989, 407–18; Wallace-Hadrill, 1989c); cf. Deniaux (Ed.), 2000, and Hölkeskamp, 2005a. Cf. Bergmann, 2000, on the general concept and the visual media of 'representation.'

[44]Cf. Hölscher, 1992; (1987) 2004; cf. the summaries of this development by Zanker, 1994, and Hölscher, 1995, 197ff., as well as their recent contributions to Borbein et al. (Eds.), 2000; Smith, 2002, 59ff. Cf. on the concrete field of Roman (Republican) 'representative art' Hölscher, 1978; 1980; 1982; 1990; 2001; 2003b and 2006; Hölkeskamp, 1987, 232ff.; idem, 1996, 305ff.; idem, 2001a and 2005a. Cf. now the interesting suggestions by Emich, 2008, on the impact of the 'visual' or 'iconic' turn of history, the role and status of 'images,' and the concept of "intermediality" (denoting an interconnected web of visual and other media).

[45]Assmann/Hölscher (Eds.), 1988; Assmann, 1992; idem, 2000, 11ff. Cf. also the relevant contributions in Wischermann (Ed.), 1996, and Burke, 1997, and idem, 2004, 65ff. Cf. the considerations in Hölkeskamp, 1996, 301ff.; 2001a, 98ff.; Fried, 2001, 561ff., and the responses by Aleida and Jan Assmann to their critics in *EWE* 13, 2002, no 2.

[46]Cf. Hölkeskamp, 2005a (on Holliday, 2002), with further references; idem, 2006b, and especially Walter, 2004a. Cf. also Gowing, 2005, 1ff.; Beck, 2008a, 111ff. Cf. also the interesting suggestions by Krasser, 2006, 9ff. on Cicero's "construction of consensual models" in the face of disintegration.

affirm values, 'rôle models,' ideal standards, expectations, and patterns of desirable behavior in an intricate web-like (sub)text—can now also be fitted into the wider (con)text of the Republican political culture.[47]

This extraordinarily dense 'ensemble' of abstract values and ideology, rules and codes of behavior, cultural practices and civic rituals, images, messages, and meanings could only unfold and develop to the full in a specific context, which one might call 'city-statehood.' Of course, a great deal of innovative, especially comparative, work has been done on (pre-modern) European as well as Near Eastern, American, and Asian 'city-state' cultures since the 1970s, and the international debate on the components of these rather artificial and even clumsy terms—'city,' 'state,' 'city-state'— as concepts and categories of description and analysis in modern research, as well as on the archaic and classical Greek *polis* as a sort of backdrop or ideal type, is by no means finished.[48]

The particular 'city-state' variant of 'statehood' cannot be adequately defined in terms of the basic but rather unspecific criteria that are considered to be constitutive of (early) 'states' in most historical, sociological, and anthropological theories. A catalogue of these criteria should include:

- a certain degree of centralization and institutionalization of de-personalized rule in the form of permanent administrative bodies or executive organs with differentiated functions and competences;
- a corresponding degree of formalized interaction between these 'institutions' (in a broad sense of the word, which needs further discussion [see below]) in the form of regular procedures for making, implementing, and enforcing binding decisions in general and for settling disputes between individuals and/or groups;

[47]Cf. Hölkeskamp, 1996; 2001a; 2005a; 2006b, and the fundamental studies by David, 1998, and Roller, 2004; cf. now also Morgan, 2007, 122ff., and Bücher, 2006 (on the uses and functions of *exempla Romana* in late Republican political discourse). On the term *exemplum* see Adolf Lumpe, in *RAC* 6, 1966, 1229ff. On the various 'texts,' levels, and dimensions of this 'memorial culture,' or rather 'culture centered on *memoria*,' see Mutschler, 2000; Stemmler, 2000, 141ff.; idem, 2001, 222ff.; Walter, 2001, 241ff.; idem, 2003, 255ff., and now the comprehensive analysis by idem, 2004a; Miles, 1995, 8f.; Chaplin, 2000, passim; Holliday, 2002, 13f. and passim; Blösel, 2003, 53f.; Beck, 2003a, 73ff.; Pina Polo, 2004; Krasser, 2005, as well as the case-studies by Flower, 2003, 39ff.; Flaig, 2003b, 69ff. Cf. on the 'invention' of exemplary 'grands hommes' Coudry et al. (Eds.), 2001.

[48]Cf. the general introductions and contributions in Griffeth et al. (Eds.), 1981, and Molho et al. (Eds.), 1991; Nichols et al. (Eds.), 1997; Hansen (Ed.), 2000, and idem (Ed.), 2002, and idem et al. (Eds.), 2004, with the review by K.-J. Hölkeskamp, in *BMCR* 2004.04.03; Hansen, 2006. Cf. also Burke, 1986.

- a certain degree of consolidation of such structures within a defined and delimited territory—although this last criterion is no longer undisputed.[49]

The main advantage of this broad, or 'minimalist,' definition is that it does not restrict 'state(-hood)' to autonomous and fully differentiated and institutionalized modern systems, and thus avoids opposing it to 'society.' In contrast with a 'maximalist' understanding of 'state,' it avoids a dualism of this type, which is not only a purely modern phenomenon as such, but could only be perceived and conceptualized as a contrast or bipolar opposition in modern political theory and philosophy. Nor is this definition laden with normative suppositions and metahistorical assumptions about 'state authority,' 'sovereignty,' and the Weberian "monopoly of the legitimate use of physical force," and it does not insist on such preconditions and/or on a fully fledged, monolithic 'centralization' and 'institutionalization' as absolutely indispensable for the existence of a 'state.'[50]

Furthermore, to come back to the related problem of the latter concept, this definition avoids a state-orientated and static understanding of the term 'institution.' On the basis of a less rigid concept of 'statehood,' one can define a (political) 'institution' more generally as a regulative system that serves to supply structures for the preparation, formulation, implementation, and enforcement of decisions that affect the whole society.[51] Such a regulative system or "ordering pattern" are normative structures that are stabilized by the 'regular' (in all the different meanings of the word) repetition of certain behavior, in the sense of acting with regard to, or re-acting in the same way to, similar problems and challenges by applying similar means and solutions. This leads to a 'solidification' of this behavior into internalized, predictable, and therefore reliable patterns. Only in a fully developed form does such a regulative system take the shape of an 'office' or magistracy, a 'council,' or an 'organization' in

[49]Cf. Runciman, 1982, 351ff.; Haas, 1982; Eder, 1990a, 17ff.; Martin, 1990, 220ff.; van der Vliet, 1990, 233ff., and Boldt et al., 1990, 5ff. However, the 'minimalist' definition proposed here is by no means undisputed: see Walter, 1998, and Feinman et al. (Eds.), 1998, on the current state of the discussion.

[50]See Walter, 1998, 9ff., with further references. Walter also mentions the origins of the 'maximalist' and 'anti-universalistic' conception (already discussed in Meier, 1996, 264)— for example, Carl Schmitt's concept of the "age of statehood" since the sixteenth century (15ff.). On the history and meaning(s) of the term 'state,' see already Julliard, 1974, 243ff. (on "l'État, cette «institution des institutions»"); Boldt et al., 1990; Koselleck, 2006, 64ff.

[51]Cf. Hölkeskamp, 2003a, 82ff. Cf. the fundamental discussions by Melville, 1992a; Acham, 1992, 33ff., as well as the contributions in Göhler (Ed.), 1994, and idem (Ed.), 1997; Blänkner, 2005, 89f.; Blänkner and Jussen, 1998a; Rehberg, 1998; Jehne, 2005, 155ff. Cf. especially on 'institution' as concept and analytical category in modern Cultural Studies Schimank, 2004, and on the characteristics of pre-modern institutions see Reinhard, 1999, 125ff.

the modern abstract sense of the concept—and this is by no means the final stage of a unilinear process at the end of which every 'primitive' institution is inevitably bound to turn into an organization.

In a general anthropological sense, institutions only have a certain life-span, which is a result of this 'solidification' or 'habitualization' of the kind of patterns of behavior mentioned above.[52] Institutions are therefore not to be perceived as stable and given over a long period of time, but rather as fluid stages in a process of 'institutionalization,' a concept that describes a process in time of a certain duration in which a regulative system achieves a minimum degree of stability for itself and at the same time generates a certain degree of social stability by supplying, as well as applying, accepted patterns of behavior and rules for cohabitation and appropriate behavior in a given society. With such a concept of 'institution,' it should become possible in the future adequately and comprehensively to describe the complex set of regulative rules encoded in the *mos maiorum*, their 'normativity' and resulting binding force.[53]

Let us return to a further general theoretical perspective. The (in a positive sense) 'minimalist' definitions of 'state(-hood)' and 'institution,' mapped out above, can certainly be applied to pre-modern sociopolitical formations of various kinds without any loss of conceptual clarity and precision. On the contrary, it is just because of their significantly fewer limitations and their openness that they can be integrated into a modern concept of political culture, which itself combines questions, approaches, methods, and models from Sociology, Social History, and Anthropology. To begin with, such a (similarly 'open') concept does not understand 'organizations' in the sense mentioned above—that is, as fully differentiated offices, administrative bodies, and highly formalized procedures—to be permanently valid, normative, and static 'orders': neither their durability, their internal and external stability, nor their status within a sociopolitical system, their conformation or configuration of functions, can be taken as given. This reservation, by the way, cannot be emphasized often and clearly enough, in view of the fact that abstract, systematic, even legalistic, and therefore necessarily static, conceptions of the so-called Roman 'constitution' are still going strong—for example, in the shape of Fergus Millar's presupposed "constitutional machinery." As 'institutions' are conceived as normative structures that have evolved out of a process of 'habitualization' as a result of a 'routinization' of recurrent behavior, they naturally have a 'history' of their own that we must explore and

---

[52]Cf. Berger and Luckmann, 1966, 65ff., 70ff. On the differentiation of the concepts 'institution' and 'organization,' see Rehberg, 1998, 390ff. Cf. on the problem of 'normativity' Willke, 1976.

[53]Cf. Linke and Stemmler, 2000a, and Bettini, 2000, 321ff. Cf. also Stewart, 1998, 1ff.

understand if we are to explain them adequately. Highly developed 'institutions' in particular are in fact the result of complex processes of 'institutionalization'—they carry and preserve the history of the process of their creation and development inside themselves.[54]

There is a further fundamental characteristic to be taken into account in this context: organs of state of the kind mentioned earlier, as well as all other types of institutions (and basically the state as such), can only survive and achieve the necessary minimum degree of stability over time if they are perceived as legitimate. This entails that they have to function as structures providing and guaranteeing order, guidance, and reliability so as to be accepted by the social group in which they evolve. Moreover, this acceptance as an indispensible prerequisite of their stabilization has to be ensured by the continuous demonstration and symbolic affirmation of their fundamental principles, values, and aims as meaningful and necessary.[55] That is why, in turn, these principles and values have to be in accord with, or even derived from, the orientations, codes of behavior, and values—that is, the 'nomological knowledge'—of the whole group in order to become and remain valid and binding. Finally, this interconnected fundament of institutional legitimacy is never self-evident or self-produced, but invariably needs some investment of active effort on the part of an 'institution' or, in concrete terms, the holders of 'institutionalized' rôles and functions.

As should be clear by now, this conception combines recent anthropological models of pre-modern 'statehood' with a set of new innovative approaches concerned with the theory, sociology, and history of institutions, on the one hand, and a modern 'culturalist' historical analysis of collective systems of values, views, and orientations, which I have mapped out above,[56] on the other. The analytical and explanatory potential of such a combination of perspectives, models, and methods has hardly been explored to the full yet—especially with regard to the complex issue of an extensive analysis of *mos maiorum* as 'nomological knowledge' and its status in the Republican political culture, also already mentioned above. This particular regulative system is after all a classic type of a meaningful 'symbolic order,' in so far as it combines normativity and an inherent claim to validity and stability, on the one hand, with a specific kind of 'legitimacy,' on the other, which is generated and reproduced by means of a whole range of media (or, yet again, an 'ensemble of texts') geared to the permanent discursive demonstration and affirmation of its main features and principles. Against such a background, more detailed

---

[54]Berger and Luckmann, 1966, 72; Melville, 1992a, 4f.; Flaig, 1998, 55ff. (whose criticism of Bleicken misses the point).

[55]Cf. Rehberg, 1998, 385ff.; Vorländer and Melville, 2002a, IX, XI and passim. For some concrete cases, see Flaig, 1998, 69ff.

[56]Cf. chapter 4, above.

work on the conceptual history and on the understanding of values and 'relational concepts' can possibly realize its full potential.

———————

The Republican variant of 'city-statehood' has some further specific characteristics—namely, the conditions under which the making of politics and acting on the political stage actually took place.[57] That is to say that in this case all institutions involved are not distant and invisible, but (not only metaphorically, but indeed physically) permanently 'present' and visible in the full sense of the word: magistrates, councils, and assemblies always confront each other 'face-to-face' and interact there with each other directly, again in the literal or 'physical' sense.[58] In other words, they meet, stand with regard to, and communicate in their various sociopolitical rôles in the public space. This concept once again is much more than a metaphor or merely a topographical place— namely, a truly 'civic space' or 'espace public' with concrete, 'visible,' social, political, as well as ritual and other symbolic functions.[59]

This is the main reason for the central importance of public or "mass" oratory that Millar (and many others) have rightly emphasized—the title of Robert Morstein-Marx's fundamental and brilliant study of oratory and "political power" is indeed programmatic.[60] This medium of communication was of primary importance for daily, practical interaction between institutions—or rather, very concretely, between individual persons as incumbents of magistracies or holders of other public functions or civic rôles, and as members of policy-deciding bodies such as councils and assemblies. One might even go yet another step further and assert that it was essentially this medium that permeated all these forms of

[57] From the point of view of theories, concepts, methods, and models, the particularly productive fields of (late) medieval and (early) modern history that focuses on the (mostly) 'Republican' city-states in Italy, on the one hand (cf. the classic works by Brucker, 1977; Martines, 1988; Trexler, 1994; Muir, 1981, and the relevant contributions in Molho et al. [Eds.], 1991; Najemy [Ed.], 2004, and Boucheron et al. [Eds.], 2005), and on cities as 'polities' and communities in Germany, on the other (e.g., the contributions in Schlögl [Ed.], 2004; Löther, 1999; Krischer, 2006; Weller, 2006; Goppold, 2007, all with ample bibliography), which seem to offer a broad range of new perspectives.

[58] I use the term 'face-to-face (society)' in a slightly different way from Finley (1973, 17; 1983, 28ff., 81ff.), who in turn had modified Peter Laslett's definition of it (outlined in idem, 1956): his concept addressed direct oral communication and interaction in very small social units alone. Cf. Goppold, 2007, 30f.

[59] Cf. especially Schlögl, 2005, 41, 50ff., and now idem 2008, 183ff., 190ff., on the one hand, and the brilliant book by Hölscher, 1998a, on the other. Cf. also Dupont, 1992, 162ff.

[60] Millar, 1998, 216ff., 224 and passim; idem, 2002a, 141f., 143ff., 178, 180ff. Cf. the general remarks by Vernant, 1982, 42ff.; Fuhrmann, 1983, 10f., 13, 23, and now Morstein-Marx, 2004, with further references.

interaction and made them possible in the first place—at least as long as these institutions, such as the Senate and the popular assemblies, as well as their many functions in the political process, from deliberation to decision as well as the whole spectrum of related and other politico-religious civic rituals, remained inseparably linked to, and indeed inscribed in, the *urbs Roma* and her particular topography. This means that institutions as well as their 'institutionalized' interactions, procedures, and rituals of collective importance were embedded in several different ways into a relatively small (at any rate, by the standards of modern states), but permanently 'present,' public audience, which was in turn itself 'institutionalized.'[61] In the first place, political action in general, as well as the actors on the political scene, their different formal or informal, but invariably public, rôles and their 'performance' in these rôles remained visible for, and could thus be immediately experienced by, all participants present— not only magistrates and senators, but also the mass of ordinary citizens. In the literal sense of the term, 'politics' took place in public, before the citizens as audience and as a public personally, and indeed physically, present in the 'forum' of a Mediterranean open-air-culture, the defining characteristic of which was, as it were, a specific immediacy of interaction (once again in the literal as well as metaphorical senses of these concepts):[62] in the Forum Romanum, the Comitium, the Capitol, and the Campus Martius.[63] Secondly, this 'public' or audience represented, and was indeed taken to be identical with, the *populus Romanus* and its *res*, the (city-)state itself—and by no means only in an abstract and detached ideological sense. Once again, the underlying idea regularly took tangible and visible shape in the large number of civic rituals and other public performances, which served constantly to reinforce this identity in public and literally under the eyes of the 'public.' Finally, this 'public' itself also regularly materialized in the form of an institution, when it assembled not only in the *comitia centuriata*, *comitia tributa*, and *concilia plebis* as formal decision-making bodies, but also and above all in the less formal and

[61] Cf. Hölkeskamp, 2003a, 81f., 85ff., with further references.

[62] Cf. Hölscher, 1998b, 14ff., and idem, 2003a, 163ff. (on his concept of a "culture of personal and physical presence," and indeed 'physicality'), on the one hand, and Schlögl, 2004, and idem, 2008, 168ff., 184ff. and passim (on "communication among personally present participants"), on the other. Cf. also now Stollberg-Rilinger, 2008, 299ff., and Schlögl, 2008a, on the concept of 'the public,' 'publicity,' and 'media' in modern Europe.

[63] The best surveys of these 'public spaces' in urbanized Rome are Stambaugh, 1988, 16ff. and passim; Kolb, 2002, and now Torelli, 2006; De Chaisemartin, 2006, and Patterson, 2006a. Cf. also Richardson, 1991; Hölkeskamp, 2001a; Dupont, 1992, 73ff., 162ff. etc., and above all Hölscher, 1978, 1998a, and 2001. The brilliant works by Filippo Coarelli remain indispensable: 1997 (on the Campus Martius); idem, 1986 and 1985 (on the *Forum Romanum*, including the *Comitium*, from the beginnings of 'urbanization' to the age of Augustus).

unstructured assemblies of the *contiones*.[64] This type of assembly was the institutional stage of public deliberation: agendas of all kinds were presented here, from everyday issues, decrees, or administrative dispositions to highly controversial bills, and from the routine reports sent in from consuls commanding armies abroad to spectacular decisions on momentous matters of foreign policy.[65] The full range of possible business on the political agenda (or, to use Meier's terminology once again, every topic that was at all 'politicizable') in this city-state and its empire could be addressed in *contiones*, since they prepared all formal decisions in public debate—or rather, in a special Roman kind of 'debate': after all, even the institution and procedures of the *contio* mirrored the omnipresent sociopolitical hierarchies.[66] Only a magistrate or a tribune of the *plebs* was entitled to call, preside over, and dismiss a *contio*; only he set the agenda to be presented to the people, and only he and the speakers named by him, virtually all of whom were themselves members of the 'magisterial' class, were allowed to take the floor (or, in this case, the platform of the *rostra*), and only they did all the speaking and debating from 'up there': that is, *de superiore loco*.[67] The symbolism implied in this term was by no means incidental—the asymmetry of the rôles of members of the political class as actors and 'addressors,' on the one hand, and of the citizens at large as audience and 'addressees,' on the other, remained inscribed in this institution.

However, this digression does not affect the main point. It is important to emphasize that a political culture of this kind, with its extraordinary degree of visibility and 'audibility,' 'publicity,' immediacy, and 'performativity,' requires a corresponding degree of 'spatial density': that is, a particular urban grid or topography of public space(s), which are specially delimited, marked off, and reserved for the different forms and media of interaction. This aspect of the symbolic or 'expressive' side of Republican political culture, which has actually become the main focus of a renewed interest in the specific 'urbanity' of the 'city-statehood' *alla Romana*,[68]

[64]Cf. Hölkeskamp, 1995, 16ff., 26ff. and passim; Pina Polo, 1996 and 2005, 141ff.; Bell, 1997, 1ff.; Laser, 1997, 138ff.; Fantham, 2000; Mouritsen, 2001, 38ff. and passim, and recently Flaig, 2003b, 193ff., and Morstein-Marx, 2004, 7ff., 34ff. and passim; Jehne, 2006, 19ff., and now Tan, 2008 (who emphasizes the character of late Republican *contiones* as major instruments of *popularis* strategy—in my opinion, in a rather one-sided way).

[65]Cf., e.g., Hölkeskamp, 1995, 32ff.; Connolly, 2007, 38, 43, 47ff.

[66]Cf. Pina Polo, 2005, 147ff. See also Deniaux, 2000, on the "image of the orator" in the Forum Romanum as "miroir topographique de la constitution romaine" (163).

[67]Hölscher, 1998a, and idem, 2001, 189ff.; Richardson, 1991, 390ff. and passim; David, 2000b; Hölkeskamp, 2001a, 122ff. and passim; more recently Edwards/Woolf, 2003b, take a somewhat expressionistic postmodern approach. Cf. on the concept of a "culture of immediate action" Hölscher, 1998b, 69ff.; idem, 2003, 164, 187ff.

consists in a close-knit web of complementary, interconnected, and, as it were, imbricated spaces and locations, 'urban' functions and purposes.[69] After all, the public areas of the city were not only the stages of political action, social interaction, and economic activity but served also as the fora (or rather, stages), as well as the scenery of spectacular *pompae*, countless religious ceremonies, and festivals: the *urbs Roma*—with its temples, altars, and procession routes—was also a 'sacral' and 'ritual landscape.'

As a matter of course, the (in fact, less than) 'private' representative urban residences of the great families had a conspicuous place and a variety of demonstrative functions in this 'text' and its 'web of meanings.' As a particular privilege, *triumphatores* acquired the right to have weapons and other spoils taken from the vanquished enemy, over whom they had triumphed, fastened at the door, or displayed in the entrance area, of his and his family's houses. Interestingly, these symbolic markers were never to be removed—according to the elder Pliny, even if the house changed hands and was sold to an "unwarlike master," who had no right to sport such spoils. In that case, it was the houses themselves that continued to celebrate triumphs for all eternity.[70] At least occasionally, this claim to an indefinite boundlessness of a triumphal memory was almost to be taken literally. By the time of Gordian, more than two centuries later, the house of the great Pompey, who had defeated the pirates in the eastern Mediterranean in a brilliantly successful campaign in the 60s BC and had thus earned this special kind of spoils—was still known as *domus rostrata*.[71] This honor obviously conveyed the same unambiguous and unmistakable message as the *columna Duilia* mentioned above and other *columnae rostratae* erected since and displayed in the public space, but also, as a remnant of a glorious past, continued to point to one man, his signal victory and his personal triumph.

---

[69]Cf. above, n. 63. Cf. also on concrete ('public,' 'civic,' or 'political') 'spaces,' cf. the collection of papers in AA.VV., 1983; AA.VV., 1987, and Coulston and Dodge (Eds.), 2000. Cf. also Patterson, 1992, 190ff., and idem, 2000, 5ff., 13ff., as well as, on a variety of particular aspects or 'spaces,' Zaccaria Ruggiu, 1995; Rykwert, 1976; Cancik, 1985–86; David, 1984, 131ff.; Rüpke, 1990, 30ff. (especially on the "sacral topography" of the city); Laser, 1997, 186ff.; Döbler, 1999, 18ff.; Zanker, 2000, 211ff., all with further references. Cf. also Laurence, 1993 (on Rome as a "ritual landscape") and, not only for purposes of comparison, Muir and Weissman, 1989 (on the concepts and concrete manifestation of 'social' and 'symbolic geography' of Renaissance Florence and Venice). Cf. on the importance of a reserved or defined (and therefore at the same time defining) 'space' for institutions and their consolidation Rehberg, 1998, 399f.

[70]Pliny, *Naturalis historia* 35, 7. Cf. now on the display of war booty in Roman houses Welch, 2006.

[71]*Historia Augusta* (Gordian) 3, 6, cf. 2, 3; 6, 5; 17, 2, and already Cicero, *Philippica* 2, 68f. Cf. Stein-Hölkeskamp, 2006, 302f.

This is a particular telling illustration of the fundamental fact that these houses, as well as temples, basilicas, honorific statues on Forum, Comitium, and Capitol, and the spate of other memorials of all kinds mentioned above, turned the city into a vast 'scenery' of imperial grandeur, which could be called a "tapestry of memory, a landscape lush with buildings and monuments that bear witness to attempts over the centuries to remember":[72] the city and the monumental constituents of its politico-sacral topography were an area where the collective 'cultural memory' of the *res publica*, people, and political class was preserved and permanently cultivated. These functions were not only closely related, and indeed cross-linked, among themselves, but also re-enforced each other in specific ways and were above all inseparably interconnected with their political functions, their technical as well as their expressive ceremonial and symbolic sides. This complex complementarity will be looked into once again from different perspectives in later chapters.[73]

To be sure, it was Fergus Millar who (among others) recently emphasized the importance of the fact that Republican politics was literally located in the limited urban center of Rome, in the area between the Capitol, Comitium, Forum Romanum, and Campus Martius. He even saw the concrete context here, of which everyone working on the history of the Republic should necessarily be aware.[74] But he has only selectively, though never systematically, tried to contextualize the various forms and levels of communication and interaction within the sociocultural framework of the Roman 'city-statehood.' This remains the most important task of serious modern interdisciplinary Ancient History.

---

[72]Gowing, 2005, 132.
[73]Cf. chapters 7 and 8, below.
[74]Millar, 2002a, 208f., cf. 90f., 101ff., 143ff.; idem, 1998, 38ff., 115, 197ff. and passim.

Chapter 6

BETWEEN 'ARISTOCRACY' AND 'DEMOCRACY'
BEYOND A DATED DICHOTOMY

AGAINST THIS BACKGROUND of a dynamic development of new questions, perspectives, theoretical models and methods, the focus of the debate about the second set of issues I mentioned at the beginning—namely, the status, structure, function, and legitimization of a political class like the senatorial aristocracy—can be sharpened. In fact, as we have seen, Fergus Millar set out radically to question the existence of this class in principle. He chose, however, not to make the effort to embark on a detailed and differentiated exploration of the intricate channels (and somewhat roundabout ways) of approaching the problem of Roman politics and political personnel that international research has taken since the seminal publications by Friedrich Münzer and Matthias Gelzer in the first half of the last century; he just contented himself with a sweeping and one-sided look back in anger. Nevertheless, Millar does deserve credit for having prompted students of Republican history to describe this political culture and re-evaluate its character, to analyze afresh its structures and concrete functioning by applying a new framework of more precise concepts and adequate categories—however, not only and exclusively, as he demanded it,[1] from a 'bottom-up' perspective, but also, as it were, from the 'top down': that is, from the uppermost level of the undeniable distinct and steep social hierarchies.

The first simple fact that we have to remember is that no one has ever claimed that this Republican ruling class, which we are used to calling the 'senatorial aristocracy' in general or 'nobility'(*nobilitas*), was a classic hereditary aristocracy in the sense of a closed and legally defined group privileged by right of birth and descent. Secondly, nobody has ever used the terms *nobilitas* and *nobilis* as technical terms—not even Münzer and Syme, let alone Gelzer.[2] On the contrary, these terms have often been employed in a deliberately loose, and therefore sometimes misleading, way. Thirdly, nobody has ever tried to define this 'aristocracy'—which it certainly was, if only in a certain sense to be discussed below—as an

---

[1] Millar, 2002a, 92f., 99.
[2] Münzer, 1920, 3f., 8ff., 98ff., 411f.; Syme, 1939, 10ff.; idem, 1986, 1ff.; Gelzer, 1912, 59ff.

'order' or 'estate' in the usual strict sense of "a juridically defined group within a population, possessing formalized privileges . . . in one or more fields of activity, governmental, military, legal, economic, religious, marital, and *standing in a hierarchical relation to other orders*"[3]—let alone as an entirely closed caste such as the old Roman patriciate, which had based its strict hereditary exclusivity on social law and religious charisma. There were many fundamental differences between this archaic "singularly inelastic order," which had already lost its monopoly on power by the end of the fourth century BC, on the one hand, and the mid- and late Republican kind of 'aristocracy,' on the other.[4]

However, this did not mean that the patrician *gentes* during the Republic ever lost their power or disappeared altogether: The new governing class consisting of old patrician and new plebeian 'aristocrats' consolidated itself in a highly complex process as the so-called struggle of the orders—itself a process that evolved on several levels and in different phases[5]—came to an end at the turn of the third century. Social pressures, internal and external developments, institutional structures (old and new), as well as events all worked together in a particular direction: The successful expansion in Italy and the creation of a hegemonic system of control was inseparably linked with the development of this new 'aristocracy of office' and its particular culture of political compromise, which was interrelated with the rise of its institutional center, the Senate, to become the 'governing body' of the Republic. These developments combined in turn fostered the consolidation of the social identity, ideological framework, and the economic basis of the new ruling class. And in the final analysis, it was this inseparable 'systemic' interconnection of dynamic external expansion and internal integration that in fact remained the preeminent characteristic of the sociopolitical order of the Republic—or, to put it in a somewhat clumsy, but precise, formula, integration-cum-hierarchization presupposed expansion-cum-empire and vice versa.[6]

To start with some basic general aspects of the problem, it should be noted that this 'aristocracy' was open in the sense that the one and only

[3]Finley (1973) 1979, 45 and 35ff. passim on 'orders and status'; idem, 1983, 12ff. Cf. Nicolet, 1977, 729ff.; Hölkeskamp, 1987, 10, and Alföldy, 1976, 50, 67.

[4]Finley, 1983, 14. Cf. Drummond, 1989b, 178ff.; Hölkeskamp, 1987, 31ff. with further references; Gabba, 1995; Cornell, 1995, 242ff. The best study of the 'patriciate' to date is Smith, 2006, 251ff.

[5]Cf. the important study by Raaflaub, (1986) 2005, and the relevant chapters in Hölkeskamp, 1987; Cornell, 1995, and Forsythe, 2005, with further references.

[6]See Hölkeskamp, 1987, 241ff. and passim; idem, 1993; Oakley, 1993, 9ff.; Cornell, 1989, 391ff.; idem, 1995, 340ff., 345ff., 364ff., 369ff. etc.; Pani, 1997, 169ff.; David, 1996, 35ff.; Raaflaub, 1996, 287ff.; Forsythe, 2005, 268ff., 324ff., all with further references. Cf. on the development in the third and second centuries BC, see Dahlheim, 1977, 170ff., 294ff.; Schulz, 1997.

fundamental condition for belonging to it was to have held certain offices, access to which was not restricted by law to a strictly defined group. The actual dominance of this group as a 'governing class' and its claim to leadership in politics and war were not based on, or derived from, established privileges of any formal kind, nor was this 'governing class' ever 'institutionalized'as such in the strict sense of the word: *nobilitas* was and always remained a matter of status rather than of class (in the Marxist sense of the concept), and the *nobiles* as a group, at least during the Republic, never solidified to become an 'estate' or 'order'—this insight was already rightly emphasized by Alfred Heuss and Moses Finley.[7] Whatever we nowadays think of their terminology and the way they conceptualized the problem, the basic point has long been generally accepted,[8] and I shall be coming back to the vexed question of clear-cut categories later. It also seems appropriate to distinguish between an inner core of especially prominent *gentes* that were able to maintain a high degree of success at elections over relatively long periods of time, and a wider circle of families that were unable consistently to win elections (at least to the highest office) and were therefore always struggling to maintain their membership in the aristocracy—and a few of these families, though never being of the first water, such as the Acilii (Glabriones) and the Calpurnii (Pisones), even managed to maintain a kind of 'gentilicial continuity' or tenacity over several centuries.[9] It was not, however, uncommon for such families to vanish from the record and possibly even from the ranks of the senatorial class, some to re-appear after a generation or even several generations, others never to resurface again, after having produced just one or two consuls.[10]

A few examples may clarify this familiar point.[11] To begin with a well-known case: the *gens Iulia*[12] produced several consuls and tribunes with consular power as early as the fifth and early fourth centuries—but only

[7]Heuss, 1963, 183; Finley, 1983, 14f., cf. idem, (1973) 1999, 45ff.; Nicolet, 1977, 727ff. Cf. on the concepts 'class' and 'status' now Morley, 2004, 76ff.

[8]Cf., e.g., Bleicken, 1981b; Astin, 1989, 169. On the terminology, see especially Alföldy, 1981, 207ff. (= idem, 1986b, 162ff., with addenda, 200ff.); idem, 1986b, 67, 72ff. with a critical discussion of Vittinghoff, 1994, and Kolb, 1982; Cf. Rilinger, 1985, 299ff.; Nicolet, 1984. Recent research on the problem of conceptualization was documented and discussed in detail by Burckhardt, 1990, and Goldmann, 2002.

[9]Cf. the detailed studies by Dondin-Payre, 1993 (on the Acilii Glabriones), and Hofmann-Löbl, 1996 (on the Calpurnii Pisones). Settipani, 2000, especially 1ff. and 76ff., stresses the general continuity of *gentes* and families, but concentrates on patrician *gentes* and uses a broad (and therefore imprecise) framework of concepts.

[10]Cf. Hopkins/Burton, 1983, 31–119, especially 112f., 117 (and the discussions of these seminal studies by Shaw, 1984; Lintott, 1999, 167f.; David, 2000a, 36f.).

[11]All dates in this and the following chapters, if not otherwise stated, are from Broughton, 1951–1952, which includes the evidence for every year; cf. the "Index of Careers," 2:524–636; Hölkeskamp, 2006d, 367ff.

[12]Friedrich Münzer, in *RE* 10, 1, 1918, 106f.

until 379 BC, when a certain L. Iulius (Iullus) was consular tribune. The next Iulius to reach the consulship was L. Iulius Libo in 267—more than a century, or at least three generations, later and the only prominent member of the *gens* for the rest of the third century. During the following century, once again only Sex. Iulius Caesar gained the *maximus honos* in 157—all other Iulii (Caesares), if at all, only reached the praetorship.[13] In the early first century, the *gens* had already produced three consuls, in the years 91, 90 and 64,[14] when the most famous scion of this old house entered the consulship of 59—the rest is history.

The next examples are of a different kind. Two families of the plebeian part of the new 'aristocracy' already rose to prominence immediately after plebeians had at last gained access to the highest offices in the years after the great 'compromise' of 367–66 BC and scored an impressive number of consulships during the phase of its emergence and consolidation in the fourth and early third centuries. To begin with the Genucii, who were among the first plebeians to reach the consulship at all: L. Genucius (Aventinensis) in 365 and 362, Cn. Genucius in 363, and another L. Genucius (allegedly with the same *cognomen*, probably a descendant of one of the previous ones) in 303.[15] A generation later, two further Genucii, both sons and grandsons of a L. Genucius and probably brothers, appear in the list: C. Genucius Clepsina, consul 276 and 270, and yet another L., once again with the same *cognomen*, consul 271—thereafter, the name all but disappears from the records.[16] The other case is different. The Popillii (Laenates) produced one of the most successful plebeian leaders of the first generation, M. Popillius Laenas, consul I 359, II 356, III 350, IV 348; his son (or possibly grandson) also reached the office in 316. It was no less than 150 years later that the line succeeded in establishing itself once again in the circle of consular families—however, once again, only for two generations. After M. and C. Popillius Laenas (the former consul 173, proconsul in the following year and censor 159, and the latter consul 172 and 158) and their respective sons M. and P. (consuls

[13] The known Iulii (Caesares) were Sex., praetor 208, and L., praetor 183; another L., praetor 166, and another Sex., praet. 123.

[14] Sex. Iulius C.f.L.n. (?) Caesar, consul 91, and L. Iulius L.f.Sex.n. Caesar, consul 90 and censor 89, were not even closely related; the son of the latter, L. Iulius L.f.L.n. Caesar, became consul in 64.

[15] An otherwise unknown C. Genucius ('Augurinus') was among the first augurs of plebeian status, co-opted under the *plebiscitum Ogulnium* in 300; as at least two other new members of this college (as well as all newly appointed plebeian *pontifices*) were probably former consuls (references in Broughton, 1951, I, 172f.; cf., however, Oakley, 2005b, 117f.), it is not impossible that this Genucius had also held some kind of (curule) office.

[16] Cf. on Clepsina Torelli, 2000, 141ff. A rather dubious Genucius with unknown *praenomen* and *cognomen* was possibly tribune (of the *plebs*) in 241, an L. Genucius is mentioned as ambassador in 210, and an M. Genucius as military tribune in 193; cf. Broughton, 1951, under the respective years.

in 139 and 132, respectively), this family disappeared from the first rank of the political class. By the way, quite a few other leading plebeian families in the third and second centuries met the same fate. The Atilii (Reguli and Serrani)[17] and the Fulvii (Flacci and Nobiliores)[18] had all but disappeared from the political stage by the turn of the century: except for Sex. Atilius Serranus Gavinus, tribune of the *plebs* 57 and never more than a minor figure on the political stage, and, not to forget her, the flamboyant Fulvia—daughter of an (allegedly) inept father and wife of P. Clodius Pulcher, then of C. Scribonius Curio, and finally of Marcus Antonius— "faithful and imperious," politically influential and versatile in her own right, a leading lady in the drama of the civil war.[19]

The three most outstanding individual plebeian representatives of the new patricio-plebeian political class—all three extraordinarily successful commanders, consuls, and censors—did not themselves stem from consular families, nor did they have at least a few successful descendants, nor were they able to establish their families in the relatively stable 'inner circle': from 339 BC onward, Q. Publilius Philo made a spectacular career, reached the consulship no less than four times, was dictator and censor and celebrated two triumphs.[20] M'. Curius Dentatus and C. Fabricius Luscinus, who in later tradition became *exempla* of the uncompromising upholding of *mos maiorum* and strict observance of the alleged traditional Roman rustic customs and frugal lifestyle, did not found a

[17]The Atilii Reguli—among them the tragic *exemplum virtutis* M. (consul 267, II 256 [*suff.*] and proconsul [?] 255); cf. Gendre et al., 2001, 136ff., 169ff.—produced consuls from the mid-fourth century to the second Punic war (335, 294, 257 and II 250, 227, 225 and II 217); the praetor 213 did not reach the consulship. Other Atilii rose to a short-lived prominence in the mid-third century with A. (Caiatinus), consul 258, II 254, dictator 249, censor 247, and C. (Bulbus), consul 245, II 235, censor 234—they were apparently neither closely related to each other, nor to the Reguli. Cf. Beck, 2005a, 229ff. The Atilii Serrani had consuls in 170, 136 and 106, as well as several praetors (218, 185, 174 and 152), who did not reach the consulship.

[18]Undoubtedly the most prominent Fulvius was Q. Flaccus, consul I 237, II 224, III 212 (and proconsul 211), IV 209 (again proconsul 208 and 207), censor 231, *magister equitum* 213, dictator 210 and also *pontifex* from 216. From the mid-third century until 125, the Fulvii Flacci fairly regularly produced consuls (264, 180 [*suff*], 179, 135 and 134), one of whom also became censor (174). The Fulvii Nobiliores scored only three consulships (189, 159, 153), but also two censorships (179 and 136). The relation of these branches to Fulvii with other *cognomina* (Curvus: consuls 322 and 305 [*suff.*]; Paetus/Paetinus: consuls 299 and 255; Centumalus: consuls 298, 229 and 211, praetor 192) is rather unclear; cf. Friedrich Münzer, in *RE* 7, 1, 1910, 229ff. and the stemma 231f.

[19]Syme, 1939, 208.

[20]He was Consul I 339, II 327 (and had his *imperium* prolonged *pro consule* for the first time), III 320, IV 315, dictator 339, praetor 336 and censor 332, he triumphed in 339 and again in 326; cf. Wilhelm Hoffmann, in *RE* 23, 2, 1959, 1912–16; Hölkeskamp, 1987, Index of persons, s.v.

'consular' line either.[21] The same is true of C. Duilius, the successful admiral and much-honored consul of 260 BC, who became censor in 258.[22] Another prominent example of a similar kind is L. Mummius 'Achaicus,' who was probably at least of praetorian stock (as son of the praetor 177BC) and made a successful career. As consul in 146, he razed Corinth and as proconsul in the following year carried out the reorganization of Greece with the assistance of ten senatorial legates, then returned to Rome to celebrate a triumph and finally became censor in 142 as colleague of P. Cornelius Aemilianus, the 'younger Africanus'—he also remained the only consul in his family.

Another famous commander—C. Lutatius Catulus, consul 242, whose decisive victory at sea at the Aegates islands finally ended the first Punic war—was also the first in his family to obtain the *maximus honos*.[23] The Lutatii then fared better than the previous examples: his younger brother, Q. Lutatius Cerco, became consul in the following year and censor in 236; his son followed in his footsteps in 220. After this spell of prominence, the family fell back into the second rank for more than a century until it returned to the inner circle of the *nobilitas* with Q. Lutatius Catulus, the colleague of the great C. Marius in the consulship 102, later proconsul and a victorious general in the German war. His homonymous son, the consul 78, censor 65 and unsuccessful candidate for the prestigious position of *pontifex maximus*, was even a prominent figure in the post-Sullan era, who lacked "brilliance and vigour," as Syme put it in his inimitable way of characterizing individual *nobiles*, but nevertheless "earned general recognition" by his "virtue and integrity," "rare in that age."[24]

Yet another example is the "dynastic house of the plebeian *nobilitas*," the Caecilii Metelli, who managed to attain signal prominence in the second half of the second century BC and were known for aristocratic haughtiness. They provided eight consuls between 143 and 109 and six more over the following fifty years.[25] Prior to this extraordinary familial

[21]On the tradition on Curius Dentatus (Consul I 290, II 275 and—this is very unusual—III 274, Censor 272) and Fabricius (Consul I 282, II 278, Censor 275): Hölkeskamp, 1987, 228ff., and recently Berrendonner, 2001, and Vigourt, 2001, both with detailed analysis of the rich source material and bibliography; Beck, 2005a, 188ff.; 204ff.

[22]Cf. on the man, his career, and the relevant tradition Beck, 2005a, 217ff.

[23]Cf. now Beck, 2005a, 125, 128, 154, 246, 353f.

[24]Syme, 1939, 21.

[25]Cf. Velleius Paterculus 1, 11, 6f.; 2, 11, 3. Syme, 1939, 20ff. etc; idem, 1986, stemma I. The consuls in the years 123, 117, 115 and 113 were sons of Q. Caecilius Metellus Macedonicus, consul 143 and censor 131 (and P. Cornelius Scipio Nasica, consul 111, was his son-in-law). The Metellan consuls of the years 119 and 109 were sons of L. Caecilius Metellus Calvus, consul 142; the family also provided consuls in the years 98, 80, 69, 68, 60 and 57. The Caecilii were also particularly well-connnected: a Metella was the wife of the

success, however, the Metelli had last obtained a consulship in 206, which is a gap of sixty-three years (or two full generations): for half a century, the family altogether disappears from sight.[26]

At that time, the family had produced but one consul per generation, beginning with the (probable) grandfather of the consul 206 and founder of the line, L. Caecilius Metellus Denter, consul 284 and perhaps praetor in the following year, who had suffered a defeat and died on the battle-field.[27] His son—also a Lucius—was more successful: as consul and pro-consul in the years 251 and 250, he won an important victory over the Carthaginian forces in Sicily, capturing more than a hundred elephants, some of which were later shown in a spectacular triumph. He went on to score further *honores*, among them a second consulship in 247 and the prestigious post of *pontifex maximus*, and at last went down in history as an *exemplum pietatis* for having saved a holy statue out of the burning temple of Vesta.[28] It was primarily his career, fame, and reputation that the pride, and indeed 'corporate identity,' of the family was based on; this is an interesting aspect of the Metellan family history, which will receive further discussion in a later chapter.[29]

General considerations as well as a detailed and careful statistical analysis[30] lead to the same (and perhaps rather unsurprising) result: that it was the plebeian 'wing' of the *nobilitas* that was subject to shifts and changes of concrete 'membership in the club' in a significantly higher degree than the patrician 'wing.' As opposed to the close caste of the patriciate, the plebeian part of the political class was, and always remained, by definition open to newcomers, *homines novi* of exceptional talent and achievement. And if quite a few of them, as Curius Dentatus,

---

influential M. Aemilius Scaurus, consul 115 and *princeps senatus* (cf. below, chapter 8, n. 6); after his death she married L. Cornelius Sulla, who was to become dictator and the most powerful man the Republic had ever seen; cf. van Ooteghem, 1967.

[26]M. Metellus, praetor 206, did not make it to the consulship. It seems unlikely (in spite of Pliny, *Naturalis historia* 7, 142) that Q. Metellus Macedonicus, consul 143, and L. Metellus Calvus, consul in the following year (and possibly Q.'s brother), were sons of Q. Metellus, consul 206, and grandsons of L. Metellus, consul 251. Neither is the filiation of the consul 143, which is assumed to be 'Q.f.L.n.,' reliably attested anywhere, nor is there any evidence for an identical filiation of the consul 142: if the epigraphic evidence refers to him (which is far from certain), he was 'Q.f.'—his grandfather's name is nowhere attested. It is therefore at least equally possible that these Metelli were 'Q.f.Q.n.': that is, sons of a Quintus otherwise unknown and grandsons of the consul 206. Cf. Friedrich Münzer. "Caecilius 94." In *RE* 3, 1, 1897, 1213; Van Ooteghem, 1967, 51, 84; Badian, 1990, 379f. with n. 7 (p. 400–1).

[27]Cf. Broughton, 1951, I 187ff., with notes, on the garbled tradition.

[28]He was also *magister equitum* of the dictator A. Atilius Caiatinus 249, *dictator comitiorum habendorum causa* 224; cf. Friedrich Münzer, in *RE* 3, 1, 1897, 1203–4, on the tradition.

[29]Cf. chapter 8, below.

[30]Cf. now Beck, 2005a, 114ff.

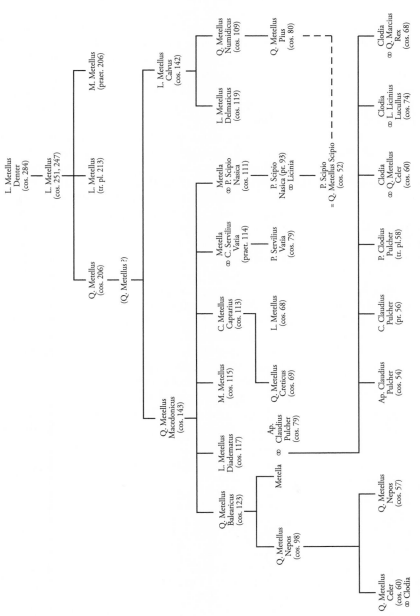

Figure 3. Family tree of the Caecilii Metelli (by the author). (Only more important members of the family mentioned in the text are included.)

Fabricius, and Duilius, did not found a 'consular' line, others were (more or less and sometimes in the long run) more successful, like the Lutatii Catuli and the Caecilii Metelli, and replaced, or even, in a way, displaced other formerly prominent plebeian families: after all, the sheer number of places—just one—in the consulship remained stable, at least until the first all-plebeian college of consuls assumed office in 172, and the number of patrician incumbents of the praetorship seems to have remained relatively high as well.[31] In this respect, patricians did indeed "wield an influence beyond all relation to their number."[32]

However, fluctuations of a similar kind as the changing fortunes, the 'ups and downs' mentioned above, also affected the inner circle of the *nobiles* proper and even established patrician *gentes maiores*, which included the Aemilii, Fabii, Valerii, Cornelii, Claudii, Servilii, Sulpicii and Manlii,[33] even though, on close examination based on statistical analysis, these *gentes* as a group within the inner circle show a rate of succession and reproduction as consular families that was regularly above the average in a given generation of the mid-Republic.[34] A good example is the famous *gens Fabia*, which had provided consuls and able commanders from the early Republic up to the second Punic war, including legendary figures such as Q. Fabius Maximus Rullianus, the most prominent general of the Samnite wars, who was five times consul as well as dictator, censor, and *princeps senatus*,[35] and his great-grandson, Q. Fabius Maximus 'Verrucosus,' who achieved a similar record and was also a member of both of the prominent priesthoods, the *pontifices* and *augures*. Moreover, he became the leading figure in the first half of the war against Hannibal and went down into history as the famous 'Cunctator.'[36] The Fabii then suddenly disappear from the lists of consuls for more than half a century, only to re-appear with Q. Fabius Maximus Aemilianus, Consul 145—and even he had been adopted by one of the Cunctator's grandsons.[37]

[31] See the *Fasti Praetorii* in Brennan, 2000, 723ff., and, on the 'dynamic' development of this magistracy, Beck, 2005a, 63ff.

[32] Syme, 1939, 10.

[33] Cf. Beck, 2005a, 115, 121f., 126f., 138f., 147 etc., with further references; cf. on the individual *gentes* Ranouil, 1975, 202ff. and "Index prosopographique," and now Beck, 2005a, (index of personal names), and Smith, 2006, Index (s.v. *gentes* and families, individual). Cf. Settipani, 2000, 61ff. for detailed stemmata.

[34] Beck, 2005a, 126f., 138f., 144, 147ff. etc.

[35] Consul I 322, II 310, III 308, IV 297, V 295, Censor 304, Dictator 315 (?). Cf. for evidence and details now Oakley, 2005b, Index s.v. (p. 623–24).

[36] Consul I 233, II 228, III 215, IV 214, V 209, Censor 230, Dictator 217, *augur* ca. 265–203, *pontifex* 216–203; cf. Rüpke et al., 2005, I, 59, 69, 74, II, No. 1595 (971f.); Beck, 2005a, 269ff. etc.

[37] Probably Q. Fabius Maximus, praetor 181, who did not reach the consulship; cf. Friedrich Münzer, "Fabius 105, 109." In *RE* 6, 2, 1909, 1790 and 1792–94, especially 1792.

It often happened that famous families or lines of *gentes* died out completely (or at least sank into obscurity), among them a substantial number of patrician *gentes*, and by no means only the less important so-called *gentes minores* of ephemeral élite status,[38] but also once famous ones such as the Furii and the Papirii. The figurehead of the former was the legendary Camillus, idolized in Roman tradition as the savior of his country after the Gallic invasion, *pater patriae*, and indeed second founder of the city.[39] However, with his less shadowy grandson, L. Furius Camillus— consul 338 and II 325, successful commander, and allegedly one of the architects of Roman hegemony after the Latin War[40]—this line of the Furii came to an end; in later times, patrician Furii of other lines rarely reached the *maximus honos* or at least the praetorship.[41] As the Furii, the *gens Papiria* had been present in the list of holders of the supreme office since the early Republic, and it produced one of the prominent commanders in the second Samnite War, L. Papirius Cursor, no less than five times consul, who went down in Roman tradition as one of the greatest generals of all time.[42] His line seems to have ended with his homonymous son, consul 293 and II 272. Another branch by the cognomen 'Maso' never became really prominent: apart from just one consul and (more than half a century later) a praetor, it apparently produced only senators of junior rank, whose names (as in many other similar cases) were handed down just by chance.[43]

A later well-known and well-documented example of a patrician line becoming extinct are the Aemilii Paulli. L. Aemilius Paullus, son and grandson of consuls and himself twice consul,[44] the victor at Pydna in

[38]Cf. Ranouil,1975, 128ff., 135ff.

[39]Livy 6, 1, 3; 3, 1; 7, 1, 10 etc.. Cf. Oakley, 1997, 376ff., and idem, 1998, 37; Coudry, 2001; Späth, 2001; Ungern-Sternberg, 2001; Walter, 2004a, 382ff. and now Gaertner, 2008.

[40]Cf. Oakley, 1998, 529, 535ff.

[41]These Furii sport several different *cognomina*, and their relation is mostly unclear: C. Furius Pacilus, consul 251; P. Furius Philus, consul 223, censor 214 and augur; L. Furius Purpurio, consul 196, and L. Furius Philus, consul 136; The following patrician Furii did not reach the consulship: L. Furius, praetor 318; L. Furius Bibalcus, praetor before 219 (?); M. Furius Crassipes, praetor 187, II 173; P. Furius Philus, praetor 174, and L. Furius Philus, praetor 171 (and *pontifex*).

[42]Consul 326, II 320, III 319, IV 315, V 313, dictator 325 or 324 and II 310 or 309; cf. Livy 9, 16, 12 and 19; 17, 7f. See Hölkeskamp, 1987, 130ff., and now Oakley, 2005a, 175ff.

[43]C. Papirius Maso, consul 231 and *pontifex*; L. Papirius Maso, praetor urbanus 176; another L. Maso was curule aedile about 290—as our knowledge of praetors' names before 218 is rather scanty (Brennan, 2000, 725f.), it is not impossible that he made it to the praetorship. Another C. and a P. Maso are mentioned as *IIIviri agris dandis assignandis* in 218 (Broughton, 1951, I, 240).

[44]He had been praetor 191 and proconsul 190–89, consul I 182, II 168 and proconsul 167, censor 164. His father L. (consul I 219, II 216) died at Cannae, his grandfather M. was consul 255, proconsul 254 and celebrated a naval triumph.

168 BC and conqueror of Macedonia, had four sons by two wives. He permitted the two sons of his first wife, Papiria (the last known descendant of the patrician Papirii mentioned above),[45] to be adopted into other famous families, the Cornelii Scipiones and the Fabii Maximi, in order to secure their male line: the first was adopted by the son of the famous P. Cornelius Scipio 'Africanus,' to become P. Cornelius Scipio 'Aemilianus,' later himself surnamed 'Africanus' (*minor*, 'the younger');[46] the second was Q. Fabius Maximus Aemilianus, also already mentioned above. Paullus's two remaining sons died young, however, at 12 and 14, and—according to a well-established tradition—did so at the time of their father's spectacular triumph over Perseus in 167. In a much-quoted speech to the people, Lucius is said to have presented himself as a tragic *exemplum*, subordinating his personal tragedy to the welfare of the city and the *res publica*. He represented his loss as a tribute to "Fate," an offering to ensure the continuing benevolence of that changeable goddess.[47]

This case is exemplary in several ways. It illustrates the relative frequency of adoption into other families of sons whose fathers were still alive. The mere development of such a legal strategy reminds us that the continuity or survival of many families in the male line could be seriously threatened in any generation[48]—after all, this case concerns no less than three large, extended patrician *gentes*, or rather their most prominent branches. One of the reasons was surely the high rate of infant-mortality and a generally low life-expectancy, which was no doubt comparable to that of other pre-modern societies.[49] In this particular kind of an aristocracy, however, there were two other factors that made the problem even more dramatic. In the first place, a young aristocrat had to face plenty of dangers during his ten years of military service: to prove oneself on the battlefield obviously involved taking some risks. At least until the late second century BC, it was only after completion of this service that he could think of *rem publicam capessere* and embark on the *cursus honorum*. Secondly, relatively high minimum ages for election to an office with *imperium* (which alone constituted personal *nobilitas* and conferred 'noble' status in the strict sense of prestige and 'honor') were made mandatory for the first time in the early second century by the *lex Villia annalis*. Though the precise content of this law will remain controversial, it

[45]She was the daughter of C. Papirius Maso, consul 231: Ranouil, 1975, 136; Astin, 1967, 12.

[46]Cf. Astin, 1967, 12ff.

[47]Polybius 31, 28, 1f.; Livy 45, 41, 1–12; Velleius Paterculus 1, 10, 3ff; Plutarch, *Aemilius Paullus* 5, 5; 35, 1ff.; 36, 2–9 (with some minor differences); Valerius Maximus 5, 10, 2 (among a whole collection of *exempla* "de parentibus qui obitum liberorum forti animo tulerunt": 5, 10 *praef.* and passim). Cf. on the tradition and his 'image' Reiter, 1988.

[48]Cf. Corbier, 1991, 63f.

[49]Cf. especially Saller, 1994, 12ff., and Hölkeskamp, 2004b, with further references.

is well possible that it introduced not only a minimum interval of two years between *honores*, but also already a minimum age of 39 years for the praetorship and 42 for the *maximus honos*.[50]

Against this backdrop, quite a few of the well-known inscriptions on the sarcophagi in the tomb of the Scipiones appear in a new light (see figure 4, below). At least four of the male members of the family buried there died before they were old enough to be allowed to run for the highest *honores*—among them (probably) the son of Africanus, mentioned above, who just held the age-old priesthood of *flamen Dialis* (or augur) and adopted the later 'Africanus (minor)' from the Aemilii Paulli. The text of his epitaph revolves around the premature death—this Scipio died about 170, perhaps at the age of 25 or 30—and its bitter consequence of cutting short a life (and possibly a promising career).[51] This is the explicit message of the inscription on the sarcophagus of Lucius Scipio, son of L. Cornelius Scipio Asiaticus, consul 190 BC, "who defeated the king Antiochus." It makes the familial predicament shortly and unambiguously clear by giving the age of the deceased—33 years—and especially by emphasizing the fact that he had progressed as far as was possible under the regulations given the age at which he died. He had just been quaestor and military tribune (probably *a populo*—that is, elected in the popular assembly).[52]

To sum up the underlying, rather inexorable general principle: The formal as well as the informal rules governing access to (the higher ranks of) this aristocracy required that in any given generation at least one (reasonably capable, well-trained, and publicly presentable) male had to live at least to the age of 40, which alone secured the position as well as the relative rank of a family in the 'senatorial aristocracy,' and especially in the inner circle of the *nobilitas*. Moreover, the combined actual effects of these rules meant that this position was always precarious and potentially in jeopardy.

Even if the actual composition of the senatorial aristocracy and its inner circle was in constant fluctuation because of a permanent "turnover of political families" and varying "rates of succession,"[53] we do not have to

[50]Cf. Kunkel/Wittmann, 1995, 45ff. and now Beck, 2005b, 51ff., with full references.

[51]*ILLRP* 311 with Degrassi's commentary; *ROL* IV, No. 5; Kruschwitz, 2002, 70ff.; Rüpke, 2005, II, Nos. 1370–71 with notes (921f.). Cf. Coarelli, 1972, 226ff.; Moir, 1986.

[52]*ILLRP* 313 = *ROL* IV, No. 7. Cf. the series 311–314 and further discussion in chapter 8, below.

[53]Hopkins/Burton, 1983, 112, 117; cf. Shaw, 1984, 454ff. and 461ff. on the concept of 'heritability' and the other discussions of Hopkins, 1983, which invariably focus on his statistical approach, its potential, limits, and results: Duncan-Jones, 1984; Susan Treggiari,

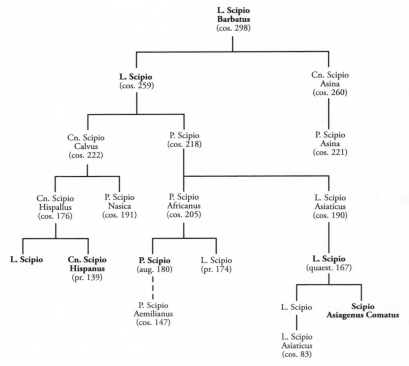

Figure 4. Family tree of the Cornelii Scipiones (by the author). (Only more important members of the family mentioned in the text are included. Persons buried in the tomb are in boldface.)

follow Millar and abandon the entire idea of an aristocratic (and, to a certain extent, even 'oligarchic') political class. On the contrary, the particular variant of this 'aristocracy of office' exposes Millar's implicitly presupposed one-sided definition of 'heredity' or 'heritability,' which is as rigidly formalist as his concept of 'constitution.'[54] On the one hand, élites

in *AJPh* 106, 1985, 256–62; Runciman, 1986; Keith R. Bradley, in *CPh* 81, 1986, 263–70; Christoph G. Paulus, in *ZRG RA* 103, 1986, 514–25; Jürgen von Ungern-Sternberg, in *Gnomon* 62, 1990, 424–28.

[54]It is unimportant which 'constitutional rights' the hereditary peers in Great Britain still have after the last reform of the House of Lords, and starting an abstract debate about Millar's understanding of aristocracy and the élite is not my intention either (although it is obviously formalist or even reductionist). On the concept of 'aristocracy' and its contents see Conze et al., 1972; Powis, 1984; Oexle, 1990, 19ff. with additional evidence, and the contributions in idem et al. (Eds.), 1997; Näf, 2001 (mainly on *nobilitas* as a topic of historiography, with selective bibliography), and now Gersmann, 2005; Asch, 2008, and the important general remarks in Beck et al., 2008b, and Walter, 2008 (who also explore the explanatory potential of comparative approaches).

or oligarchies, which are not formally closed, display a kind of inherent tendency toward exclusivity—even if it is never fully attainable via the total closing of its ranks. *A fortiori*, this tendency was even very pronounced in the Republican aristocracy of office: The number of consuls with consular ancestors never dropped below 70 percent after the beginning of the second century BC. In the last generation of the Republic (between 80 and 50 BC), it was actually as high as 80 percent, which is a rather impressive rate of self-reproduction.[55]

On the other hand, once again, we must not understand the notion of 'exclusivity' in a rigid and formalist way, such as would imply that collective membership of the group remained stable over a long time and that, vice versa, all individual members invariably retained their status. The 'exclusivity' of the Republican aristocracy was mainly derived from, as well as defined by, its collective identity and the underlying narrow and consistent self-definition as a genuinely political class. "Being involved in politics meant being part of the aristocracy, and being part of the aristocracy meant being involved in politics"—this dictum of Christian Meier's is only apparently circular, and it is by no means merely a banal tautology, as Millar suggests.[56] Rather, it is to be understood as an attempt precisely to circumscribe the complex character of a 'status group' that was based not only on the interdependence and indeed interpenetration of political office and social status,[57] but also on a concomitant collective ideological orientation of 'exclusive' devotion to politics and war in permanent service to the *res publica*.[58] It was a Republican aristocracy in the original sense of the concept—in other words, it identified itself utterly, completely, and exclusively with the *res publica*. In turn, this (self-)identification was the basis, on the one hand, of its collective claim to leadership and guidance, to rank, authority, and prestige, to appreciation and acceptance of superiority and, on the other, of its permanent demand of strict obedience, docility, and discipline, deference and respect on the part of the *populus* at large—it was this interdependence that was the very core of its legitimacy as an 'aristocracy.' It developed a corresponding, ideologically coherent, as well as cohesive collective ethos that it fervently upheld as its very own (in that sense 'exclusive') system of orientations and values. The sole focus of this system was the glory and grandeur of

[55] Cf. Badian, 1990, passim, summary on 411f. The statistical data in Hopkins/Burton, 1983, 32, 112, 117 and table 2.4 (p. 58) do not contradict this concept; cf. Nicolet, 1977, 733; Shaw, 1984, 456ff., and now Beck, 2005a, 17ff., 405ff.

[56] Meier, 1966/1980, 47, and Hölkeskamp, 1987, 248f.; Pittenger, 2008, 286. Contra: Millar, 1998, 4f., and idem, 2002a, 95, 205.

[57] Hopkins/Burton, 1983, 108, 116 etc.

[58] Comparing this 'ideology of service' to the idea of 'noblesse et service' in other premodern societies—for example, in late medieval France—could perhaps be interesting: cf. Contamine, 1997.

the *populus Romanus*—its superiority, dignity, and majesty—denoted by the terms *imperium* and *maiestas*, as well as the global power of its empire, which could tangibly be measured in extent, victories, and nations conquered and subdued.[59]

Meier's dictum also implies that all members of this aristocracy had to devote themselves individually and, once again, 'exclusively' to the service to this system. This entails that they had to subordinate themselves to a strict, and indeed severe, kind of discipline, to meet high demands and exacting standards of personal performance arising from the collective ethos and the code of behavior—this was the price for access to membership, personal rank, and recognized reputation in this self-defined 'exclusive' club. Nonpolitical or apolitical criteria of status and prominence, or even decidedly individualistic strategies of self-fashioning, could never have a place in this mentality—in stark contrast to the societies of Archaic and Classical Greece, in which a splendid lifestyle and ostentatious extravagance, victories at the Olympic Games and other festivals, elegance, physical beauty, and pure, 'philosophical' knowledge without practical relevance were highly appreciated.[60] Not even wealth was worth much in Roman Republican society—at any rate not for its own sake. Wealth and its accumulation was the result of success in politics and war (or perhaps a highly desirable and welcome side-effect), but it was not an end in itself: it always served as a means to another end.

This end was the success of the individual member of this aristocracy in the permanent and pervasive internal competition over positions, rank, and prestige in the service of the *res publica*.[61] Obtaining such positions—above all in the shape of the senior magistracies, which were understood to be honors and accordingly referred to as *honores*, which carried the most important political and administrative functions and above all military command under one's own *imperium auspiciaque*—did not only just constitute the individual's membership in the aristocracy. The rise into

[59] Cf. Harris, 1979, 9ff. This book is still one of the most important contributions to our understanding of Republican 'political culture' since Meier's *Res publica amissa*; cf. North, 1981, and the contributions in Harris (Ed.), 1984b (especially Gabba, 1984); Rich, 1993, with further references. Cf. also Richardson, 1991; Hopkins, 1978, 25ff.; Hölkeskamp, 1987, 204ff., 244ff.; idem, 1993, 25ff. Cf. on the terminology Awerbruch, 1981; Lind, 1986, 52ff., 59ff., and on the 'theology of victory' see Fears, 1981a, as well as Brunt, 1978 (= idem, 1990, 288ff., with additions 506ff.).

[60] On the Greek aristocracy, and their lifestyle as constituents of prominent status, see Stein-Hölkeskamp, 1989, and—partly on the basis of this fundamental study—Flaig, 1993a, 203, 214ff.; idem, 1999b, 99ff. Cf. Elke Stein-Hölkeskamp. "Adel [2, griechisch]." In *DNP* 1, 1996, 107–9, and recently Duplouy, 2006; Schmitz, 2008, and Boschung, 2008, 184ff.

[61] Cf. on the concept of a 'competitive culture' Hopkins/Burton, 1983, 107ff. Wiseman, 1985a, 3ff.; Astin, 1989, 169, 174ff.; Beard/Crawford, 1985, 53ff., 68ff.; Hölkeskamp, 1987, 1993, and 2006d, with further references. Cf. also Yakobson, 1999, and recently Farney, 2007.

higher offices was also the only means of obtaining prestige and influence within this élite. The hierarchy as such, as well as the criteria for gaining higher ranks, was firmly, if informally, inscribed in the collective code of values: They had begun to evolve during the consolidation of the new patricio-plebeian élite in the fourth century BC and did not take their final form until the late third century—the *lex Villia annalis*, mentioned above, only marked one step in this long and complex process.[62] By that time, it had become the fundamental principle that former consuls and censors formed the uppermost rank, with the highest *dignitas* and *auctoritas*; as the *principes civitatis*, they were the recognized opinion leaders in the Senate. Next came the former praetors—as holders of *imperium*, they had served as commanders and governors of the provinces and had long been considered 'colleagues' of the consuls. After them came the former aediles and finally the former *tribuni plebis* and quaestors.

The informal rules for rising through the ranks of the senatorial aristocracy were just as deeply ingrained: good performance and recognized success in lower offices constituted a claim to higher *honores*. Once again, the inscriptions from the tomb of the Scipiones provide the earliest authentic evidence for this: The epitaphs for L. Cornelius Scipio Barbatus, consul in 298 BC, and his son, consul in 259, explicitly state that they had both been consuls, censors, and (curule) aediles *apud vos*—"with you" or "among you"—mentioning the most important function first and, in the same context, showing the extent of ingrained orientation toward the *populus Romanus*, as the instance that had conferred these 'honors' through popular election.[63]

To repeat a fundamental fact of Roman aristocratic life: There were no alternative career options available that would have promised anything comparable in the way of ideal and material rewards in the form of social prestige, political influence, and also wealth. The *curriculum vitae*, the personal identity and the 'persona' of an aristocrat were 'exclusively' defined and completely determined by his *cursus honorum*, and, at least in principle, this was still true after the Republic had long since fallen and the imperial aristocracy was no longer a 'political class' in the strict sense of a '(self-)governing class.'[64]

[62]On this complex process, see the survey by Nicolet, 1979, 397ff.; Hölkeskamp, 1987, 114ff., 170ff., 241ff. and passim; idem, 1993, as well as Bleckmann, 2002, and now the detailed study by Beck, 2005a.

[63]*ILLRP* 309 and 310 = *ROL* IV, 1–2 and 3–4; Kruschwitz, 2002, no. 2 (33ff.) and no. 3 (58ff.), with further references. Cf. Hölkeskamp, 1987, 225; Flower, 1996, 166ff.; Beck, 2005a, 329ff. Cf. figure 5, below.

[64]Cf. Alföldy, 1982, 380ff.; Eck, 1984, 149ff.; idem, 1999, 39ff., and recently idem, 2005a and 2005b; Eich, 2008. However, the complex change of 'mentality' and ethics, set of rules, and criteria of social distinction under the early *principes* (which cannot be discussed here) necessarily had consequences for the status and relative importance of the traditional 'political' orientation; cf. Roller, 2001, and Stein-Hölkeskamp, 2003.

Figure 5. Sarcophagus of L. Cornelius Scipio (Barbatus), consul 298, with epitaph (Quasar, 1996, courtesy of Edizioni Quasar, Rome).

As a matter of course, this hierarchization and its dynamics had ramifications—eventually only the highest honor, the consulship, the *maximus honos* as apex of the hierarchical order of the *cursus honorum*, and the political and military success required, could enable a man to rise up into the inner core of the aristocracy, which we still, and with some justification, may call the *nobilitas*. It also entails the fact that the senatorial aristocracy had a vertical inner structure, which was increasingly consolidated and clearly defined: that is, we are dealing with the historically rather uncommon variant of an aristocracy with a strict internal hierarchy of ranks.[65]

It was this particular character of the senatorial aristocracy that assigned crucial, and indeed constitutive, functions in this political culture to the *populus Romanus*, especially in the form of its assemblies. These functions were not restricted to an abstract, center-stage rôle in an ideology, already mentioned above, that revolved around the 'sovereignty' and *maiestas* of the Roman people. *Populus* or *plebs* in their respective assemblies had to play a much broader range of different, but indispensable, rôles, reaching from the symbolic to the very concrete functions in the Republican structure of institutions and procedures.[66] In the first place, it was the essential right and duty of the *populus Romanus* to award the *honores* in the annual elections—and this was not only a mere

[65]Cf. Flaig, 1993a, 197ff., as well as idem, 2003b, 27ff. and passim, and also, from a different point of view, Badel, 2005, 53ff.

[66]Cf. generally Yakobson, 1999, 20ff. and passim; idem, 2006a and 2006b.

ritual reaffirming the close connection between and interdependence of the Roman citizen body and its politico-military leadership and the legitimacy of this élite based on their shared code of collective values.

Moreover, elections had a tangible function. Even though the people could never express its 'sovereign' will—in any meaningful sense of the term—by independently and freely voting or electing. Even though the assemblies were only allowed, as it were, to 'take their pick' of candidates who were all coming from the privileged classes in general (and therefore potential or actual members of the political élite, who were eligible to run for the office and vice versa and who had at last been formally accepted and presented by a magistrate) election as such, as a mode of recruiting the holders of the institutionalized positions of power in the shape of public offices, was in principle and in structure indispensable. This is to say that a political class that defined itself by means of these offices and needed the formalized *cursus* continuously to sort out its internal ranking necessarily needed a procedure that itself had the main advantage of 'formalization' and 'institutionalization'—namely, being regulated by uncontroversial norms and rules, in principle accepted by the respective competitors or contestants involved in any actual election. Thus the principle of 'election' could become part and parcel of the fundamental pattern of neutral norms governing the recruitment, promotion, and allocation of status and rank in an aristocracy that constructed itself ideologically as a 'meritocracy' defined by *honores* (in both senses of the concept).

In this context, we have to remind ourselves that elections by the people were indeed very frequent: already in the second century, there were more than seventy official positions of one kind or another that had to be filled every year, not only the six to eight most important and powerful *honores* with *imperium*, the consul- and praetorships, which were always elected in the old, strictly hierarchically structured *comitia centuriata*, with its lengthy and awkward procedure. It is a strange distortion if Fergus Millar dismisses this assembly as relatively less important than the *comitia tributa*, because the former assembly "had only very restricted functions"—namely, it met "*only* to elect consuls and praetors" and (every five years) the two censors.[67] Moreover, the latter assembly was also by no means only (or even mainly) a legislative body, but also met regularly to exercise important elective functions. Not only were the junior magistrates of the *cursus* proper, such as the aediles—two curule and two plebeian— and probably well over a dozen quaestors, elected in the *comitia tributa*, but also a substantial number of lower officials in different colleges, such

[67]Millar, 1998, 206, and idem, 2002b, 179 (my italics, K.-J. H.); cf. also Millar, 1998, 204, and idem, 2002a, 94, where he explicitly criticizes "the excessive emphasis on elections, above all elections to the consulship."

as the *tresviri capitales* or *nocturni*, as well as a certain number of junior officers of the legions (*tribuni militum a populo*). Last but not least, the assembly by tribes in the shape of the *concilia plebis* elected the ten tribunes of the *plebs*.

The competition for the *honores* was regularly keen and sometimes downright fierce, as the senior offices at the end of the *cursus honorum* were only available in far lower numbers than the junior ones.[68] Statistically, only every third or fourth praetor could become consul, and by no means all quaestors or *tribuni plebis* went on to win a praetorship. Against this backdrop, it was obviously vital for the political system as a whole and its functioning in particular that the procedure of selection of 'winners' had to be located in a neutral area—and that necessarily meant, outside the political class itself. No institution with sufficient authority, impartiality, and acceptance could have existed inside such a highly competitive class: the usual rivalries, and the permanent infighting over positions, rank, and prestige that were inscribed in such a highly competitive system, would immediately and automatically have caused perpetual conflicts regarding the status and competence of, and above all the right of participation in and access to, an internal institution with the power to award the *honores*; personal membership in such a 'super-institution' would necessarily have become the true *maximus honos* in the system.

A similar kind of serious or 'systemic' disadvantage also made the second mode of recruitment of leadership personnel unsuitable—namely, the co-optation of new members of a college by the college itself. Even as the traditional procedure to fill the vacancies in the important colleges of priests, it was partly and gradually repressed until the late Republic.[69] And the third mode of recruitment was obviously out of the question for an oligarchy—namely, appointment by a superior power, as a favor granted from above. It was this mode, introduced in the first decades of the principate, that brought about a complex process of adaptation and assimilation of the senatorial aristocracy as 'governing' (but no longer 'ruling') class.[70]

As a consequence, the principle of election remained the only procedural mode that was able to reduce the potential for conflict and channel the resulting centrifugal forces that would otherwise soon have overburdened the capacity for regulation and de-escalation of the system, and

[68]Cf. Beck, 2005a, who deals with this 'pyramid of offices' in detail. Earlier surveys include Nicolet, 1979, 393ff., and Evans, 1991.

[69]Cf. Mommsen, 1887–88, II, 27ff.; Wissowa, 1912, 487f., 523, etc.

[70]Cf. the fundamental studies by Roller, 2001; Stein-Hölkeskamp, 2003; and now also Eich, 2008, which approach this process from different perspectives.

would thus have severely jeopardized the capacity to function and rule, and therefore in turn the very survival of the political class. As a result, which is only seemingly paradoxical, 'election' was at least the relatively best way to ensure stability and a necessary minimum level of homogeneity and consensus in this 'aristocracy of office.'

However, from the point of view of this aristocracy—or rather, of its individual members— the principle of popular election and its inevitable ramifications demanded a high price. Given that the offices that constituted aristocratic status and rank were regularly redistributed by means of open and public competition, they could never be truly—that is, legally—hereditary, and this in turn entailed the consequence that individual membership of, and rank in, this aristocracy could also never become formally and 'exclusively' hereditary.

Secondly, as I have already mentioned, not only the individual membership, but also the status and relative position of the whole family was always precarious, a fact that entails another apparent paradox: in spite of the relatively high rate of succession in the 'consular' families, only a very small number of families managed to provide consuls regularly and continuously over three (or even more) generations. In fact, not even all 'noble' houses of the first water, which constituted the inner circle of the *nobilitas* mentioned above, managed to remain permanently and equally prominent during the whole period from the emergence of the new patricio-plebeian aristocracy in the fourth century to the fall of the Republic in the middle of the first century BC. For example, as shown above, neither the great patrician clan of the Fabii Maximi nor the plebeian families that initiated the integration of the new aristocracy, or later the 'dynasty' of the Caecilii Metelli or, to give yet another example, the Claudii Marcelli, managed to maintain the maximum rate of success(ion). M. Claudius Marcellus, it is true, who reached the consulship three times (166, 155 and 152 BC) and was later praised for his *summa virtus, pietas, gloria militaris*, had an inscription put up at his family monument—it was, perhaps unsurprisingly, the temple of *Honos* and *Virtus*—that proudly claimed a successful succession: it read III MARCELLI NOVIES COS., referring to himself, his father, and above all his grandfather, who had been consul five times and a famous general of the second Punic war, conqueror of Syracuse, and the founder of the temple just mentioned.[71] However, in the generation before the legendary Marcellus, on the one hand, and in

---

[71]Cf. now Valvo, 2005, 77f., and McDonnell, 2006a, 206ff.

the whole hundred years after the grandson, on the other, no other Marcellus appears in the list of consuls: it took no less than three generations
for the next Marcelli to reach the *maximus honos*, in the years 51, 50 and
49, in the twilight of the Republic at the outbreak of the civil war.[72]

Fluctuations of this kind were not at all unusual—the one remarkable exception was the patrician *gens Claudia*, or rather, to be more precise, the branch of the Claudii Pulchri.[73] Until the last decade of the
Republic, this family "persisted, unchanged in their alarming versatility"
and "intolerably arrogant," as Syme (and already his favorite forerunner
Tacitus) saw it,[74] and was as prolific as earlier generations of the clan:
Ap. Claudius Pulcher, consul 79, not only had three sons—by a wife be-
fitting his illustrious station, Caecilia Metella, of the famous plebeian
family mentioned above, daughter and sister of consuls and niece of another three Metellan consuls.[75] Their offspring included another Appius,
consul 54 and censor 50, C. Pulcher, praetor 56 and proconsul in Asia in
the following years, and the notorious tribune of 58, P. Clodius; Pulcher
père also left three daughters, "whose birth and beauty gained them ad-
vantageous matches and an evil repute," as Syme put it in his typical
old-fashioned way of elegantly characterizing families and individuals.
They were married to (and got divorced from or survived) another Caecilius Metellus, consul 60, L. Licinius Lucullus, consul 74 and of luxury
and gourmet fame, and Q. Marcius Rex, consul 68, respectively. Until
this generation, the *gens* had managed to provide a consul in virtually
every generation since the early Republic—and another, for several generations less successful branch of this noble house, the Nerones, eventually supplied the first dynasty of the Principate. This makes the *gens
Claudia* one of the most successful aristocratic families in the entire history of Europe: Suetonius counts twenty-eight consulates, five dictatorships, and seven censorships. This unparalleled continuity ended in tragedy: Ti. Claudius Caesar Britannicus—the rather unlucky 14-year-old

---

[72]Asconius, *In Pisonianam* p. 18 Stangl. The grandfather of the famous Marcellus, consul
I 222 (cf. Chapter III, n. 11), was consul in 287. The father failed to obtain the *maximus
honos*; his son was consul 196 and censor 189, cf. Broughton, 1951–1952; Domenico Palombi, "Honos et Virtus, Aedes." In *LTUR* 3, 1996, 31–33.

[73]Cf. Tatum, 1999, 32ff.; Ungern-Sternberg, 2006, with further references.

[74]Syme, 1939, 19. Tacitus, *Annales* 1, 4, 3 commented on the "old and inbred arrogance"
of the *gens* ("vetere atque insita Claudiae familiae superbia"); cf. also Suetonius, *Tiberius*
1, 1ff.

[75]See fig. 3, above. Her father was Q. Metellus 'Balearicus,' consul 123, her brother Q.
Nepos, consul 98, and her uncles were consuls in 117, 115 and 113—and Cicero extolled
this "highly esteemed woman" for her "sense of duty" of old, her *honos* and *dignitas* in her
own right (*Pro Roscio Amerino* 27; 147). The details of the complex family connections of
the Claudii and the Caecilii Metelli are, however, controversial: Wiseman (1976) 1987, and
Tatum, 1999, 33ff.

boy who was murdered on Nero's orders (who was in fact only his adopted step-brother) in the year AD 55—was the last scion of a long line of patrician Claudii that had begun more than five hundred years earlier with the consul of the year 495 BC.[76] But to make this absolutely clear, the Claudii, their gentilicial continuity—if not their reputation of notorious arrogance—provide the exception that proves the rule.

[76]Suetonius, *Tiberius* 1, 2 and Tacitus, *Annales*, 12, 25, 4. Cf. the relevant chapters in Wiseman, 1979, and idem, 1985b, 15ff.

Chapter 7

CONSENSUS AND CONSENT

NECESSARY REQUIREMENTS OF A COMPETITIVE CULTURE

THESE FACTS, WHICH ARE WELL KNOWN, if not uncontroversial, suggest a number of ramifications that, I hope, will inspire and guide further discussion, not only on the concrete problem, but also on our framework of descriptive concepts and analytical categories. Let us look at these facts once again and then focus on their particular structural interdependence. If, on the one hand, the assignment of ranks in this hierarchically structured aristocracy did not take place automatically by formalized rules of inheritance; if, on the other, individual rank, and indeed, at least in principle, 'membership in the club' had to be asserted individually; and if, at last, this social system of recruiting and reproducing a ruling class is at the same time not only radically void of alternative options, but also (therefore and necessarily) highly competitive—then we must conclude that such a system requires an extraordinary consensus about its basic principles and rules. As a consequence, we have to turn to the issue of this collective consensus, its nature, depth, and breadth—and, in particular, its highly specific complementarity between competition and consensus.[1] In this context, it will be fruitful to take into account some fundamental reflections and basic considerations about this peculiar relationship that were suggested a century ago by the German sociologist Georg Simmel.[2] Until recently, his sociological and philosophical works on the constitution of societies, forms of 'sociability,' and culture had not received the degree of attention that they deserve in modern social and cultural history of the kind mapped out in previous chapters,[3] which aims to provide a new complex analysis of key terms, traditional models of interpreting the world, systems of values, and orientations, as well as a more satisfactory explanation of their particular strongly developed binding nature. Especially the peculiar and ingrained

---

[1]Cf. Hölkeskamp, 1993 and 2006d, 377ff., for earlier attempts to describe the particular complementarity of 'competition' and 'consensus'; cf. also Beck, 2008a, 119ff., and Krasser, 2006, who highlights the disintegration of this complementarity in the late Republic.

[2]See especially Simmel, 1992 (new edition in German); many of the studies included had also been published in English as *The Sociology of Georg Simmel*, compiled and translated by Kurt Wolff (Glencoe, Ill., 1950).

[3]Cf. Oexle, 1996, 17ff., 22f., as well as idem, 1995, 194ff. and passim, and Daniel, 2001, 53ff. with further references.

'depth of obedience,' which seems to have been characteristic of the *pop-ulus Romanus* and its behavorial patterns, needs to be re-evaluated in this context, given that it was the most essential resource for this aristoc-racy of office, its régime, and its legitimacy as a 'meritocracy,' based as it was on reproduction by popular election and therefore dependent upon a high level of acceptance.

Against this backdrop, it seems only natural to ask what shape this fundamental consensus might take in a social context of omnipresent and pervasive competition? Simmel's framework of sociological categories provides a useful definition of this concept of competition. At first, this category only includes "conflicts that consist of the parallel efforts" of the competitors "for the same prize," and this prize (this is an indispens-able precondition, according to Simmel, of the functioning of competi-tion as a mode of social action) must not already be in the possession of one of the competitors. In this "special form of fighting," the "parties" engaging and participating in it do not struggle "directly against each other" but rather "for the success of their merits in the eyes of a third party" as a kind of instance of reference or even arbitral authority.[4] Un-like many other sociological approaches, which emphasize the socially disintegrating, destructive, or even "venomous" effects of competition as a form of fighting, Simmel's concept revolves around its "immense social-izing effect" and a particular "synthetic power": as the objective of this kind of competition is always to obtain the favor of a third party (consist-ing of one or several people), the two competing parties are necessarily driven or even forced to get as close to the "third party" as possible. This "third party" may also be the mass of the people (or, for that matter, a citizen body in assembly), if it is called to choose among a number of ap-plicants or candidates competing for the respective "prize."[5] In this case, "competition within society" is always competition for, and therefore focused on, the individual person (or a defined and definable concrete group as "third party"); it is a struggle for acceptance, approval, ap-plause, allowances, and attention of all kinds, "a struggle of the few for the many just as of the many for the few": in short, a complex pattern, in Simmel's terms, made of "a thousand interwoven sociological threads," generated by the multiple ways and refined means of cultivating contacts and gaining favors. Thus, competition forces "the competitor who is con-fronted with other competitors" (which is usually the constellation that makes him a competitor in the first place) to make advances and offers to the 'third party,' to establish as many and as close contacts as possible and to "search out or create every possible connection between himself,

---

[4]Simmel, 1992, 323ff., quotes from pages 323 and 340 (translations K.-J. Hölkes-kamp).

[5]Simmel, 1992, 327f.

his own abilities and achievements on the one hand and the 'third party,' its desires and expectations on the other."[6]

This throws a new light on the sustained effort with which the political class and its members cultivated an extraordinarily intensive, as well as extensive, communication with the people and the citizens. The collective orientation toward, and fixation on, the people as audience and addressee that was inherent in many forms of self-presentation and self-fashioning of the political class had already been acknowledged in the field,[7] but until recently this phenomenon had never really been perceived as a specific dimension of Roman political culture, and indeed a field of research *sui generis*. Under the influence of new trends, ideas, and impulses from contemporary social and cultural history, however, the Roman (Republican) variant of a 'culture of spectacles' seems to call for a more differentiated analysis. The collective concentration on public presentation and the permanent pressure upon every member of the political class to make himself publicly 'present,' 'visible' in person (and as a personality) and thus 'known'—which is implied in the very concept of *nobilis* itself, its original meaning as well as secondary connotations—emerges, to use Simmel's terms, as an inevitable corollary inscribed in the social logic and practical dynamics of an agonal system. It is this logic that not only generated and drove forward the (re-)production of the extensive and refined repertoire of rituals and ceremonies, such as the *pompae* in the context of games and festivals, the opulent triumphal processions, and the symbolically highly charged funerals of large families, during which the aristocrats presented themselves to the Roman people in a variety of rôles constitutive for their status, as representatives of 'Romanness,' as donors and organizers, patrons and benefactors—we shall have to look at this accumulation or aggregation of functions once again later in another context.[8] The similarly differentiated spectrum of locations, places, and spaces reserved and marked out for the interaction between the participants—the Forum Romanum, the Comitium, the Sacra via and the Capitol, the Campus Martius, the Circus Maximus, and Circus Flaminius[9]—is also to be realized as an integral part of this system, as well as the enormous range of other 'spectacular' occasions for public presentation located in them, ranging from triumphs and other *pompae*, theater productions, and other performances, such as gladiatorial combats and animal chases, to public executions.[10]

[6]Simmel, 1992, 328 and 327, respectively (quotations).

[7]Hölkeskamp, 1987, 219ff., cf. 248ff., and idem, 2006d, 378ff., with further references. Cf. Nicolet, 1980; Flaig, 1993a, 207ff. and passim; Patterson, 2000, 29ff.; Flower, 2004a, 338ff.; Connolly, 2007, 30ff. and passim.

[8]Cf. chapter 8, below, and now generally Beck, 2008a and 2009.

[9]Cf. chapter 5, above.

[10]Cf. Flaig, 1995a, 100ff., 118ff.; idem, 2003b, 232ff., and now idem, 2007, with further references. Cf. already, among others, Laser, 1997, 92ff.; Döbler, 1999, 67ff. Cf. also Stambaugh, 1988, 225ff.; Gruen, 1992, 183ff., and Benoist, 2005, 245ff.

The rapid increase in the frequency of such occasions is also covered by the logic of Simmel's agonal system. We can identify at least one specific cause for this development in the political culture of the middle and late Republic—and this cause is not just derived from the simple assumption of a general dynamic increase, inherent in any system of this kind. Rather, the ever higher degree of frequency is to be seen as a kind of compensation for the fact that another important level of interaction—namely, the traditional system of patronage and *clientela*—entered its 'third phase,' in which the web of personal bonds between the élite and the people dwindled in importance and usefulness for direct communication and immediate interaction. This process has largely been described in negative terms since Meier's work on the subject was published: that is, in a terminology connoted with loss, growing deficits, and deprivation.[11] It is true that we have to understand the sheer quantitative growth and accumulation of *clientelae*, the multiplication and differentiation of relationships and the resulting increase in hierarchical difference and distance between a patron and most of his clients, on the one hand, and the inevitable concomitant decrease in the frequency and regularity of direct contacts and communication between the parties involved in this mode of interaction based on personal presence, on the other, as an indication of a rapid decline in social proximity and in the intensity of relationships.[12] It was this decline that had to be substituted, and in a way compensated for, by increased resort to other media of communication and interaction between the *populus Romanus* and its political class. Therefore, the importance of publicly demonstrated 'joviality' and 'political euergetism,' the variety of its forms in the shape of splendid games and other festivities, generous '*largesses*,' and 'symbolic gifts' (as defined and described in the classic book by Paul Veyne) was bound to increase.[13]

The various forms of *comitia* and the plebeian *concilia* taking place on the Campus Martius, in the Comitium, or the Forum were of course among the most important fields or spaces of direct political interaction between the élite and the people. The electoral, legislative, or judicial assemblies mentioned earlier—in their important expressive and symbolic function as

[11] Meier, 1966/1980, 30ff., 41ff. Also see Hölkeskamp, 1987, 253ff.

[12] Cf. Flaig, 1995a, 103ff.; idem, 1993a, 210f.

[13] Veyne (1976) 1990, 201ff.; cf. the (partly critical) discussion of Veyne's key concepts by Andreau, Schmitt, and Schnapp, 1978. Cf. Jehne, 2006, 12f., who highlights the innovative impact of Veyne's and Nicolet's work (1980), about which cf. also Andreau, 1977, and Hölkeskamp, 2009b, 16; cf. the seminal study by Jehne, 2000b, on 'joviality' as a pattern of behavior, which, by its inscribed attitude of condescension, emphasizes superiority of social rank and standing.

rituals representing and affirming, on the one hand, sociopolitical hierarchies or, on the other, a kind of civic equality[14]—were also instruments of communication, given that they provided the institutional as well as physical and 'spatial' context of a regular—and at times even frequent, if only implicit—(re-)negotiation of the relationship between aristocracy and the people and about their respective expectations and obligations to reaffirm each other's position within the sociopolitical system of the Republic.

As a matter of course, the *contio* as particular kind of assembly was also an integral part of the communicative system of this political culture of personal presence, and obviously a most important, and indeed vital, part. It was in this institutional context that the daily business of the *populus Romanus*, its *res*, its empire (and therefore the business in which its political class was permanently engaged), was debated, discussed, and, in a way, negotiated between persons and groups as parties involved in this business. It was also the institutional 'forum' on which everyone who was, or wanted to become, a member of the political class regularly fulfilled his most important public function as an orator in public debate, arguing for (or against) motions or measures in controversies over urgent current issues on the political agenda, taking sides for (and/or against) other representatives of his class in the process, or acting as advocate in lawsuits, as prosecutor or defense counsel.[15] Every active member of this class was permanently obliged to fulfil this social rôle: young senators from old families as well as ambitious *homines novi* without an ancestral background, craving the attention of the citizens (and potential electors) present, junior magistrates keen on rising up into the higher ranks, as well as established former consuls asserting (and sometimes defending) their *dignitas*. This rôle was pragmatically and structurally constitutive for membership in the élite and was no less important than the functions of senator and patron, magistrate and priest, or even military commander. After all, it was impossible to obtain any of the senior positions of the *cursus honorum* without being 'well known' (in the full sense of that descriptor) through one's public appearances, and without having attained, as a result of, or reward for, these efforts, a particular kind of 'high profile' as a public *persona*[16]—this was an essential requirement for gain-

[14]Jehne, 2006, 21; cf. idem 2001, 108, and Yakobson, 2006b, 385ff.

[15]Cf. Hölkeskamp, 1995, 16ff., 48ff. and passim; idem, forthcoming a; Laser, 1997, 138ff., 186ff.; Fantham, 1997, 111ff., and eadem, 2004, 102ff., 209ff.; May, 2002a, 53ff.; and especially Jehne, 2000a, 170ff., who highlights the differences between the various functions of an orator. Cf. also David, 1980; 1992, and now idem, 2006a; Rosenstein, 2006, 369; Astin, 1978, 131ff. (on M. Porcius Cato 'Censorius' as orator), as well as the comprehensive studies by Morstein-Marx, 2004, and Bücher, 2006, especially 20ff., 41ff., 52ff., 81ff.

[16]Cf. also Beck, 2008a, 109f. Flaig, 2003b, 99ff., 123ff., and idem, 2005, has highlighted another important aspect of this permanent personal presence and 'visibility' in and before a public; cf. on the crucial rôle and culture-specific functions of (performative) gestures, poses, and postures Aldrete, 1999.

ing promotion into higher *honores* with *imperium* and thus achieving or (re-)asserting one's rank as *nobilis*. The rôle of the orator as constituent part and prerequisite of social prominence, as well as the range of "technical" and "expressive" functions of oratory as medium and as an "instrument of personal self-fashioning and social apprenticeship," was thus deeply embedded in the communicative system, and thus in the political culture, of this city-state, based as it was on permanent and intensive interaction between the political class and the people.[17] This interaction manifested itself in two ways: as an appeal to, and negotiation with, the *populus Romanus* as the formal forum for decision making and as the ultimate source of legitimacy; and as the reaffirmation, reproduction, and renewal of the political class by the *populus* in elections and in other forms of asserting assent by acclamation.

Institutions and procedures that permitted participation of the citizen body at large—the *comitia* and *contiones*, elections, legislation, and popular jurisdiction, the ingrained 'publicity' of politics, the perpetual presence and conspicuous visibility, 'audibility,' and activity of members of the political class in public and in all civic spaces—are thus not only possible in a democratic political culture, as Millar would have it.[18] We have seen that the media and forms of a 'hierarchical communication' are structurally essential requirements of an aristocratic political culture of a particular kind, with an institutionalized citizen body central to the process of constituting and reproducing a specific variant of an aristocracy as a genuinely political class.

At this point of the argument, we have to remind ourselves that there is an indispensable requirement for the particular kind of competition typical of this 'meritocratic' system—namely, a consensus about its rules and conditions. Not only does such a consensus maintain, control, and balance the various social forces; it is also a fundamental pre-condition for the very evolution of such a competitive system as well as for its continuous "real-world" functioning and also, in the final analysis, for its "immense socializing effect" attributed to it by Georg Simmel. He himself has therefore emphasized that the parties involved in his ideal type of competition have to enter it "under the governance of a mutually accepted body of norms and rules"—and the keener and the hotter the competition, the more "rigorous, impersonal, and binding" the observance of rules must be, "to a degree of strictness like a code of honor." One of these fundamental rules

---

[17]Connolly, 2007, 131f. (quotation) and passim, who offers an interesting 'reading' of the complexity of functions connected with the rôle of the orator and the cultural status of rhetoric: she even claims that oratory was indeed "more than a means by which members of the Roman élite fashioned themselves according to élite ideals." Cf., however, Hölkeskamp, forthcoming a, and now Morstein-Marx, 2004, and already idem, 1998, and Tatum, 2007 (on the *Commentariolum petitionis* as a source highlighting these aspects of Republican political culture).

[18]E.g., Millar, 2002a, 141f., 181f.; idem, 1998, 9ff. and passim.

is that the competitors, their chances and hopes for success, must be equal. Only then can the participants accept all possible outcomes of the competition (victory or defeat) as fair, as based entirely on their individual achievement and merit. The victor has the same chances as the loser, who thus, to put it bluntly, has only himself to blame for his own failure.[19] In this context, however, Simmel seems to underestimate an important factor: if competition as a pattern of social interaction is to function continuously and smoothly, the loser must always have the hope of becoming a winner at last. He must be given a second (and even, as in the Roman case, a third) chance[20]; in other words, the prize must be made available, or rather achievable, at regular, foreseeable intervals—by annual elections, for example, in the Roman case. This is a vital precondition for the acceptance of the outcome of any single concrete competition on the part of the losers, as well as for the continuing validity, binding force, and pacifying effect of the general rules and regulations governing competitions.

These facets of competition are closely connected to a second basic requirement: that the performance and achievements of the individual competitors had to be able to be compared. The 'third party' awards its favor in the shape of the valuable and coveted prize solely on the basis of this comparison, and in doing so makes not only defeat acceptable to the loser, but also the competition itself, as the regulated, or even ritualized, mode of fight over the scarce resource of the prize. In our case, the acceptance of the procedure by the protagonists is made possible, and even increased, by placing it in the hands of the 'third party' of the electoral assemblies of the sovereign *populus Romanus*, the procedures of which are governed by a complex code of conventions and time-honored traditions, which are not only not a matter of debate or negotiation between the protagonists, but are also (in fact, if not in 'constitutional theory') beyond the actual decision-making powers of the 'third party' and the magistrate presiding over the assembly.

This acceptance was further increased by another peculiarity of the traditional system of rules, which Martin Jehne has aptly called a "clearly consensual element" of the electoral system and taken it to be a characteristic trait of this political culture.[21] As is well known, it was a fundamental general principle that the procedure of voting came to a halt as soon as the majority of voting units, *tribus* or *centuriae*, was reached. This was also true of elections, which were invariably broken off at the point when the

---

[19]Simmel, 1992, 204f., 343, cf. 335 (translations K.-J. Hölkeskamp).

[20]A systematic analysis of the known 'losers'—that is, the 'also-rans' in elections—and their (previous and later) careers remains a desideratum, although the prosopographical material has long been available: Broughton, 1991; Konrad, 1994, and recently Farney, 2004; cf. also Evans, 1991.

[21]Jehne, 2001, 108ff.; cf. also Flaig, 1995a, and idem, 2003b, 167ff.

last candidate of the number of candidates required to fill a college of magistrates had gained the minimum number of votes necessary. In the case of the most important annual elections, those for the consulship, that means that as soon as two candidates had the necessary ninety-seven *centuriae* votes, the procedure was brought to a halt and the votes of the other centuries were not taken into account at all (depending on the degree of unanimity of the upper classes, the votes of many, or at least of some, *centuriae* of the lower classes). When the results of the election were finally announced, all that was made public by the solemn declaration of the presiding magistrate was the names of the candidates who had been elected; however, the number of votes they had obtained, let alone the number of votes for the unsuccessful candidates, was never revealed. This means that narrow results, slim majorities, or strong minorities could never become openly and publicly visible. This particular procedure had the effect of suggesting a very high degree of unanimity, which was the basis of a peculiar 'fiction' of general 'consensus' between voters and candidates.[22] And it was this fiction that in turn could be (and was) not only accepted, but actively supported by successful candidates as well as defeated 'also-rans.'

This parallelogram of socio-institutional conditions and resulting forces allows us to conceptualize the factors that underlay the typical homogeneity and the extraordinary degree of coherence of the senatorial aristocracy, which in itself is familiar enough, with greater clarity and in more precise terms.[23] Competition and its central importance for maintaining and continuously reproducing this 'meritocracy,' its omnipresence and intensity, had to be embedded in, and thus contained by, a consensus about its preconditions, rules, and aims—a consensus that had to be based on a correspondingly high degree (or depth and breadth) of acceptance and collective consent. This in turn was an indispensable precondition of competition as a pacified (and continuously pacifying and stabilizing) mode of contending for a valuable resource: during the actual

[22]Jehne, 2001, 109; cf. Flaig, 2003b, 155f., and, for some basic insights into the functions of a "(façade of) consensus" and the strategies to construct it, see Stollberg-Rilinger, 2001b, 22f., and eadem, 2005, 20. Cf. also Williamson, 2005, who frequently emphasizes the "central position" and indeed "unique rôle of public lawmaking assemblies," a rôle that was an important "institutional instrument for developing communitywide consensus that was unprecedented in ancient Mediterranean societies" (xiii, 19, 228, 275; cf. 33, 96, 315, 420 etc.); cf. the critical remarks by Elizabeth A. Meyer, in *BMCR* 2005.09.68, on her concept of 'consensus': Williamson herself seems to realize (at least occasionally) that it was just "a façade of public agreement" (2005, 358).

[23]Cf. Meier, 1966/1980, 49ff., 119f.; Hölkeskamp, 1987, 241ff., with further references; Blösel, 2000, 46ff.

competition, the consensus about its norms and rules had to remain undisputed between all parties involved, the contenders as well as the 'third party.' As a result, this consensus could not just manifest itself in noncommittal appeals to such abstract values and 'noble' virtues as *virtus*, *fortitudo*, *gravitas*, and *sapientia*, but had to include much more practical rules for the 'real-world' application of these values: that is, conventions about adequate behavior, proper (and improper) practices, and even about the social or legal sanctions against the latter in the official functions of magistrate, senator, priest, and patron, as also of contender and competitor for such functions. It was again the *mos maiorum* that included such practical instruction and rules in the form of traditional *exempla*, thus encoding and affirming the 'ideal types' and maxims of truly aristocratic behavior.[24] These rules had to be obeyed, and were enforced by the consensus, because such conformity was the indispensable precondition for the maintenance of the norms and criteria that determined the hierarchy of rank and reputation, superiority and seniority, authority and influence. In other words, the constant competition for rank and predominance in this hierarchy could never be allowed to affect the ranking process as such, its criteria, principles, and procedures. They had to remain untouched, and more than that, they had to be part of the inner core of the consensus.

In application, this general rule meant that not only did the hierarchy of the *cursus honorum* as such have to remain undisputed, but it had to remain beyond any doubt that former consuls were higher in the hierarchy than former praetors, that the older ex-consuls had more influence than younger ones, and finally, all other criteria being equal, that those of patrician ancestry were senior to plebeian ex-consuls. Moreover, the concrete criteria and requirements that a junior senator had to meet in order to attain the next higher rank had to be uncontroversial as well—and by no means only with the senatorial class itself, which produced individual competitors and candidates for promotion year in year out, but also with the *populus Romanus* and the citizens as voters, the 'third party' awarding the coveted *honores*. The consensus about the criteria for status and rank, their relative value and importance, was after all the fundamental precondition for comparison between, and comparability of, individual competitors, their *res gestae*, concrete achievements and services to the *res publica*, and the claims that they could make in the struggle for the favor of the *populus Romanus* in the *comitia*. To refer to Simmel's model once again and complement its conceptual framework with new categories, comparison and comparability of competitors must always be a central part of the consensus about the rules of competition.

---

[24]Cf. Hölkeskamp, 1996, 312ff., and recently Flaig, 2003b, 76ff. Cf. also the relevant contributions in Coudry et al. (Eds.), 2001.

Chapter 8

SYMBOLIC CAPITAL AS SOCIAL CREDIT
LOCATING THE CORE OF THE CONSENSUS

AMONG THE RELEVANT and legitimate criteria for 'promotion' to higher office were not only the concrete achievements and personal merit of the individual candidate, but also—in the form of a particular kind of 'recommendation' or an 'advance payment' or 'credit'—the rank and reputation of his family. At last, we are getting to the core of the matter—namely, the really essential, and indeed defining, characteristics of this meritocracy: if the *honores* themselves and as such were not hereditary (which they could not be because of the ideology of reciprocity of service and achievement, excellence and honor), other attributes, properties, advantages, and privileges that were hereditary could and did become correspondingly more important for the individual's self-presentation. This leads us to yet another basic question: under these conditions, what exactly *was* constitutive of status, rank, and pre-eminence, for *dignitas* and *auctoritas*?

In the last few decades, scholars have provided quite a few plausible answers to this question. These answers, however, are in need of further differentiation and elaboration. What the specific type of 'recommendation' by hereditary attributes revolved around can best be described as the typically Roman Republican variant of "social" or "symbolic capital," both of which are concepts developed, applied, and tested by the French sociologist Pierre Bourdieu. In general, social capital consists of "all current and potential resources that are connected, and contribute, to the possession of a permanent network of more or less institutionalised relationships of mutual acknowledgement or acceptance." By definition, therefore, these resources are based upon membership in a group. Further, he writes that "the accumulated total capital that the individual members (of such a group) possess serves as a security for all of them and grants them credibility in the broadest sense of these concepts." The symbolic capital is acquired through respect and appreciation and includes prestige and honor, fame and reputation. These two forms can usually hardly be separated or even notionally distinguished, because the "social capital" always functions as "symbolic capital" (and vice versa), because the former functions according to the same specific "logic of acquaintance and acknowledgement" as the latter.[1]

In the case of the Republican 'meritocracy,' it was the specific symbolic capital of this group that constituted an indirect, secondary, and rather precarious type of inheritance or inheritability of individual aristocratic status: this 'capital' was created by 'the ancestors' and their steady accumulation of those achievements that were universally acknowledged as prestigious and constitutive of pre-eminence, on the one hand, and the visible manifestation and formal recognition of these achievements in the form of *honores* (once again in both senses of the Latin word) over generations, on the other; it was only this interconnected reciprocity that essentially made aristocratic status quasi-inheritable. The core of the matter is epitomized in the classic brief inscription on the sarcophagus of yet another member of the aforementioned Scipiones, Cn. Cornelius Scipio Hispanus, from the second half of the second century BC. Not only did he increase the *virtutes* of his famous *gens* by his own *mores* and try to equal the achievements of his father, but he also passed on this 'heritage': *stirpem*, which in this context is to be understood to mean 'family,' 'clan,' 'stock,' and 'descendants'—*nobilitavit honor*.[2] What this *honor*—or rather, these *honores*—were in this specific case is of course listed in detail: praetor, curule aedile, and quaestor. He had been military tribune twice, a member of a board of judges and also of the important priesthood of the *decemviri sacris faciundis*.[3]

In the case of the Republican political class, it was the careful collecting and 'filing' of the ancestors' *honores* in the family's fund of memories, which in fact amounted to the continuous accumulation of the particular heritage of a family or *gens*. In the competition for current *honores*, this heritage could then be called up, as it was inseparably linked to the one single personal characteristic of a candidate that was indeed hereditary in the strictest sense of the word: his name, which against the backdrop of the family heritage was a 'great name' in Roman eyes. This is the gist of the peculiar idea of the 'recommendation by the ancestors' (*commendatio maiorum*) that substantially increased a candidate's chances of being elected. With his usual mixture of envy and contempt, Cicero (habitually

---

[1]Bourdieu, 1983, 190f., 194f. and passim; idem, 1993, especially 215ff. Cf. Fröhlich, 1994, 35ff.; Flaig, 2004, 362ff., with additional evidence and references. For the basics and the context of Bourdieu's categories, cf. the relevant contributions in Mörth et al. (Eds.), 1994; Gilcher-Holtey, 1996, 111ff.; Reichardt, 1997, especially 79f. Göhler et al., 1998, 37ff.; Daniel, 2001, 179ff.; Raphael, 2004; Flaig, 2004, all with additional references. Also see David, 2000a, 23, 31 etc.; Burke, 2004, 56f.

[2]*ILLRP* 316 = *ROL* 4, No. 10. Cf. figure 4, above.

[3]Dates and evidence can be found in Friedrich Münzer, "Cornelius (No. 347)." In *RE* 4, 1, 1900, 1493; cf. on the priesthood Rüpke et al., 2005, 2, No.1378.

posing as the quintessential *homo novus*) explicitly observed of the bearers of such 'great names' that they had been born to become consuls.[4]

In other words, it was part and parcel of the general consensus that the symbolic capital of a *gens* was a legitimate criterion when it came to the determination of individual status and assignment of rank. The next concern must be to describe the specific character of this capital in this culture by exploring its concrete contents in more detail: what exactly was the symbolic capital in this unique sociopolitical system with a leading class that permanently constituted itself as a meritocracy? What forms could it take, which 'input' or 'deposits' could be used as symbolic capital? How does one deal with this symbolic capital under these circumstances and under the particular conditions of a pervasive competition? How is it used, what rules apply, when and where is it invoked and to what ends? Moreover, do different facets of, or 'deposits' in, the symbolic capital have different effects? Are there different contexts that allow individuals, as it were, to 'tap' specific contents or 'reservoirs' of their family's capital? By no means all of these questions have been answered—and some of them have hitherto not even been asked.

The symbolic capital of any *gens* obviously and necessarily included straightforward 'deposits' in the shape of simply and easily countable figures, such as the number of *honores* (in the strict as well as broad sense) and especially the number of triumphs. To take once again the most prominent family as an example, apart from the consulships, dictatorships, and censorships accumulated over centuries, the *gens Claudia* had six proper and two minor triumphs (*ovationes*) to its name.[5] There seem to have been differences and subtle distinctions in value between the various 'deposits' in the vaults of 'symbolic capital,' which were, as a matter of course, the basis of one-to-one comparisons and of comparability in general. This is certainly true for the simple or primary *commendatio maiorum* gained from the easily ascertainable number of accumulated consulates and other higher magistracies. More recent and fresh 'deposits' of this kind were obviously worth more than old and dusty ones. A close look at the sources provides quite a lot of support for this assumption. To quote a particularly prominent example: The famous (or perhaps

---

[4]Cicero, *De lege agraria* 2, 100; cf. 2, 1ff. passim, especially 2, 3, where he characterizes the consulship as "eum locum, quem nobilitas praesidiis firmatum atque omni ratione obvallatum tenebat"; Sall. *Bellum Iugurthinum* 63, 6 (about the conditions at the end of the second century BC): ." . . consulatum nobilitas inter se per manus tradebat"; Cic. *Pro Plancio* 18, etc. Cf. Hölkeskamp, 1987, 205 with additional evidence.

[5]Suetonius, *Tiberius* 1, 2.

notorious) M. Aemilius Scaurus, who had been consul, censor, and *princeps senatus* (and was later denounced as arrogant and conniving, as well as corrupt and greedy), was among the most influential political players of his time, one of those who were able to "well-nigh control the world by his nod." At the beginning of his career, however, he had to work "as hard as a *homo novus*," according to Cicero, in order to "resuscitate the almost extinct memory of his family by his own *virtus*" (*memoriam prope intermortuam generis sua virtute renovare*). For although being a *homo nobilissimus* born into the well-known aristocratic *gens Aemilia*, Scaurus derived little from their symbolic capital because he belonged to a rather undistinguished line most often remembered for their ineptitude and inertia (*propter tenues opes et nullam vitae industriam*) than any accomplishments of his father, grandfather, and even great-grandfather, all of whom had attained few *honores*.[6] The dictator L. Cornelius Sulla, who was to become even more famous (and controversial) than Scaurus, had to deal with similar disadvantages "because the fame of his family had been on the wane" for more than four generations (*cum familiae eius claritudo intermissa esset*). Although he belonged to a family of the highly renowned patrician *gens Cornelia*, this particular branch was not at all in the same league as the Scipios. The last consul among Sulla's direct lineage—P. Cornelius Rufinus, consul in 290 and 277 and possibly dictator at some point—had even disgraced the family: in 275, he was expelled from the Senate by the censors for greed and extravagance. Rufinus's male progeny—probably Sulla's great-grandfather and grandfather—managed to attain praetorships, but Sulla's father apparently failed to secure even that.[7]

The idea that symbolic capital at Rome could be exhausted in a few generations is supported by Cicero's telling comment in his defense of L. Licinius Murena, who—after having been elected to a consulship in 62 BC—found himself charged with electoral 'bribery' (*ambitus*) by an unsuccessful competitor, Ser. Sulpicius Rufus.[8] Rufus as prosecutor—directly opposing Cicero, working for the defense—seems to have based his case on the assumption that the victory of a *homo novus* over a noble candidate of ancient lineage at consular elections was as such and *prima facie* an indication of corruption and 'malpractice.' Interestingly, Cicero concedes (15f.) that his opponent in this trial does indeed not only pos-

---

[6]Asconius, *in Scaurianam*, p. 25 Stangl; Cicero, *Pro Fonteio* 24; *Pro Murena* 16 (quotes); Sallustius, *Bellum Iugurthinum* 15, 4.

[7]Sallustius, *Bellum Iugurthinum* 95, 3; Velleius Paterculus 2, 17, 2 (quote); Plutarch, *Sulla* 1, 1ff. Cf. Friedrich Münzer, "Cornelius (No. 302, 379, 382f.)." In *RE* 4, 1, 1900, 1422f., 1517f.; Broughton, 1951–1952 (under the respective years and Index of Careers).

[8]Cf. the interesting observations by Badel, 2005, 1ff. (on what he describes as "le 'paradoxe de Murena'"). Detailed discussions of this speech include Classen, 1985, 120ff.; Adamietz, 1989; May, 1988, 58ff.; MacKendrick, 1995, 75ff., and especially Yakobson, 1999, 91ff.

sess integrity, character, and all other necessary qualities to be expected in a consular candidate, but also *summa dignitas generis* and even *summa nobilitas*—a less-than-sophisticated strategy to disarm the prosecution, conjure up traditional rules of precedence, and highlight the particular *virtus* of his opponent.[9] But in this case, Cicero—himself consul at the time and *homo novus*—then continues his refutation in highly polemical terms: he not only dismisses out of hand Rufus's (alleged) insinuation that only a patrician is truly "well born" (*bono esse genere natus*), but goes on to disparage Rufus's inherited "nobility" as "better known to men of letters and antiquarians" than to the people and the voters, to whom it is rather "more obscure" (*Tua ... nobilitas ... hominibus litteratis et historicis est notior, populo vero et suffragatoribus obscurior*). For Rufus's father had only been of "equestrian rank" (*equestri loco*), meaning that he had not even attained a lower magistracy (and the senatorial status that went with it); the same was true of his grandfather, who was "not particularly distinguished" (*avus nulla inlustri laude celebratus*). This allowed Cicero to sum up this important part of his argument for the defense by observing rather exaggeratedly, "so evidence for your *nobilitas* has to be dug up not from the actual talk of people, but from ancient annals" (*itaque non ex sermone hominum recenti sed ex annalium vetustate eruenda memoria est nobilitatis tuae*). This polemical conclusion would have failed to hit the mark if it did not command some degree of plausibility and acceptance. Therefore, it has to be read as a further indication that there must have been a kind of consensus about the hierarchy and relative importance of different kinds of 'deposits' of symbolic capital—and this particular hierarchy also reflects all the other hierarchies that form the basis of the criteria of status and rank.

Cicero's remark implicitly evokes yet another specific feature of the Roman Republican variant of aristocratic political culture: in order to remain effective, socially 'profitable,' and available for concrete purposes of political advancement in a competitive environment, the symbolic capital of individuals and families had to be carefully cultivated and constantly renewed. The 'power of a great name' as a criterion of aristocratic status could only be effectively used if it was up to date, present—as it were, in living memory—and well known: in Cicero's terms, *ex sermone*

[9]Some years later, Cicero was to pursue the same strategy in his defense of Cn. Plancius, who had won the election to curule aedile and was prosecuted by the 'also-ran' M. Iuventius Laterensis "of consular rank," according to Cicero, on both sides—that is, from his father's as well as his mother's family (*Pro Plancio* 17f.); cf. May, 1988, 116ff.; Yakobson, 1999, 97ff.

hominum recenti. This was the case not only among the members of the peer group, but also in the *memoria* of the *populus*: after all, it was the *populus* as public and assembly that awarded the most important prizes in this competition. Moreover, it was therefore also the *populus* that was capable of increasing the stock of their symbolic capital by providing the families of successful competitors with fresh 'deposits' in the shape of these prizes.

Symbolic capital had to be cultivated and regularly refreshed not only by updating it by new 'deposits,' but also and at the same time by renewing the memory of the previously accumulated capital, recently acquired as well as that of old—and it was precisely to this end that a good part of the well-known repertoire of practices and media of public self-representation of the major families was geared. This function is particularly obvious in the ritual of the *pompa funebris*.[10] This particular variant of a funerary procession was carefully regulated and always followed the same specific kind of choreography or normative syntax, serving the representation, affirmation, and symbolic continuation of rank and status.[11] The procession started from the residence of the deceased *nobilis*, whose body had been lying in state in the most representative, accessible, and 'public' room of the 'private' residence, the *atrium*.[12] It will be immediately clear that this preliminary stage was as symbolically meaningful as the following constituent parts of the ritual syntax. From this starting point, the procession invariably led to the Forum Romanum: that is, to the main political and religious center of Rome and her empire. The main intention of this procession was not so much to provide a conventional opportunity for the surviving descendents to pay their last respects to the deceased man. The primary function, rather, was to mark his ritual entry into the ranks of his predeceased ancestors and to allocate to him a henceforth permanent position in their line, this line being the very backbone of the family's symbolic capital accumulated over generations. To this end, the ancestors were made symbolically 'present' during the procession, a particularly powerful symbolic act in this 'culture of personal presence.' This meant that the waxen portrait-masks of the ancestors (*imagines*),[13]

[10]Cf. Hölkeskamp, 1996, 320ff., and now idem, 2008, 104ff.; Dupont, 1992, 23ff.; Flaig, 1995b, 121ff.; idem, 2003b, 49ff.; Flower, 1996, 91ff. and passim; eadem, 2006b. Cf. also Bodel, 1999, 259ff.; Blösel, 2000, 37ff.; Walter, 2003, 260ff.; Beck, 2005b; Sumi, 2005, 41ff.; Benoist, 2005, 110ff.

[11]A systematic comparison with funerary processions as public and political rituals in other (pre-)modern cultures, which invariably show a specific sophisticated 'taxonomy,' may be fruitful: cf., e.g., Weller, 2006, 230ff. on this 'stage' of the complex *'theatrum praecedentiae'* in a German city from the fifteenth to the eighteenth centuries.

[12]Cf. Flower, 1996, 93ff. with references; Dupont, 1992, 95ff. on the *atrium*.

[13]Cf. the basic work by Flower, 1996, 185ff. Also see the detailed reviews by McDonnell, 1999, and Flaig, 2000: the latter combines (rather harsh) criticism of the theoretical and conceptual basics with important additional considerations; also see Belting-Ihm, 1996.

usually kept in their shrines in the *atrium* of the house—that is, the very starting-point from which the *pompa* had set out—were carried by people dressed to represent the 'deposit' of symbolic capital that the specific ancestor had contributed. Depending on which rank and *honores* an ancestor had attained, the person representing him wore the purple-bordered *toga praetexta*, which denoted a praetor or a consul, or even the gold-embroidered purple attire worn by triumphators.[14] He was accompanied by the number of lictors appropriate to the rank in the *cursus honorum* that he represented. Thus, the 'ancestors' literally escorted their newly deceased scion, and did so in a strictly chronological order: the oldest ancestor, who had first achieved curule *honores*, and by so doing established the rank and 'name' of the family and thereby laid the foundation for its symbolic capital, being always at the head. As a consequence, such processions never staged the family's entire ancestry but only a select few: ancestors who had failed to achieve *honos/honores* in the competition for rank and standing were simply omitted in this parade of successful contributors to the family's symbolic capital.

The climax of this ritual was the *laudatio funebris*,[15] a speech that was usually delivered by one of the dead man's sons from the *rostra* in the Forum. The *laudatio*, being the central element of the syntax of the *pompa funebris*, followed a highly conventionalized pattern. The best (and earliest extant) example is the speech by Q. Caecilius Metellus, who held it for his father, Lucius, at the latter's funeral in 221 BC. One part was invariably focused on the countable *honores* and *res gestae* of the deceased: as mentioned before, Lucius Metellus had been consul and proconsul, *magister equitum* and dictator (in order to preside over the elections), *pontifex* and *pontifex maximus*, and the first general who was able to display elephants at his triumph. Moreover, according to the *laudator* Quintus, Lucius had managed to attain the "ten most important and highest aims," which all "prudent men" tried to fulfil in the course of their life, to such a degree of perfection as no one had attained since the founding of Rome. This canon of typical aims for a *nobilis* included, on the one hand, exhibiting extraordinary personal prowess in battle, as *primarius bellator*, and skill and steadfastness as a commander, as *fortissimus imperator*, under whose auspices some military operations of the utmost importance had been (successfully) carried out (*auspicio suo maximas res geri*). On the other hand, this catalogue also included 'civic' virtues. Lucius had excelled as *optimus orator*; he had enjoyed the highest 'honor' (*maximus honos*). Further, he was deemed

---

[14]Cf. now on the 'symbolism' of clothing and costumes in general Scholz, 2005, 414ff., 419ff., and also, from a different perspective, Koortboijan, 2008.

[15]Polybius 6, 53, 2f.; and 54, 1f. Cf. Kierdorf, 1980; Flower, 1996, 128ff. (both with full references).

the most eminent member of the senate (*summus senator*), who had displayed supreme wisdom (*summa sapientia*) in counsel. At the same time, this exemplary *nobilis* had also ensured the prosperity, status, and continuity of his family by making a large fortune in a "respectable" and appropriate way—whatever that meant (*pecuniam magnam bono modo invenire*)—and by having several (male) children. All this culminated in his being highly renowned within the whole citizen body (*clarissimus in civitate*).[16]

A *laudatio* of this kind—and its characteristic series of superlatives—was the final, explicit, and ultimate affirmation of the claim that the deceased had been successful in the life-long competition for *honores* and rank and whose posterity therefore deserved to be part of the glorious history of his *gens*. This message was highlighted by the rules of the performance: a *laudatio* was not only delivered to the assembled people but also directly addressed to the symbolically represented ancestors, whose 'images' had taken their places on the official chairs of the curule magistrates. As a matter of course, a further section of the typical *laudatio* would focus on the glorious family record as such by recalling the *honores* and *res gestae* of the ancestors present (once again in chronological order, beginning with the feats of the oldest ancestor present). Symbols and words, representation and images, ritual and speech, performance and discourse thus created a dense network of cross-references and mutually affirming allusions, all embedded in the concomitant and equally dense topography of places and spaces, from the 'private' *domus* as shrine of familial *memoria* centered on the *atrium*,[17] to the 'public' Forum Romanum, as 'museum' of the Roman collective memory. It was this network, its density and irresistible suggestiveness, that allowed (and obliged) the public present at the occasion, *plebs* and peers alike, to comprehend the tradition of a single family as an integral, and indeed constituent, part of the history of the Republic itself.[18]

For the individual family in question, a glorious *pompa funebris* not only meant a kind of 'realization' of the fresh 'profits' that its deceased member had earned by his *honores* and *res gestae* and 'deposited' in its symbolic capital. The ritual recalling of this capital as a whole was also and above all particularly suited to confirm, and in a way even increase, the overall value of the capital accumulated by the symbolically present

[16]Pliny, *Naturalis historia* 7, 139–140. Cf. Kierdorf, 1980, 10ff.

[17]Cf., e.g., Dupont, 1992, 90ff., 146ff., and now von Hesberg, 2005, and Stein-Hölkeskamp, 2006, 301ff., on the multiple symbolic functions of the urban residences of senatorial families.

[18]Hölkeskamp, 1996, 321ff.; idem, 1995, 11f., 22, 30ff.; and recently Blösel, 2000, 41ff.; 2003, 53ff.; Pina Polo, 2005, 152ff.; Beck, 2008a, 111ff.

ancestors of previous generations. This important effect has to be taken literally and needs to be repeated in this context: a symbolic capital of this kind had to be frequently renewed in order to prevent it from dwindling. In other words, the value of symbolic capital did not remain constant; it could not be relied on to yield 'interest' automatically, let alone at a steadily increasing rate. An ancestor of consular rank who had lived several generations ago was worth much less than a father or an uncle of the same rank. As a consequence, symbolic capital had to be carefully cultivated, continuously renewed, and (if at all possible) regularly increased by new achievements and *honores* in each generation. This principle is yet another part of the 'hidden agenda' to which Cicero implicitly referred in his defense of Murena: he not only pours scorn on the patrician Rufus's claim to *nobilitas* and a *dignitas* superior to Murena's standing, but also extols the latter's descent from a plebeian family "of distinction and honor." He goes out of his way to emphasize that, in stark contrast to Rufus's signally undistinguished paternal ancestry, Murena's great-grandfather and grandfather had at least made it to the praetorship, and his father as praetor had even "celebrated a magnificent and thoroughly deserved triumph" (an audacious claim), and therefore left to his son "an easier path to consular rank," which had indeed already been "his father's due."[19]

There is yet another message implied in this strategy of argumentation: the subtle rule of hierarchy and the law of supply and demand played an important rôle here, too, as the scarce resource of the *maximus honos* was of course the most valuable, prestigious, and profitable one. This meant, *mutatis mutandis*, that the lower *honores*, even the praetorship, became correspondingly less and less important during the second century BC, so that only consulates, and the corresponding commands and triumphs, contributed significantly to a family's symbolic capital.[20] The aforementioned inscription on the tomb of Scipio Hispanus fervently emphasizes the fact that he had (at least) tried to equal his father's greatness and had (at least) produced male children, so that the outstanding, indeed larger than life-size, *maiores* of his *gens* would not have to feel ashamed of him: the apologetic tone is by no means a coincidence. For despite the elaborate listing of all his *honores*, it cannot conceal a glaring

---

[19] *Pro Murena* 15. L. Murena, the consul of 62, was L.f.L.n. His father was praetor by 87, held command (probably *pro praetore*) in Asia under Sulla, fought the so-called 'Second Mithridatic War' until recalled by Sulla and celebrated a triumph in 81 (Brennan, 2000, 556f.; Itgenshorst, 2005, No. 244).The consul's grandfather L., otherwise unknown, must have been praetor by 101; his great-grandfather was probably another L., praetor 147 (Broughton, 1951–1952, for the dates; cf. 1952, 2, Index of Careers).

[20] This 'ranking' is also suggested by Cicero, *Pro Plancio* 14f.

deficit: this son and grandson of consuls, related to the great Africanus and to Scipio Aemilianus, had only managed to reach the praetorship.[21]

But was the code of internal ranking criteria really limited to the mere enumeration or bookkeeping of consulates, triumphs, and other countable *honores*? How important were the successes and exploits, capabilities and 'virtues' (actual or ascribed, assumed or alleged) of the men who held these offices: did they complement, shade, illustrate, and represent values? Did they (at least in case of need) even compensate for current deficits in 'tangible'—that is, countable—capital? Perhaps it is possible to fit the fictitious genealogies of more or less famous families into this context; the well-known practice of sporting the Trojan Aeneas (or his mythical descendants) as the family's progenitor was only one variant.[22] Widespread though such fabulous family trees seem to have been, however, myths of the kind could evidently never establish themselves as an important, let alone decisive, factor when placed beside the real 'Republican' family record of a *gens*. Even descent from gods, goddesses, or heroes could not generate aristocratic status. It is significant to note that the famous *gens Claudia* seems never to have construed any Greek or other heroic or divine descent in its entire glorious history, but rather maintained its original down-to-earth Italian progenitor, Atta Clausus; with two dozen consuls, several dictators, and famous censors in the family tree, the *gens Claudia* did not really need a god.[23]

Moreover, there were quite distinctive traditions of a different kind that also played an important part in constructing the collective image of a considerable number of patrician *gentes*, as well as plebeian families whose 'grand name' was immediately associated with, and inseparably

---

[21]*ILLRP* 316, Z. 5f.: "progeniem genui, facta patris petiei. Maiorum optenui laudem ut sibei me esse creatum laetentur..." His father was Cn. Cornelius Scipio Hispallus, *pontifex* since 199 and consul 176 (Broughton, 1951–1952, under the years and Index of Careers; Rüpke et al., 2005, 2, No. 1377); his grandfather was Cn. Scipio Calvus, consul 222 and uncle of the later Africanus. Cf. Flower, 1996, 169f., and Kruschwitz, 2002, 86ff. Cf. fig. 4, above.

[22]Cf. Wiseman, 1974, and Hölkeskamp, 1999. Cf. now Bettini, 2006, *passim*, and Farney, 2007, 54ff. etc., on the complexity and ambivalence of this tradition. Farney deals with the related aspect of (Italian) 'ethnic identity' in more detail—cf., e.g., Cicero, *Pro Plancio* 19ff., where a kind of implicit 'hierarchy' of different ethnic identities is suggested. Cicero claimed that coming from the "municipium antiquissimum" Tusculum was particularly prestigious. Cf. also, again for comparative purposes, Schreiner, 1997, 408ff., on fictitious genealogies as a form of legitimation in the Middle Ages.

[23]Cf. Hölkeskamp, 1999, 20 (*pace* Wiseman, 1979, 57f.), and now Farney, 2007, 78ff.; 88ff. on the Sabine background of the Claudii and some other *gentes*.

connected to, legends and stories of spectacular feats and/or specific traits and characteristics. For example, to begin once again with the aforementioned Claudii, this most prominent patrician *gens* was famous (or rather, notorious) for their *superbia*, a particular kind of pride, aristocratic arrogance, a rude and ruthless haughtiness toward the common people.[24] We have, however, to bear in mind that 'arrogance' as such may have been considered less outrageous, if not acceptable, in a society in which steep hierarchies and an insurmountable distance between *nobiles* of the first water and the vast majority of ordinary Romans was universally taken for granted. It is, however, also true that, in contrast to the Claudian 'image,' the Valerii were traditionally known for being well disposed toward the *plebs*: Their legendary early representatives—among them one of the first consuls of the *libera res publica*, P. Valerius, surnamed 'Publicola'—were credited with the fundamental legislation *de provocatione*, guaranteeing and protecting the *libertas* of the man in the Roman street.[25] As this right of individual Roman citizens to appeal to *populus* and assembly against arbitrary action and unjust rulings by magistrates was a cherished part of the ideological core of the collective identity of the Roman citizen body,[26] this reputation must have been of considerable value.

The Manlii (Torquati) enjoyed a somewhat ambivalent reputation for their merciless severity (*severitas*) and unrelenting 'imperious' strictness as holders of *imperium* and/or bearers of *patria potestas* in the face of insubordination or disgraceful demeanor by junior family-members. Interestingly, it was the very same T. Manlius (consul in 347, 344, and 340, and allegedly also three times dictator) who laid the foundations of both elements of their 'corporate identity.' According to a well-established tradition, he was named 'Imperiosus' because as commander and holder of *imperium*, he ordered his own son to be executed who, against explicit orders, had fought and vanquished an enemy in single combat,[27] a feat of

---

[24]Tacitus, *Annales* 1, 4, 3 mentions the "vetus atque insita Claudiae familiae superbia"; cf. Livy 9, 33, 3; 34, 1ff. etc.; Suetonius, *Tiberius* 2, 2ff. How far back this 'family image' goes is still disputed: according to Alföldi, 1965, 159ff., it originates from the third century BC; Wiseman, 1979, 125ff., cf. 57ff., claims that it was only established in the middle of the first century (which seems to be too radical); cf. now Ungern-Sternberg, 2006.

[25]Cf. on this tradition (Cicero, *Pro Flacco* 1; 25; Livy 2, 8, 1f.; 3, 55, 1ff.; 10, 9, 3ff. etc.) Wiseman, 1979, 113ff., with additional evidence (and somewhat idiosyncratic speculations about a much later origin); cf. now the detailed discussion by Oakley, 2005b, 120ff. (on Livy 10, 9, 3–6); Walter, 2003, 267ff., and idem, 2004b, 416f.

[26]Cf., e.g., Cicero, *De oratore* 2, 199, on *provocatio* as "patronam illam civitatis ac vindicem libertatis"; Livy calls it "unicum praesidium libertatis" (3, 55, 4). Cf. now Jehne, 2002, on this aspect of the ideological 'construction' of the Republic as a community based on liberty.

[27]Cf. Oakley, 1998, 436ff. (on Livy 7, 1–22) about this image (Cicero, *De finibus* 1, 23f.; 34f.; Livy 7, 7, 22; Valerius Maximus 5, 8, 3 etc.); cf. Hölkeskamp, forthcoming b.

virtus that he himself had accomplished as a young man: as military tribune (and after having requested explicit permission of his commander) he had killed a gigantic Gaul and stripped him of his typical piece of decoration, worn around the neck (*torques*), which earned him the honorary *cognomen* 'Torquatus.'[28] Perhaps unsurprisingly, it was this 'deposit' in their symbolic capital that the family cherished in the first place.[29]

The 'corporate identity' of the Caecilii Metelli, the most successful plebeian family in the second half of the second century BC,[30] was based on a rather extravagant kind of combination of myths of divine descent and tangible 'Republican' merits of recent memory: on the one hand, the family claimed to be descended from Caeculus, son of the god Vulcanus and founder of the family's original Latin home town of Praeneste; however, they also claimed a 'Trojan' ancestry in the shape of a certain Caecas, one of the many companions of the founder-hero Aeneas on his long way to Italy.[31] On the other hand, they apparently took every opportunity to remind their peers and the people at large of two particularly memorable feats in their 'Republican' record of *res gestae*: The victory of L. Caecilius Metellus, consul 251 and honorand of the famous *laudatio funebris* discussed above, over the Carthaginians at Panormus in Sicily, where he captured a huge number of elephants; and the Greek victory of Q. Caecilius Metellus, after his triumph surnamed 'Macedonicus,' who built the Porticus Metelli and lavishly adorned it with spectacular works of art, such as the twenty-five equestrian statues by the famous Lysippus of the companions of Alexander the Great killed in the battle on the Granikos.[32] Several members of the family made good use of the opportunity that the (junior) position of a member in the college of moneyers (*tresviri monetales*) offered:[33] from the second century BC onward, coinage and

[28]Livy 7, 9, 6–10, 14; cf. for further references and detailed discussion of the episode Oakley, 1998, 113ff.; Walter, 2004b, 420ff.

[29]Cf. Itgenshorst, 2005, 207f.

[30]Cf. chapter 6 and figure 3, above.

[31]Cf. Hölkeskamp, 1999, 7, with references; Farney, 2007, 62f. etc. Cf. also Bastien, 2007, 381ff., who deals with yet another aspect of the complex 'corporate identity' of the Metelli.

[32]Cf. Coarelli, 1997, 529ff.; Viscoglioso, "Porticus Metelli." In *LTUR* 4, 1999, 130–32, with references.

[33]Cf. Crawford, *RRC* 2, 598ff., on the "monetary magistrates" in general. The Metelli, who held the position in an early stage of their career and later rose to prominence, presumably include Q. Metellus Macedonicus, consul 143, and his sons Q. Metellus Balearicus, consul 123, M. Metellus, consul 115, and C. Metellus Caprarius, consul 113, as well as (L.) Metellus (either Delmaticus, consul 119, or Diadematus, consul 117) and another Q. Metellus (either Numidicus, consul 109, or—probably—Nepos, consul 98); as Sullan commander in 81, Q. Metellus Pius, consul 80, also issued coins with the typical Metellan symbol: the elephant on the reverse, in this case unsurprisingly combined with a head of *Pietas* as goddess on the obverse. His adopted son Q. Metellus Pius Scipio, consul 52, fol-

Figure 6. Macedonian shield decorated with an elephant's head; the laurel-wreath border also alludes to the triumphs of the Metelli: reverse of a *denarius* of the moneyer M. Metellus Q.f. (probably M. Caecilius Metellus, son of Q. Metellus Macedonicus and consul 115); the obverse shows the helmeted head of Roma as goddess (courtesy of Freeman & Sear, Los Angeles).[35]

the imagery on coins—in the shape of mythological and historical allusions, visual signals and symbols of all sorts—became an ever more important medium of advertising their familial symbolic capital and specific 'corporate identity.'[34]

This selection shows that what we call symbolic capital could be a complex, multilayered, and occasionally even highly ambivalent heritage. What is more—what was the status and value of these 'deposits' in the familial symbolic capital? After all, they could hardly be counted, classified into a clear-cut hierarchy of *honores* and thus made comparable to the stock of merits of other families. Evidently, however, some of the most valuable items of symbolic capital with a particularly high 'yield' could be of this kind, such as well-known *res gestae* of famous ancestors, which may even had earned fixed places as shining *exempla* of (some kind of) *virtus* in the collective memory of the people and the aristocracy alike. Such items could carry a particular potency by being automatically associated with the name of the *gens* as such and turning it into a 'household name' in the literal sense of the term (even if this could occasionally mean, as apparently in the case of the Manlii Torquati, that the burden

lowed the tradition as commander in the civil war: cf. Crawford, *RRC* I, Nos. 211 (cf. p. 55), 256, 262, 263, 269 (cf. p. 64f.), 284, 374, 459. Cf. chapter 6, above, and the stemma, figure 3.

[34]The classic treatment is Alföldi, 1956. Cf. recently Boschung, 2008, 18ff., with further references.

[35]Cf. Crawford, *RRC* I, No. 263/1a; Itgenshorst, 2005, 133ff. Cf. also Bastien, 2007, 216ff. on triumphal symbols on coinage in general.

of the 'grand name' overshadowed everything else). In this context, it is certainly significant that a very large part of these *res gestae* was performed in those countable and (in principle) datable rôles of prominence that formed the chronological backbone, and generally the main structure of the system, of a family's symbolic capital—namely, as consuls, dictators, and commanders with *imperium*, or even as junior military tribunes. This is emphasized in the inscription on the honorific monument of the consul and admiral Duilius, discussed in a previous context,[36] as well as in the votive inscription that Lucius Mummius, consul in 146 BC, had put up on the temple for Hercules Victor that he had founded: The *res gestae* enumerated in this inscription—the conquest of Achaia and the destruction of Corinth—were performed "under his command and auspices" as consul (*ductu auspicio imperioque eius*), as the second line of the inscription emphasizes, before he returned to Rome in triumph (*triumphans*).[37] The precise placing and dating of such deeds and the virtues that they indirectly connoted—such as *virtus, fortitudo,* or even *severitas*—allowed them to be integrated into, and at the same time ranked according to, the value system of this meritocracy. In turn, this contextualization allowed these 'deposits' to be easily quoted—or rather, to be withdrawn from the family's accumulated stock of symbolic capital, for example, in the context of a *laudatio funebris*, as discussed above, or in the inaugural speech of a consul on the occasion of taking up office. According to Cicero, it was a long-established ancestral custom that those who by the favor of the Roman people—that is, by having been elected to high office—have also gained the right to have *imagines* in their family should, when addressing the assembly for the first time in their new capacity, not only express their gratitude for this new *beneficium*, but also praise their ancestors (and their rank obtained by *honores*).[38]

These time-honored practices—as well as all the other forms and media of public self-(re)presentation of individual members or families of the senatorial aristocracy—implicitly suggest, or even explicitly emphasize, that the symbolic capital of an individual family always represents the consolidated contribution of many generations of ancestors to a much greater and more important whole—namely, the collective tradition of the entire class. In other words, the grand total of accumulated family achievements is also part of the collective heritage of the *res publica* and the *populus Romanus*. This means that the *maiores* of an individual aristocrat were always part of the totality of *maiores*. In other words, the

[36] Cf. chapter 5, above.

[37] *CIL* I² 626 = VI 331 = *ILS* 20 = *ILLRP* 122, see Kruschwitz, 2002, 139ff.; Domenico Palombi. "Hercules Victor, aedes et signum." In *LTUR* 3, 1996, 23–25, both with full references; Valvo, 2005, 79ff.

[38] *De lege agraria* 2, 1, 1; cf. Hölkeskamp, forthcoming a.

founders of, and subsequent successful contributors to, a family's symbolic capital were always an integral part or subset of that group of 'ancestors' (*maiores* as an abstract collective) who had laid the basis of the empire's later grandeur, and in fact of Rome herself, in their position as idealized, demanding, but always unsurpassable rôle models—the men and (their) *mores* 'of old,' to expand on Ennius's famous phrase, are the rock-solid foundation of Rome's cause.[39] At the same time, this self-positioning of the great *gentes* is itself a result of (but also a precondition for) the general consensus within the ruling class as a whole about ideological contents and messages, legitimate strategies and media of their public self-construction.

One of these messages, the *pompa funebris*, has already been mentioned in another context.[40] The perpetual creation and renewal of this kind of *memoria* was an important integral part of the continuous process of affirming the collective superiority of the political class as well as reproducing the legitimacy, validity, and stability of the underlying sociopolitical hierarchies. Moreover—and in this context this is the most important aspect of these strategies of familial self-identification with the history of the *res publica*—there is the welcome side-effect that this emphatic focus upon continuity helped to construct a (precarious) heritability of the membership of the individual *gens* in the political class or even in the *nobilitas*; this is, so to speak, the socially profitable 'yield' of a family's accumulated symbolic capital.

This particular strategy of self-definition had a downside, however, in so far as it fostered increasingly sharp competition as a matter of course. That is to say, if the *honores* and the resulting status as exclusive criterion of rank could only be obtained by individual achievement, on the one hand, and if the *commendatio maiorum* nevertheless provided certain advantages in this competition, on the other, then it is this apparent paradox that obviously exerted high pressure on the individual members of every politically ambitious and active family. Not only could and did a young *nobilis* never escape this pressure, he could not even afford to arouse the faintest suspicion that he lacked the necessary *industria* or energy to distinguish himself: the smallest rumor of this kind could damage a reputation and threaten a fledgling career. This 'iron law' of meritocracy is

[39]The famous expression is: "Moribus antiquis res stat Romana virisque" (Ennius fragm. 156 Skutsch). On this topic see the most recent work by Blösel, 2000, 27; Stemmler, 2000, 141f. On the concept of *mos maiorum* cf. Hölkeskamp, 1996, 308ff., and recently Mencacci, 2001, 421ff.

[40]On the *pompa funebris*, see above.

reflected in the well-known conversation between Polybius and the young Scipio Aemilianus about the latter's fear of being considered a quiet and indolent young man lacking a truly Roman energetic character and therefore unworthy of his noble house and famous forefathers. In the ideological world of his peers this would inevitably have meant failing the obviously very high expectations that male Cornelii Scipiones in general, and the aspiring head of the family in particular, had to meet.[41]

The symbolic capital of such a family, which was the precondition for gaining the advantages of the *commendatio maiorum*, consisted solely of countable, visible, and (in the full sense of the word) memorable achievements by individual family-members—and those had to be accomplished before they could be used and yield the aforementioned social profit. The epitaphs on the tombs of those Scipiones who died early and were therefore unable to enter the *cursus honorum* or did not manage to proceed to higher *honores*—at least by the high standards of a family of the first water, as the Scipiones certainly were in the two generations following Scipio Africanus—give a very clear impression of how self-evident, and indeed inescapable, these norms and the resulting expectations and claims really were. Interestingly, these epitaphs are the only ones in which the deceased men's age is explicitly emphasized or even precisely stated: They were between sixteen and thirty-three years old.[42] "So do not ask"—as the elogium on Lucius, son of Gnaeus, consul 176 BC, demands—why he was never entrusted with the *honos* (of a magistracy): The young man had died at the tender age of twenty. Once again, the implied addressee is the community, the *populus Romanus*, that had been directly addressed in earlier elogia on more successful Scipiones. Another inscription also invariably emphasizes that the prematurely deceased man (possibly a son of Scipio Africanus) undoubtedly had the rich talents and skills required to pursue such a fitting career: it was death that tragically deprived him of the chance to ascertain and make good use of his (inbred) *honos, fama virtusque, gloria atque ingenium*. In a longer life, "you" (in this case the honorand) would "easily have surpassed the *gloria* of your ancestors by (your own) deeds."[43] This telling assertion and its typical se-

---

[41]Polybius 31, 23, 6–24, 12. Cf. Astin, 1967, 18ff., 245f.; Hölkeskamp, 1987, 206, 211f.

[42]*ILLRP* 312 (which is probably referring to the son of the consul in 176 BC, Cn. Cornelius Hispallus); 313 (referring to L., son of L. Scipio, consul 190); 314 (probably referring to the son of the man in *ILLRP* 313, and the grandson of the consul 190 BC, L. Cornelius Scipio Asiagenes). Cf. chapter 6 and figure 4, above; Eck, 1981, 127ff.; idem, 1999, 35ff., with further references; Kruschwitz, 2002, 86ff.; Alföldy, 1982, 381.

[43]*ILLRP* 311: "mors perfecit tua ut essent omnia brevia, honos, fama, virtusque gloria atque ingenium. Quibus sei in longa licuiset tibe utier vita, facile facteis superases gloriam maiorum." Cf. Kruschwitz, 2002, 73ff. Also consider the typical wording (in Greek) of the conversation between Polybius and Aemilianus that was mentioned before: The older man

mantics of comparison with the ancestors conveys yet another message: competition was truly omnipresent, as it even defined and determined one's position (and rank) within one's own family and above all among one's own ancestors.

Moreover, the elogium on Lucius Scipio embarks on a particularly interesting kind of explicit wordplay: in his short life, this promising young man had not only never been outdone in (the competition for) *virtus*, and not only had he already shown *magna sapientia* and *multas virtutes*—his life "lacked not *honos*, but *honos*." Almost never does one find the double meaning of this term so clearly expressed.[44] These inscriptions, their explicit messages and implicit meanings, make clear how apt Bourdieu's differentiation of his concept of 'symbolic capital' really is. He emphasizes that it is always a *"loan* in the widest sense, a kind of advance, discount or credit order, that the group grants to those of its members who can (or at least promise to) provide the most material and virtual assurances,"[45] in the hope of benefiting the entire group.

This conception of symbolic capital leads on to another consideration concerning a fundamental condition of competition as a mode of social behavior (as described by Simmel)—namely, the perpetual comparison and general comparability of achievements and merits. This prerequisite of its functioning required the consensus to be extended to the whole spectrum of forms, means, and media of public presentation of these achievements. In this competitive culture, all the rituals and modes of self-advertisement had to follow reliable and recognizable patterns; therefore, they had to be regulated on the basis of an accepted and appropriate set of rules. It was this 'subcode' of rules that made the necessary comparability of achievements possible, which was based on the 'countability' of accumulated *honores*, on the one hand, and their relative importance in an undisputed framework of hierarchies, on the other: consulates, dictatorships, and censorships are worth more than praetorships, triumphs always 'count' a lot, *res gestae* in (high) office are particularly 'memorable' (and therefore valuable). It is the need for comparability that not only explains the aforementioned patterns and stereotypes of the Republican 'epigraphic habit,' which invariably occur in different contexts, public and funerary, and different genres of inscriptions. The same fundamental need is also the common denominator of the set order of the individual elements of the *pompa funebris*, on the one hand, and the complex syntax

---

offers his help because the younger one has to prove himself "worthy of his ancestors in word and deed" (Polybius 31, 24, 5).

[44] *ILLRP* 312: "Quoiei vita defecit, non honos honore, is hic situs, quei numquam victus est virtutei." Cf. Kruschwitz, 2002, 93ff. Generally see already Hölkeskamp, 1987, 211 and 206, with additional (literary) sources.

[45] Bourdieu, 1993, 218.

124   CHAPTER 8

of the triumphs, on the other: These particularly spectacular rituals (and all other processions) consisted of typical—that is, recognizable—basic elements in a paradigmatic order, which, however, allowed a certain amount of variation, addition, accentuation, and intensification. But even the keen competitiveness of the aristocratic class, with its peculiar vicious circle (or perhaps rather, spiral) of increasing bitterness and wasting of economic and social resources could not be allowed to break up the framework of reference, comparison, and comparability. This was also (or, in the final analysis, perhaps even especially) true in the case of the triumphal processions of Pompey, Caesar, and later the future Augustus, their unprecedented scale, opulence and, at least in the case of the former two figures, somewhat scandalizing messages.[46] Even in the unbalanced and confused situation at the end of the Republic, comparability always remained the essence of competition. It was after all—to use the combination of concepts coined by Tonio Hölscher—a particular type of willful "provocation" and "transgression"[47] that characterized these dramatic and truly memorable celebrations of victories of (once again) unprecedented scale, as well as the public (and private) demeanor of these and a few other grandees, and set the tone in the last decades of the Republic. Once again, this 'competition' of record breaking, of outdoing and outbidding one another and everybody else, as well as its inherent 'provocative' potential and 'transgressive' momentum, could only be perceived as such against the backdrop of established and time-honored practices—once again and still only by comparison.

[46]See, e.g., Velleius Paterculus 2, 40, 3; Appian, *Mithr.* 116, 568–117, 578; Plutarch, *Pompeius* 45, 1ff.; Eutropius 6, 16 etc. (on Pompey's triumph in 61 BC); Velleius Paterculus 2, 56, 2; Appian, *Bella civilia* 2, 101, 418–102, 422; Suetonius, *Divus Iulius* 37; Plutarch, *Caesar* 55, 2ff.; Cassius Dio 43, 19, 1ff. etc. (on Caesar's five triumphs in 46 and 45, four of which were in fast succession); Cassius Dio 51, 21, 5ff. etc. (on Octavian's threefold triumph in 29 BC). The complete references can be found in *Inscr. It.* XIII 1, 566f., 570. Cf. Itgenshorst, 2005, Nos. 258, 262–66, 287–89; Beacham, 1999, 49ff., 74ff.; Sumi, 2005, 57ff.; Hölkeskamp, 2006a; (2006) 2007 and now also Beard, 2007, 7ff.
[47]Hölscher, 2004, and idem, 2009. Cf. also David, 1993, and Krasser, 2006, 7 and passim.

Chapter 9

AN END OF THE BEGINNING

A NEW ANCIENT HISTORY AND ITS TOPICALITY

B Y THE TIME FERGUS MILLAR began his all-out attack on what he characterized (in occasionally highly rhetorical terms) as an old, outmoded, and obdurate orthodoxy, a shift of paradigm had already been well under way in the field of ancient (Roman as well as Greek) history, not only in American, British, and French Classics and History departments, but also in German classic(al) academe. This shift was not restricted to the history of the Roman republic and has certainly not come to an end—whatever that could mean in this context (and an 'end' of any kind is probably not desirable at all, as it may mean nothing else but the consolidation and solidification of yet another 'orthodoxy'). The first criticism of Millar's position must therefore be fairly general: he failed to take into account a broad spectrum of attempts at a revision of whatever 'orthodoxy' was still in place in the mid-1980s—attempts that had long since been put forward in publications. He thus passed up the chance to pursue and enrich an already ongoing and open discussion with a promising innovative and productive potential, as it began to concern, beyond a mere revision of received wisdom, general theoretical and methodological issues and their far-reaching implications. This sweeping process of change can well be labeled 'paradigm shift,' as it not only involved a search for new categories and concepts, new patterns and models for the description, analysis, and explanation of political and social structures in the *libera res publica* from the fourth century BC to the beginning of the Principate—structures that had once been considered to be well known and widely accepted. Whereas their stability, unchanging character, and function had previously been taken for granted, they and their inherent dynamics were now being seen in a new light. Moreover, and at the same time, the discipline of Ancient History as such had also begun to break out of the 'ghetto' of its traditional fixations and restrictions: on the one hand, it was gradually overcoming its narrow, and even meta- or ahistorical, understanding of 'law' and 'constitution,' institutions, and formal procedure in the tradition of *Staatsrecht*. On the other hand, it began to abandon the equally traditional antiquarian concentration on a strictly positivist "histoire historisante" and the abundantly examined "histoire traités-et-batailles,"[1] the all-too-familiar history of great men, their deeds and feats, from Camillus to Caesar. At the same time, the discipline was slowly emancipating itself from its one-sided methodological fixation upon a conservative classical philology. In the wake of discussions in the neighboring fields of Medieval, Early Modern, and Modern History—not only about abstract programs of social, 'structural,' and cultural history, but also about completely new issues, theories, and methods, about forms of presentation and cognitive aims[2]—an increasing number of ancient historians are now attempting to rejuvenate, and even reinvent, their field by reformulating specifically historical questions and problems, on the one hand, and, on the other, by repositioning it and extending its horizons in interdisciplinary contexts of neighboring historical and archaeological disciplines.[3]

Initially, discussions within other major fields of history were probably the first factors to have a perceivable impact on the historical approach to the ancient world—at least, in France[4] and in Germany.[5] In the course of the 1970s, a great individualist such as Alfred Heuss (a German ancient historian with an untypical interest in theories, methods, and issues

[1]Febvre, (1947) 1953, 114ff.; Veyne, 1974, 70 (cited by Meier, 1976, 44): Veyne defined it as "une histoire narrative, écrite au niveau de la vision des sources, c'est-à-dire au niveau de la vision que les contemporains, auteurs de ces sources, avaient de leur propre histoire"—and, as a consequence, that "vision" was necessarily "confuse et incomplète"; cf. idem, 1976, 40ff. Cf. Raphael, 1994, 59ff. and passim; idem, 2003, 96ff.; Burke, 1990; Jacques Revel in Eibach et al. (Eds.), 2002, 23–37, with references: 86–88 (on the intellectual background of the *Annales* school in general); Clark, 2004, 63ff.

[2]Important surveys of modern (and postmodern) developments include Cartledge, 2002, and Eibach, 2002 (on 'Social History'); Rubin, 2002, and Dinges, 2002 (on 'Cultural History'); Pedersen, 2002, Schlögl, 2002, and Rexroth, 2009 (on 'Political History'); Clark, 2004, 106ff. (on the 'new Intellectual History'), and also individual chapters on concrete developments in Eibach et al. (Eds.), 2002, with bibliographies. Cf. also the introduction into Twentieth-Century History as a discipline by Raphael, 2003.

[3]Cf. the surveys by Morley, 1999 and 2004; Jehne, 2006; cf. also Hölkeskamp, 2009a, for further references and concrete examples.

[4]The important and (at least indirectly) influential volumes by Le Goff et al. (Eds.), 1974, included substantial contributions by leading ancient historians (Paul Veyne, Pierre Vidal-Naquet), an archaeologist (Alain Schnapp), and a Greek 'classicist' (Marcel Detienne).

[5]It was again at first Christian Meier (and later Wilfried Nippel) who contributed papers to a six-volume series on "*Theorie der Geschichte*" ("theory of history"), or rather on the spectrum of theoretical and methodological approaches to 'history'—for example, the problem of 'objectivity,' 'process,' and 'structure,' history as 'narrative,' etc.: Koselleck et al. (Eds.), 1977; Faber et al. (Eds.), 1978; Kocka et al. (Eds.), 1979; Koselleck et al. (Eds.), 1982; Meier et al. (Eds.), 1988; Acham et al. (Eds.), 1990. This series, which (if only indirectly) provided quite a few innovative impulses for History as a discipline, its general orientation and standing in Germany, was never really taken notice of in the Anglo-American (or, for that matter, the French) academic universe.

of universal history) was not quite as alone as he had been (and as he had continued to deplore). As late as 1965, however, Heuss could justifiably complain that the works of Max Weber, their manifold theoretical implications and rich methodological potential for a modern social and economic history of antiquity, had hardly been taken notice of.[6] A decade later, this had begun to change, when Weber's concept of the "occidental" (and not simply "ancient") "city" was taken up and developed by the internationally best-known and most influential ancient historian of his day, Sir Moses Finley.[7] It was mainly his oeuvre that initiated a process that—if only slowly and hesitantly—led from vague awareness to cautious acceptance, and finally to an increasingly widespread pragmatic and empirical employment of individual models and categories that Weber had explicitly proposed, implicitly suggested, or even indirectly inspired.[8] Whether we can expect more concrete work making empirical use of his conceptual framework and whether Weber's work still holds a productive potential and further possibilities of practical application is not my main concern in this context: this important issue certainly requires a thorough discussion in its own right. At any rate, the fundamental debate, which has now already been going on for more than two decades, about the potential of Weber's work for the renewal of the subject and for a systematic widening of its horizons—by means of 'ideal types' as analytical categories and models, as well as by means of methodologically controlled synchronic and/or diachronic comparisons between different cultures and historical epochs—is still not at an end.[9] So far, however, the influence of this debate on the current discussion about Rome as a 'city,' (Republican) 'state,' or 'city-state,' and about its political culture seems to have been indirect at most.

Since the mid-1970s, there has been a much greater willingness on the part of more and more historians of the Greek and Roman world to question received wisdom, traditional preconceptions, and old assumptions— such as, for example, established 'periods,' 'ages,' and 'epochs' and the

[6]Heuss, 1965, 538 and 554 (= idem, 1995, III, 1844 and 1860).

[7]Finley, 1977, 305f. (= idem, 1981, 3ff.); idem, 1986a, 90ff. Cf. Deininger, 1989, 269ff.; Nippel, 1991, 19ff.; idem, 1999a, 1ff., as well as the contributions in Meier (Ed.), 1994, Bruhns et al. (Eds.), 2000, and now Morley, 2004, 13, 22ff. etc.

[8]Cf. Dahlheim, 1977, 4f., and Hantos, 1983, 4f. (on the use and applicability of Weber's concept of *Herrschaft* ['rule,' 'power']). The recent study by Hatscher, 2000, not only ignores essential aspects of the more recent research on the Roman republic, but also fails to realize that Weber's concept of 'charisma' seems only to be of limited use for (new and original) analyses of the claim to power of the *'nobilitas'* (70ff.) and of Sulla's and Caesar's careers (106ff.; 162ff.).

[9]Cf. above, n. 7, as well as Nippel, 1986, 112ff.; idem, 1999a, 15ff. and passim; idem, 2000, 240ff., with additional evidence. Also see Breuer, 1982, 174ff.

general habit of 'periodization.'[10] At last, German historians have followed suit and also learnt to think about theories and methods, problems
and perspectives of historical research, and also the general functions and
aims of historiography in the modern world.[11] They have increasingly
become conscious of the perpetual tension between 'events,' 'structures,'
and 'processes'; between the making and implementation of concrete decisions by individual and collective actors in the past and present, on the
one hand, and the prerequisites and conditions of these actions—which
were not at the disposal of, and therefore could not be influenced by and
put on the agenda of politics by these actors, on the other; between stability, continuity, and evolution, on the one hand, and the dynamics of
rapid, or even revolutionary, change, on the other.[12] One illustration for
this pervasive tension might be the debate about the form, character, and
interpretation of Roman 'imperialism' that began as early as the 1970s
and soon led to new and fundamental questions about the conditions,
causes, and driving forces of Roman expansion in general:[13] the character
of 'power'; the impact of Roman '(élite) culture'; 'Romanization' and (or
as?) 'acculturation'[14]; the structure of the empire; and the organization of
imperial hegemony.[15] Just in recent years, this debate has once again been

[10]Cf. recently the (at least) thought-provoking contributions in Golden et al. (Eds.),
1997.
[11]Cf. Gehrke, 1993, 1995 and 2004, with further references; cf. on modern tendencies of
research on the Roman republic Jehne, 2006.
[12]Cf. already Julliard, 1974, 246f. and passim; Nora, 1974. Jehne, 2009 and 2009a, offers an interesting case-study—namely, on Caesar as a leading figure or 'individual,' whose
options and alternatives of political decisions and actions were determined by 'major,' general 'feuds' of sociopolitical development and by concrete or 'minor' 'practical constraints'
of Roman politics in the late Republic.
[13]Cf. Werner, 1972, 501ff., and Hampl, 1977, 48ff. The basic work remains Harris,
1979. Its importance has generally been recognized, even by reviewers who do not (fully)
share Harris's views: cf., e.g., Sherwin-White, 1980; North, 1981; Stewart I. Oost, in CPh
77, 1982, 81–83; Leandro Polverini, in RFIC 110, 1982, 83–89, and the literature cited in
chapter 6, above, as well as Harris, 1984a, 13ff. Other important contributions, again with
different perspectives, include Brunt, 1964–1965 (= idem, 1990, 110–33), which is still useful today, as well as Nicolet, 1978, 883ff., and (as usual) Veyne, 1975, and 1976, 15ff. Cf.
the recent contributions in Webster et al. (Eds.), 1996, and Mattingly (Ed.), 1997, as well
as Raaflaub, 1996; Giovanni Brizzi, in Hinard (Ed.), 2000, 443–501; Sidebottom, 2005
(whose perception of positions and relevant publications is, however, rather selective and
Anglocentric); Eich and Eich, 2005, 4ff.; Eckstein, 2006b, and the bibliography in Hölkeskamp, 2007.
[14]Cf. also Torelli, 1995; Woolf, 1998, 1ff.; Le Roux, 2004; Hingley, 2005, 49ff.; Roth,
2007, 9ff., and the relevant contributions in Mattingly (Ed.), 1997, Huskinson (Ed.), 2000,
Keay et al. (Eds.), 2001, and Roth et al. (Eds.), 2007.
[15]Cf., e.g., the different approaches and perspectives of Dahlheim, 1977; Gruen 1984 and
2004; Braund, 1988a; Schulz, 1997; Kallet-Marx, 1995. Cf. also Richardson, 2008, and
(not only for comparative purposes, but also for discussions of concepts and approaches)

invigorated by a 'realist' approach (inspired by a certain school of American political science) that emphasizes the "persistence, pervasiveness, and ferocity of international competition" in a "multipolar" anarchic system of necessarily aggressive and expansionist "actors," whose inherent "competitive imperative" necessarily creates an "interstate environment of unavoidable and continual friction."[16]

After all, the central issue was (and still is) the question of the particular dynamics of the interdependence between (political) rule and (social) integration, between imperial expansion and the basic structure of the city-state. Once again, it was Sir Ronald Syme who set the tone in his inimitable magisterial style: "the governing of all Italy and a wide empire under the ideas and system of a city state was clumsy, wasteful and calamitous."[17] As usual, this was a dictum elegantly put, but not a detailed diagnosis, let alone a differentiated analysis and a satisfactory explanation. Once again, it was Christian Meier who offered a fresh conceptual approach to the problem: against the backdrop of 'city-statehood,' Roman imperial expansion necessarily caused a problem of, as it were, 'extensivity' or even '(over-)extensification,' which (not only in Meier's view) brought about its crisis, and ultimately its disintegration. It is obvious that, because of its complexity, the description of the interconnectivity of integration and expansion posed new problems of conceptualization, and even describability. The concrete topic as such, as well as the creation of an adequately precise conceptual framework, constitutes of course a very wide field of its own, and both dimensions of one and the same problem have therefore been on the agenda of a corresponding international discussion, which has long since gone beyond a mere tentative criticism of the traditional terminology and conventional concepts of 'imperialism'—this debate is once again certainly not completed. In this context, it is worth mentioning that the fundamental specific feature of city-states (in Greek as well as Roman antiquity, the medieval and early modern periods alike)—namely, their 'territoriality' as a constitutive aspect of 'city-statehood'[18]—has already been systematically discussed by German and American historians in a comparative context: such approaches are one (though not the only) promising strategy to come to terms with the irresolvable tension between their restricted spatial dimensions,

---

the survey of the variety of "rewritings of British and other imperial histories," Colley, 2002 (quotation on 145).

[16] Eckstein, 2006a, 18, 30, and passim; cf. Manuel Tröster, in *Gnomon* 81, 2009, 41–45; Karl-J. Hölkeskamp, "The Emergence of Empire." In *CR* 59, 2009, 211–14; cf. also now Eckstein, 2008.

[17] Syme, 1939, 387.

[18] Cf. Hölscher, 1998a, and Hölkeskamp, 2004c, with further references, as well as the literature cited in chapter 5, at nn. 48ff., above.

the imperial claims of powers like the Roman republic (or Athens, Renaissance Florence, and Venice), and the various forms of hegemonic political organization.[19]

As far as the discussion about the internal 'architecture' of the *res publica* was concerned, it also did not end with a general, but futile, programmatic demand to overcome the pervasive state of solidification and sterility of the historiography of the Roman republic, which was easy to blame on the traditional brand of prosopography mentioned in an earlier chapter,[20] obsessed as it was with the *arcana* of dynastic and factional maneuvering within a governing class whose character, basis, and power were taken for granted. In fact, Matthias Gelzer himself had been one of the first to try to determine in detail and in precise conceptual terms the full range and complexity of the social relations in which politics, political institutions, and political action were embedded. Some years later, it was Christian Meier who put forward the innovative program of a systematic and comprehensive 'political grammar' that collected and focused various ideas and approaches, most of which had previously been isolated and tentative. The term (coined well before metaphors of this kind became fashionable in the wake of the so-called 'linguistic turn') may have failed to establish itself, but the core of the matter was, is, and will certainly remain on the agenda of a modernized Ancient History. It is still appropriate to acknowledge that he was the first who not only outlined the general issues at stake and their implications, but also provided new perspectives and—last, but not least—made clear that it was a challenge that the discipline as such would have to address. From that point on, the objective could not be but a truly comprehensive 'structural history' of the Republic, which would have to overcome both the traditional restrictions imposed by an outdated concept of 'constitutional' history, as well as the equally dusty orthodox dogmas about a self-contained, self-sufficient, and self-stabilizing oligarchy and its unchanged and unchallenged *arcana imperii*, running the *libera res publica* for a good four hundred years.

In the following years, an increasing number of scholars not only began to apply the rather general ideas that had arisen from the aforementioned theoretical debates within the wider field of History, but also the equally

[19]Cf. Raaflaub, 1990, 511ff.; idem, 1991, 565ff.; Chittolini, 1991, all three of which provide additional evidence, as well as the comments by Hartmut Galsterer and Anthony Molho, in Molho et al. (Eds.), 1991, 619ff. and 627ff. On this topic see also Dahlheim, 1977, passim; Schulz, 1997, 289ff.
[20]Chapter 1, above.

important impulses from neighboring disciplines within the Classics. A school of 'new' archaeology set out to analyze and explain monuments and all sorts of material remains, images, and their messages within the framework of their specific cultural, social, and also political contexts, and emphasized the integral and interconnected functions of visual 'languages' in the process of construction and reproduction of these contexts themselves. It was important (if not quite fortuitous) that one of the first major achievements of this new 'school' was a comprehensive and sustained interpretation in terms of a 'semantic system' comprising not only typical genres of representative art, such as statues, portraits, friezes, and reliefs, and the architecture of temples and public buildings, but also the topography as such and the dynamic urban development of Rome in the middle and late Republic and early Empire.[21] This development in turn opened doors that had hitherto been closed: representatives of a modern Ancient History became aware of monuments and material remains as sources *sui generis*, in their own right and above all as material of immense historical interest, which shed completely new light on, and sometimes even provided the only access to, their social and cultural backgrounds. In an interdisciplinary dialogue, these historians have been learning to draw upon these sources (and to apply the modern methods of 'reading' them) as fresh material toward, and vital impulses for, a new 'structural' history of the (middle and late) Roman republic.

In recent years, a reformed Classical Philology (sometimes revamped according to intellectual fashions) has joined the field by redefining its notion of a (or rather, the) literary 'text' and taking account of categories such as 'con- (sub-, or hyper-)text,' 'communication,' and 'culture'—which in turn not only generated a new interest in the position of 'literature' in Roman life, but also provided fresh views of, and original insights into, the social and intellectual conditions for its production.[22] Under the influence of English and American Classics, which had never known the entrenched traditional borders between the different academic subfields of 'Philology' and 'Literary Studies' (*vel. sim.*), 'History' and 'Archaeology' that Germany has had to overcome in the first place, such inspirations may create incentives and offer new chances for an interdisciplinary

[21] One of the most eminent representatives of the new direction of archaeology has also provided a series of thoughtful (if sometimes somewhat pessimistic) theoretical and methodological contributions: Hölscher, 1992, 1995, 2000 and 2001a, and especially idem, (1987) 2004, on the "language of images" as a "semantic system." Cf. also Bergmann, 2000, and the remarks in chapter 5, above.

[22] Some titles that are also relevant for a historical analysis of political culture are: Wiseman, 1985b; Classen, 1985; Vasaly, 1993; Miles, 1995, passim; Edwards, 1996; Fantham, 1996; Jaeger, 1997; Feldherr, 1998; Chaplin, 2000; Mutschler, 2000; Rüpke, 2000, 31ff. (with further references); Roller, 2001 and 2004; May, 2002a; Cape, 2002; Riggsby, 2002; Krasser, 2006.

approach to a 'classical civilization'—even though it is to be regretted, at least in the eyes of a historian with a typical scepticism, that eminent representatives of Classics seem to have gone astray and become ensnared in 'poststructuralist,' 'postmodernist,' and 'deconstructivist' temptations.[23]

So far, at least in my opinion, the historical 'sciences' in general—though they did open themselves (and rightly so, in many respects!) to a variety of new 'histories,' unconventional topics, views, and approaches, and even extravagant 'his-' and 'herstories'[24]—seem to have been more resistant to the radicalism (and the aberrations) of these fashionable theories than have other fields, such as literary criticism.[25] One is tempted to go a step further and say that the inherent conservatism of the field of ancient history may well have had its advantages—if only in this respect. Be that as it may, the threat represented by postmodernist arbitrariness can be countered by going on the offensive and actively promoting a concept of 'political culture,' based on modern (social and cultural) history, as well as political science.[26] Such a strategy could provide a strong link between the various perspectives and methodological approaches, ideas, and interpretations and finally place them in a new, differentiated, and complex context. The nodal points here are the two fundamental sides of politics, political systems, and the 'political' as such: the side of content or matter (*Inhaltsseite*)—which includes not only the concrete themes and topics on the political agenda of a given society, but also the rational or 'technical' framework of institutions and formal procedures of decision making —on the one hand, and the side of 'representation' or 'manifestation' (*Ausdrucksseite*), on the other, which not only include the media, symbols, visual and other symbolic languages, and discursive strategies, but also the collective repertoire of values, attitudes, and 'mentalities' of a given society.[27] Above all, a holistic model of a political culture in general

[23]See, e.g., Henderson, 1997, whose title is rather misleading, and Dench, 2005, who attempts to explain "Roman identities" in general and the "character of Roman citizenship" in particular by a kaleidoscopic combination of inspiration, ideas, and interpretations in a postmodern sort of glass-bead game.

[24]The three volumes by Le Goff et al. (Eds.), 1974, have been fairly influential, not only in France, and remain an important survey of new "problems" (1), "approaches" (2) and "topics" (3); cf. more recently the contributions in Cameron (Ed.), 1989; Golden et al. (Eds.), 1997; Mergel et al. (Eds.), 1997; Bonnell et al. (Eds.), 1999, and Cannadine (Ed.), 2002, and now Bachmann-Medick, 2006, on different '(cultural) turns.'

[25]Cf. the brilliant surveys by Daniel, 1997, 259ff., and eadem, 2001, 120ff. (on poststructuralism) and 167ff. (on postmodernism), with further references; Clark, 2004; Marcus Sandl, in Eibach et al. (Eds.), 2002, 329–41, who highlights the innovative potential of postmodern perspectives; Burke, 2004, 96ff. Cf. for a different view Evans, 1997, and, in a less defensive argument, idem, 2002, 7ff., 10ff.; Flaig, 1999a, 458ff., with further references, to which add Kablitz, 2006.

[26]Cf. chapter 5, n. 2, above.

[27]The conceptual differentiation between *Inhaltsseite* and *Ausdrucksseite* was coined by Rohe, 1990, 334, 336ff.

(that is, pre-modern or modern, historical, or contemporary)—in other words, a modern "cultural history of politics"[28]—must highlight the specific interfaces and interconnections of these formal and social, ideological, and symbolic layers, as well as their complex cross-referencing. Such an approach could certainly profit by other modern models of middle-range explanatory reach, such as a systems-theoretical model of institutionalization or 'institutionality,'[29] or by comparative approaches, which focus on a whole variety of equivalent global and particular sociopolitical structures in different cultures in different (especially pre-modern) epochs.[30] A carefully developed and controlled theoretical underpinning of such a comprehensive concept of political culture, its systematic empirical testing and practical application in an interdisciplinary research environment, would certainly have a beneficial integrative and regulative effect on the field of ('new' political) History in general and Ancient History in particular.

This is exactly why creating this kind of discourse is an important challenge for a modern discipline of Ancient History that has now (re-)discovered the history of the Roman republic. In the last few years, the general character of this political culture and its peculiar complexity have just been outlined—a detailed overall account that would meet the (admittedly exacting) new standards remains a desideratum. But at least some central points and coordinates seem to be established: the most important is the extraordinary combination—or rather complementarity—of the pervasive patterns of hierarchies deeply inscribed in this culture, on the one hand, and the striking degree of ideological agreement, social homogeneity, and coherence, on the other.[31] For such a combination is far from being self-evident, let alone natural: not only were hierarchy and dominance, power and its exertion deeply inscribed in the greatest of all social divides, that between free and slave and between rich and poor;[32] not

[28]Cf. chapter 5, above, and also Burke, 2004, 103ff. on new (and old) problems, themes, and topics.

[29]Cf. Hölkeskamp, 2003a, 82ff. with further references.

[30]On comparative approaches in general, see Haupt et al., 1996a, with additional evidence. However, the contribution in Haupt et al. (Eds.), 1996b, that focuses on Ancient History (Meier, 1996) only addresses this field indirectly.

[31]A systematic comparison with the construction of "order, hierarchy, and subordination in early modern society" (Braddick and Walter, 2001; Freist, 2005, and the other contributions in Asch et al. [Eds.], 2005) may provide interesting perspectives: cf. now the individual contributions on the 'power of the few' and its construction in different pre-modern societies in Beck et al. (Eds.), 2008, and especially Walter, 2008, for comparative approaches to the description and analysis of traditional élites.

only were they institutionalized in the formal status differences between *populus Romanus*, Italian 'allies,'[33] and foreign 'friends,'[34] and subjects in the provinces; and not only were the society (or societies) of Rome, Italy, and the empire as a whole suffused by steeply asymmetrical power relations between the ruling classes and the lower—the principles of power and hierarchy also openly and even demonstratively structured all political institutions and procedures, assemblies and Senate alike, and above all the relations between magistrates and citizens.[35] Last but not least, the same principles were underpinned, affirmed, and legitimized by political and social ideology, and even Roman myths and legends revolved around them.[36] In other words, there simply were no institutions that would have been capable (or were even intended) to create and guarantee 'civil' or 'civic' equality *in politicis*: in Rome, there was absolutely no one—no *popularis* tribune and no self-professed champion of the *plebs*, no political philosopher, and certainly not the notoriously elusive 'man in the street'—who would even have dreamt that 'equality' between all and for all could ever be a desirable value *sui generis*. The fact as such does not, however, provide the answer to the all-important question: how could the system have created and sucessfully upheld such a high degree of acceptance and assent, which was the necessary requirement for subordination and obedience and, in the final analysis, for the functioning of the system itself, so as to achieve this peculiar Roman kind of self-stabilizing 'monistic' coherence?

One contributing sociological factor that we can pin down with some confidence is the dense and stable network of structures and mechanisms mentioned above,[37] which guaranteed, reproduced, and sanctioned the vertical and horizontal integration of classes, status groups of all kinds, and individuals. Interestingly, this network did not shatter in the crisis of the Roman republic, and even outlasted its fall. Another basic factor is that the coherence of the political system of the Republic was based upon, and continuously affirmed by, a deeply rooted consensus that was diligently, permanently, and, as it were, polymorphically tended by a political class at the summit of all hierarchies: that is, by means of an extraordinarily diversified range of discursive strategies. The identity of this class

---

[32]Cf., e.g., Dupont, 1992, 16, 30ff., 56ff.; Hope, 2000b, 128ff.; and most recently Robert, 2008, 113ff.

[33]Cf. Galsterer, 1976; Nicolet, 1979, 279ff.; Hantos, 1983, and now the contributions in Jehne et al. (Eds.), 2006.

[34]Cf. Dahlheim, 1977; Braund, 1984; Schulz, 1997.

[35]Cf. already, e.g., Nicolet, 1977, 732ff. and passim; Hope, 2000b, and Hölkeskamp, forthcoming b, with further references.

[36]Cf. now Morgan, 2007, 63ff., 95ff. etc., and Hölkeskamp, 2009a, on 'myth' as a specific "figure of discourse" in (pre-)modern political cultures (with further references).

[37]Cf. chapter 3, above.

as a 'meritocracy' was reproduced by a rich repertoire of performative practices, rituals, ceremonies, and other symbolic forms of representation that made their culture-specific symbolic capital visible, which was thus used as social 'credit' or 'creditability,' and thereby served the manifestation and indeed the constitution of order by hierarchy.

'Manifestation' and 'visibility' can certainly be taken literally because all these aforementioned performative modes and media of representation had to be situated in the public spaces of a city-state "culture of personal physical presence"—a very precise descriptive term coined by Tonio Hölscher. These spaces were the 'fora' (both meanings of the word apply) of an extraordinarily high degree of civic communication and direct interaction. As such, they were in turn indispensable, and indeed constitutive, parts of the characteristic political and sacral topography of city-statehood: The immediacy and actual 'visibility' of all procedures and practices, rituals and ceremonies (even for passive spectators) were themselves an integral part of the repertoire of consensus-creating mechanisms in this—as again Tonio Hölscher has aptly put it[38]—"culture of immediate action."

Another facet of this specific form of collective consensus, which I have described in other contexts,[39] was also an essential factor supporting the social coherence between the *populus Romanus* and its political class: it was this consensus that helped to defuse and channel the omnipresent and pervasive competition within this class for positions of 'power' and its inherent centrifugal and potentially disintegrating tendencies. This consensus limited and restricted competition and its concomitant patterns of behavior by means of regulations and rules, prohibitions and sanctions. Moreover, in the case of the Roman republic, competition among the members of the political class as a pattern of social action even became an integral part of the consensus and actually constantly affirmed it as the legitimate and accepted procedure of the permanent (re-)positioning of its individual members and their respective families within its own inherent hierarchy. A fresh and critical re-reading of the relevant work of Georg Simmel may contribute to a further precision and refinement of our terminology here: the practical application of his brilliant ideal-typical conception of the sociological phenomenon of 'competition' is only one example of the possible explanatory potentials that remain to be unearthed here. This is yet another reason why a continuation and even extension of this discussion may be worthwhile.

But already in the last decade, the debate has produced one important insight that every scholar can agree on, however critical he or she may be

[38]Cf. chapter 5, with n. 62, above.
[39]Cf. chapters 6 and 7, above.

of Fergus Millar's view of the Roman Republican political world[40]—or, for that matter, of the alternative reconstruction(s) of this political culture proposed in the present work.[41] The ongoing international discussion about presuppositions, conditions, and characteristics of politics, policies, and policy making gloriously proves that Ancient History after—and even, *horribile dictu*, to a certain extent, rejuvenated by—the 'cultural turn' is and remains a modern, thriving, and not only merely academic discipline at the beginning of a new century.[42]

[40]Rogers, 2002, xvi; cf. Fergus Millar, author's prologue, in: idem, 2002a, 6ff., 18ff. This message is also implied by North, 2002.

[41]Critical discussions include David, 2006b; Yakobson, 2006b, and Zecchini, 2006. Cf. also Morstein-Marx, 2004, 7f., 32 with n. 115.

[42]This claim is now brilliantly corroborated by Harriet Flower's innovative and stimulating new book on the different "Roman Republics" (Princeton 2010).

ABBREVIATIONS

GWU	Geschichte in Wissenschaft und Unterricht
HA	Historische Anthropologie
HZ	Historische Zeitschrift
IJCT	International Journal of the Classical Tradition
JRA	Journal of Roman Archaeology
JRS	Journal of Roman Studies
JDAI	Jahrbuch des Deutschen Archäologischen Instituts
KZSS	Kölner Zeitschrift für Soziologie und Sozialpsychologie
LCM	Liverpool Classical Monthly
MDAI(R)	Mitteilungen des Deutschen Archäologischen Instituts— RömischeAbteilung
MEFRA	Mélanges d'archéologie et d'histoire de l'École Française de Rome–Antiquité
MH	Museum Helveticum
NECJ	New England Classical Journal
P&P	Past and Present
PCPhS	Proceedings of the Cambridge Philological Society
OP	Ordia Prima. Revista de Estudios Clásicos
QS	Quaderni di Storia
RAL	Rendiconti dell'Accademia dei Lincei
RArch	Revue archéologique
REL	Revue des Études Latines
RFIC	Rivista di filologia e di istruzione classica
RH	Revue historique
RhM	Rheinisches Museum für Philologie
RJ	Rechtshistorisches Journal
SBWGF	Sitzungsberichte der Wissenschaftlichen Gesellschaft an der Universität Frankfurt
SCI	Scripta Classica Israelica
SHAW	Sitzungsberichte der Heidelberger Akademie der Wissenschaften, Philosophisch-historische Klasse
SIFC	Studi italiani di filologia classica
StStor	Studi storici. Rivista trimestrale dell'Istituto Gramsci
TAPhA	Transactions of the American Philological Association
TRG	Tijdschrift voor Rechtsgeschiedenis
ZHF	Zeitschrift für Historische Forschung
ZPE	Zeitschrift für Papyrologie und Epigraphik
ZPW	Zeitschrift für Politikwissenschaft
ZRG RA	Zeitschrift der Savigny-Stiftung für Rechtsgeschichte, Romanistische Abteilung

CORPORA, COLLECTIONS, COMMENTARIES, ENCYCLOPEDIAS, ETC.

Adamietz, Joachim. 1989. *Marcus Tullius Cicero. Pro Murena* (Darmstadt)

Broughton, T. Robert S. 1951–1952. *The Magistrates of the Roman Republic*, vols. 1–2 (New York)

———. 1991. *Candidates Defeated in Roman Elections: Some Ancient Roman "Also-Rans"* (Philadelphia)

CAH 7.2   *The Cambridge Ancient History*², vol. 7.2: *The Rise of Rome to 220* BC (Cambridge 1989)

CAH 8   *The Cambridge Ancient History*², vol. 8: *Rome and the Mediterranean to 133* BC (Cambridge 1989)

CAH 9   *The Cambridge Ancient History*², vol. 9: *The Last Age of the Roman Republic* (Cambridge 1994)

CIL I²   *Corpus Inscriptionum Latinarum antiquissimae ad C. Caesaris mortem*, Editio altera (Berlin 1893)

Crawford,   Crawford, Michael. *Roman Republican Coinage*, vols. 1–2
RRC   (Cambridge 1974, repr. with corrections 1983)

DNP   Cancik, Hubert; Schneider, Helmuth, et al. (Eds.). *Der Neue Pauly*. Vols. 1– (Stuttgart 1996)

Elster, Marianne. 2003. *Die Gesetze der mittleren römischen Republik. Text und Kommentar* (Darmstadt)

EnzNZ   Jaeger, Friedrich, et al. (Eds.). *Enzyklopädie der Neuzeit*. Vols. 1– (Stuttgart 2005)

GGr   Brunner, Otto, et al. (Eds.). *Geschichtliche Grundbegriffe. Ein Lexikon zur politisch-sozialen Sprache*. Vols. 1–8 (Stuttgart 1972–1997)

HbKW 1–3 Jaeger, Friedrich, et al. (Eds.). *Handbuch der Kulturwissenschaften*. Vol. 1: *Grundlagen und Schlüsselbegriffe*; vol. 2: *Paradigmen und Disziplinen*; vol. 3: *Themen und Tendenzen* (Stuttgart 2004)

ILLRP   Degrassi, Atilio (Ed.). *Inscriptiones Latinae liberae rei publicae* (Florence 1965)

ILS   Dessau, Hermann (Ed.). *Inscriptiones Latinae Selectae* (Berlin 1892–1916)

Inscr. It.   Degrassi, Atilio (Ed.). *Inscriptiones Italiae*, vol. 13.1 (Rome 1947)

Kruschwitz, Peter. 2002. *Carmina Saturnia Epigraphica. Einleitung, Text und Kommentar zu den saturnischen Versinschriften* (Stuttgart)

LTUR   Steinby, Eva Margareta (Ed.). *Lexicon Topographicum Urbis Romae* (Rome 1993–2000)

Oakley, Stephen. 1997. 1998. 2005a. 2005b. *A Commentary on Livy, Books 6–10*, vols. 1–4 (Oxford)

RAC   *Reallexikon für Antike und Christentum* (Stuttgart 1950)

RE   Wissowa, Georg; Kroll, Wilhelm, et al. (Eds.), *Paulys Real-Encyclopädie der classischen Altertumswissenschaft* (Stuttgart 1893–1978)

ROL 1–4   Warmington, E. H (Ed.). *Remains of Old Latin*, vols. 1–4 (Cambridge, Mass. 1935ff.)

Rotondi,   Rotondi, Giovanni. *Leges publicae populi Romani* (Milan
LPPR   1912, repr. 1962)

Rüpke, Jörg, et al. 2005. *Fasti sacerdotum. Die Mitglieder der Priesterschaften und das sakrale Funktionspersonal römischer, griechischer, orientalischer und jüdisch-christlicher Kulte in der Stadt Rom von 300 v. Chr. bis 499 n. Chr.*, vols. 1–3 (Stuttgart)

Skutsch   Skutsch, Otto. *The Annals of Quintus Ennius* (Oxford 1985)

Stangl   *Ciceronis orationum Scholiastae*, recensuit Thomas Stangl (Vienna 1912, repr. 1964)

ThesCRA *Thesaurus Cultus et Rituum Antiquorum*. Vols. 1ff. (2004)

BIBLIOGRAPHY

AA.VV. 1983. *Architecture et société de l'archaïsme grec à la fin de la République romaine* (Rome).

AA.VV. 1987. *L'Urbs. Espace urbain et histoire (Ier siècle av. J.-C.-IIIe siècle ap. J.-C.)* (Rome).

Acham, Karl. 1992. "Struktur, Funktion und Genese von Institutionen aus sozialwissenschaftlicher Sicht." In Melville (Ed.), 1992b, 25–71.

Acham, Karl, and Winfried Schulze (Eds.). 1990. *Teil und Ganzes. Theorie der Geschichte: Beiträge zur Historik*, vol. 6 (Munich).

Aldrete, Gregory S. 1999. *Gestures and Acclamations in Ancient Rome* (Baltimore, etc.).

Alföldi, Andreas. 1956. "The Main Aspects of Political Propaganda on the Coinage of the Roman Republic." In *Essays in Roman Coinage, presented to H. Mattingly* (Oxford), 63–95.

———. 1965. *Early Rome and the Latins* (Ann Arbor).

Alföldy, Géza. 1976. "Die römische Gesellschaft—Struktur und Eigenart." In *Gymnasium* 83: 1–25 (= idem, 1986b, 42–68, with additions).

———. 1981. "Die Stellung der Ritter in der Führungsschicht des Imperium Romanum." In *Chiron* 11: 169–215 (= idem, 1986b, 162–209, with additions).

———. 1982. "Individualität und Kollektivnorm in der Epigraphik des römischen Senatorenstandes." In *Tituli* 4: 37–53 (= idem, 1986b, 378–92).

———. 1986a. "Die römische Gesellschaft: Eine Nachbetrachtung über Struktur und Eigenart." In idem, 1986b, 69–81.

———. 1986b. *Die römische Gesellschaft. Ausgewählte Beiträge* (Stuttgart).

———. 2001. "*Pietas immobilis erga principem* und ihr Lohn: Öffentliche Ehrenmonumente von Senatoren in Rom während der frühen und hohen Kaiserzeit." In idem and Silvio Panciera (Eds.), *Inschriftliche Denkmäler als Medien der Selbstdarstellung in der römischen Welt* (Stuttgart), 11–46.

Althoff, Gerd. 1997. *Spielregeln der Politik im Mittelalter. Kommunikation in Frieden und Fehde* (Darmstadt).

———. 1999. "Rituale—symbolische Kommunikation. Zu einem neuen Feld der historischen Mittelalterforschung." In *GWU* 50: 140–54.

———. 2003. *Die Macht der Rituale. Symbolik und Herrschaft im Mittelalter* (Darmstadt).

Andreau, Jean. 1977. "Servitude et grandeur politiques dans la Rome républicaine." In *AESC* 32: 756–63.

Andreau, Jean, Schmitt, Pauline, and Schnapp, Alain. 1978. "Paul Veyne et l'évergétisme." In *AESC* 33: 307–25.

Asch, Ronald G. 2008. *Europäischer Adel in der Frühen Neuzeit* (Cologne etc.).

Asch, Ronald G., and Freist, Dagmar (Eds.). 2005. *Staatsbildung als kultureller Prozess. Strukturwandel und Legitimation von Herrschaft in der Frühen Neuzeit* (Cologne etc.).

Assmann, Jan. 1992. *Das kulturelle Gedächtnis. Schrift, Erinnerung und politische Identität in frühen Hochkulturen* (Munich).

———. 2000. *Religion und kulturelles Gedächtnis* (Munich).

Assmann, Jan, and Hölscher, Tonio (Eds.). 1988. *Kultur und Gedächtnis* (Frankfurt).

Astin, Alan E. 1967. *Scipio Aemilianus* (Oxford).

———. 1968. *Politics and Policies in the Roman Republic* (Belfast).

———. 1978. *Cato the Censor* (Oxford).

———. 1989. "Roman government and politics." In *CAH* 8: 163–96.

Awerbruch, Marianne. 1981. "IMPERIUM. Zum Bedeutungswandel des Wortes im staatsrechtlichen und politischen Bewußtsein der Römer." In *ABG* 25: 162–84.

Bachmann-Medick, Doris. 2006. *Cultural Turns. Neuorientierungen in den Kulturwissenschaften* (Reinbek).

Badel, Christophe. 2005. *La noblesse de l'empire romain. Les masques et la vertu* (Seyssel).

Badian, Ernst. 1958. *Foreign Clientelae (264–70 BC)* (Oxford).

———. 1990. "The Consuls, 179–49 BC" In *Chiron* 20: 371–413.

———. 1996. "*Tribuni Plebis* and *Res Publica*." In Linderski (Ed.), 187–213.

Barnes, Timothy D. 2007a. "Prosopography Modern and Ancient." In Keats-Rohan (Ed.), 71–82.

———. 2007b. "Prosopography and Roman History." In Keats-Rohan (Ed.), 83–93.

Barton, Carlin A. 2001. *Roman Honor. The Fire in the Bones* (Berkeley).

Bastien, Jean Luc. 2000. "Le triomphe et la voie sacrée. Quelques réflexions sur les interactions d'un espace et d'une cérémonie." In Deniaux (Ed.), 149–61.

———. 2007. *Le triomphe romain et son utilisation politique à Rome aux trois derniers siècles de la République* (Rome).

Beacham, Richard C. 1999. *Spectacle Entertainments of Early Imperial Rome* (New Haven etc.).

Beard, Mary. 2003. "The Triumph of the absurd: Roman street theatre." In Edwards et al. (Eds.), 2003c, 21–43.

———. 2007. *The Roman Triumph* (Cambridge, Mass.).

Beard, Mary, and Crawford, Michael. 1985. *Rome in the late Republic. Problems and Interpretations* (London).

Beck, Hans. 2003. "'Den Ruhm nicht teilen wollen'. Fabius Pictor und die Anfänge des römischen Nobilitätsdiskurses." In Eigler et al. (Eds.), 2003, 73–92.

———. 2005a. *Karriere und Hierarchie. Die römische Aristokratie und die Anfänge des* cursus honorum *in der mittleren Republik* (Berlin).

———. 2005b. "Züge in die Ewigkeit. Prozessionen durch das republikanische Rom." In *GFA* 8: 73–104.

———. 2008a. "Die Rollen des Adeligen. Prominenz und aristokratische Herrschaft in der römischen Republik." In idem et al. (Eds.), 2008c, 101–23.

———. 2009. "Die Rollen des Adligen und die Krise der Republik." In Hölkeskamp et al. (Eds.), 53–71.

Beck, Hans, Scholz, Peter, and Walter, Uwe. 2008b. "Einführung: Begriffe, Fragen und Konzepte." In idem (Eds.), 2008c, 1–13.

——— (Eds.). 2008c. *Die Macht der Wenigen. Aristokratische Herrschaftspraxis, Kommunikation und 'edler' Lebensstil in Antike und Früher Neuzeit* (Munich).

Behne, Frank. 2002. "Volkssouveränität und verfassungsrechtliche Systematik. Beobachtungen zur Struktur des Römischen Staatsrechtes von Theodor Mommsen." In Spielvogel (Ed.), 124–36.

Bell, Andrew J. E. 1997. "Cicero and the Spectacle of Power." In *JRS* 87: 1–22.

———. 2004. *Spectacular Power in the Greek and Roman City* (Oxford).

Belting-Ihm, Christa. 1996. "*Imagines Maiorum.*" In *RAC* 17: 995–1016.

Benoist, Stéphane. 2004. "Un parcours d'«évidence»: Fergus Millar et le monde romain, de la République au Principat." In *RH* 128: 371–90.

———. 2005. *Rome, le prince et la cité. Pouvoir impérial et cérémonies publiques (Ier siècle av.—début du IVe siècle apr. J.-C.)*(Paris).

Berger, Peter L., and Luckmann, Thomas. 1966. *The Social Construction of Reality: A Treatise in the Sociology of Knowledge* (New York).

Bergmann, Bettina, and Kondoleon, Christina. 1999a. "Introduction: The Art of Ancient Spectacle." In eadem (Eds.), 1999b, 9–35.

——— (Eds.). 1999b. *The Art of Ancient Spectacle* (New Haven).

Bergmann, Marianne. 2000. "Repräsentation." In Borbein, Adolf et al. (Eds.), 166–88.

Bernstein, Frank. 1998. *Ludi publici. Untersuchungen zur Entstehung und Entwicklung der öffentlichen Spiele im republikanischen Rom* (Stuttgart).

Berrendonner, Clara. 2001. "La formation de la tradition sur M'. Curius Dentatus et C. Fabricius Luscinus: un homme nouveau peut-il être un grand homme?" In Coudry et al. (Eds.), 97–116.

Bettini, Maurizio. 2000. "*Mos, mores* und *mos maiorum*: Die Erfindung der 'Sittlichkeit' in der römischen Kultur." In Linke et al. (Eds.), 2000b, 303–52.

———. 2006. "Forging Identities. Trojans and Latins, Romans and Julians in the *Aeneid.*" In Jehne et al. (Eds.), 269–91.

Blänkner, Reinhard. 2005. "Historizität, Institutionalität, Symbolizität. Grundbegriffliche Aspekte einer Kulturgeschichte des Politischen." In Stollberg-Rilinger (Ed.), 71–96.

Blänkner, Reinhard, and Jussen, Bernhard. 1998a. "Institutionen und Ereignis. Anfragen an zwei alt gewordene geschichtswissenschaftliche Kategorien." In idem (Eds.), 1998b, 9–16.

——— (Eds.). 1998b. *Institutionen und Ereignis. Über historische Praktiken und Vorstellungen gesellschaftlichen Ordnens* (Göttingen).

Bleckmann, Bruno. 2002. *Die römische Nobilität im Ersten Punischen Krieg. Untersuchungen zur aristokratischen Konkurrenz in der Republik* (Berlin).

Bleicken, Jochen. 1962. "Der Begriff der Freiheit in der letzten Phase der römischen Republik." In *HZ* 195: 1–20 (= idem, 1998, 2: 663–82).

———. 1968. *Das Volkstribunat der klassischen Republik. Studien zu seiner Entwicklung zwischen 287 und 133 v.Chr.* (Munich).

———. 1972. *Staatliche Ordnung und Freiheit in der römischen Republik* (Kallmünz) (= idem, 1998, 1: 185–280).

———. 1975. *Lex publica. Gesetz und Recht in der römischen Republik* (Berlin).

———. 1976. "Freiheit II.2: Römische libertas." In *GGr* 2: 430–35 (= idem, 1998, 1: 156–61).

———. 1978. "Staat und Recht in der römischen Republik." In *SBWGF* 15, 4: 143–62 (= idem, 1998, 1: 281–300).

————. 1981a. "Das römische Volkstribunat. Versuch einer Analyse seiner politischen Funktion in republikanischer Zeit." In *Chiron* 11: 87–108 (= idem, 1998, 1: 484–505).

————. 1981b. "Die Nobilität der römischen Republik." In *Gymnasium* 88: 236–53 (= idem, 1998, 1: 466–83).

————. 1994. *Die athenische Demokratie* (Paderborn).

————. 1995. *Die Verfassung der römischen Republik* (Paderborn). Orig. ed.: 1975. (Substantially revised and extended seventh edition, 1995).

————. 1995a. *Gedanken zum Untergang der römischen Republik* (Stuttgart) (= idem, 1998, 2, 683–704).

————. 1996. "Im Schatten Mommsens." In *RJ* 15: 3–27 (= idem, 1998, 1: 526–50).

————. 1998. *Gesammelte Schriften*, ed. by Frank Goldmann et al. (Stuttgart).

Bleicken, Jochen, Meier, Christian, and Strasburger, Hermann. 1977. *Matthias Gelzer und die römische Geschichte* (Kallmünz).

Blösel, Wolfgang. 2000. "Die Geschichte des Begriffes *mos maiorum* von den Anfängen bis zu Cicero." In Linke et al. (Eds.), 2000b, 25–97.

————. 2003. "Die *memoria* der *gentes* als Rückgrat der kollektiven Erinnerung im republikanischen Rom" In Eigler et al. (Eds.), 2003, 53–72.

Bödeker, Hans Erich (Ed.). 2002. *Begriffsgeschichte, Diskursgeschichte, Metapherngeschichte* (Göttingen).

Bodel, John. 1999. "Death on Display: Looking at Roman Funerals." In Bergmann et al. (Eds.), 1999b, 259–81.

Boldt, Hans, Conze, Werner, Haverkate, Görg, and Koselleck, Reinhart. 1990. "Staat und Souveränität." In *GGr* 6: 1–154.

Bonnefond-Coudry, Marianne. 1989. *Le Sénat de la République romaine de la guerre d'Hannibal à Auguste* (Rome).

Bonnell, Victoria E., and Hunt, Lynn (Eds.). 1999. *Beyond the Cultural Turn. New Directions in the Study of Society and Culture* (Berkeley etc.).

Borbein, Adolf H., Hölscher, Tonio, and Zanker, Paul (Eds.). 2000. *Klassische Archäologie. Eine Einführung* (Berlin).

Boschung, Dietrich. 2008. "Adlige Repräsentation in der griechischen und römischen Antike." In Beck et al. (Eds.), 2008c, 177–206.

Boucheron, Patrick, and Mattéoni, Olivier (Eds.). 2005. *Les espaces sociaux de l'Italie urbaine (XIIᵉ-XVᵉ siècles). Recueil d'articles* (Paris).

Bourdieu, Pierre. 1983. "Ökonomisches Kapital, kulturelles Kapital, soziales Kapital." In Reinhard Kreckel (Ed.), *Soziale Ungleichheiten* (Göttingen), 183–98.

————. 1993. *Sozialer Sinn. Kritik der theoretischen Vernunft* (Frankfurt). Orig. ed.: 1980. (Paris).

Bowman, Alan K., Hannah M. Cotton, Martin Goodman, and Simon Price (Eds.). 2002. *Representations of Empire. Rome and the Mediterranean World* (Oxford).

Braddick, Michael J. 2005. "State formation and political culture in Elizabethan and Stuart England." In Asch et al. (Eds.), 69–90.

Braddick, Michael J., and Walter, John. 2001. "Introduction. Grids of Power: Order, Hierarchy and Subordination in Early Modern Society." In idem (Eds.), *Negotiating Power in Early Modern Society. Order, Hierarchy and Subordination in Britain and Ireland* (Cambridge), 1–42.

Braun, Maximilian, Haltenhoff, Andreas, and Mutschler, Fritz-Heiner (Eds.). 2000. *Moribus antiquis res stat romana. Römische Werte und römische Literatur im 3. und 2. Jh. v. Chr.* (Munich).

Braund, David. 1984. *Rome and the Friendly King. The Character of Client Kingship* (London etc.).

———. 1988a. "Introduction: The Growth of the Roman Empire (241BC–AD193)." In idem (Ed.), 1988, 1–13.

———. 1988b. "Client Kings." In idem (Ed.), 1988, 69–96.

———. 1989. "Function and dysfunction: personal patronage in Roman imperialism." In Wallace-Hadrill (Ed.), 1989b, 137–52.

——— (Ed.). 1988. *The Administration of the Roman Empire (241BC-AD193)* (Exeter).

Brennan, T. Corey. 2000. *The Praetorship in the Roman Republic.* Vols.1-2 (Oxford).

———. 2004. "Power and Process under the Republican 'Constitution'." In Flower (Ed.), 2004b, 31–65, 369–70.

Breuer, Stefan. 1982. "Max Weber und die evolutionäre Bedeutung der Antike." In *Saeculum* 33: 174–92.

Brilliant, Richard. 1999. "'Let the Trumpets Roar!' The Roman Triumph." In Bergmann et al. (Eds.), 1999b, 221–29.

Briscoe, John. 1972. "Flamininus and Roman Politics, 200–189 BC." In *Latomus* 31: 22–53.

———. 1982. "Livy and Senatorial Politics, 200–167 BC: The Evidence of the Fourth and Fifth Decades." In *ANRW* 2, 30, 2: 1075–1121.

———. 1992. "Political Groupings in the middle Republic: a Restatement." In Deroux (Ed.), 6:70–83.

Broughton, T. Robert S. 1972. "Senate and Senators of the Roman Republic: The Prosopographical Approach." In *ANRW* 1, 1: 250–65.

Brucker, Gene. 1977. *The Civic World of Early Renaissance Florence* (Princeton).

Bruhns, Hinnerk, David, Jean-Michel, and Nippel, Wilfried (Eds.). 1997. *Die späte römische Republik. La fin de la République romaine* (Rome).

Bruhns, Hinnerk, and Nippel, Wilfried (Eds.). 2000. *Max Weber und die Stadt im Kulturvergleich* (Göttingen).

Brunner, Otto. 1959 [1943]. *Land und Herrschaft. Grundfragen der territorialen Verfassungsgeschichte Österreichs im Mittelalter*, 4th edition (Vienna).

Brunt, Peter A. 1964–1965. "Reflections on British and Roman Imperialism." In *CSSH* 7: 267–88 (= idem, 1990, 110–33).

———. 1971. *Social Conflicts in the Roman Republic* (London).

———. 1978. "Laus Imperii." In Peter D.A. Garnsey and Ch. Richard Whittaker (Eds.), *Imperialism in the Ancient World* (Cambridge), 159–191 (= idem, 1990, 288–323, with additions 506ff.).

———. 1988. *The Fall of the Roman Republic and Related Essays* (Oxford).

———. 1990. *Roman Imperial Themes* (Oxford).

Bruun, Christer (Ed.). 2000. *The Roman middle Republic. Politics, Religion, and Historiography c. 400–133 B.C.* (Rome).

Bücher, Frank. 2006. *Verargumentierte Geschichte. Exempla Romana im politischen Diskurs der späten römischen Republik* (Stuttgart).

Bunse, Robert. 1998. *Das römische Oberamt in der frühen Republik und das Problem der "Konsulartribunen"* (Trier).

Burckhardt, Leonhard A. 1988. *Politische Strategien der Optimaten in der späten römischen Republik* (Stuttgart).

———. 1990. "The Political Élite of the Roman Republic: Comments on Recent Discussion of the Concepts *nobilitas* and *homo novus*." In *Historia* 39: 77–99.

Burke, Peter. 1986. "City-States." In John A. Hall (Ed.), *States in History* (Oxford), 137–53.

———. 1987. *The Historical Anthropology of Early Modern Italy* (Cambridge).

———. 1990. *The French Historical Revolution. The Annales School, 1929–1989* (Cambridge).

———. 1997. *Varieties of Cultural History* (Cambridge).

———. 2004. *What is Cultural History?* (Cambridge).

Busse, Dietrich. 1987. *Historische Semantik. Analyse eines Programms* (Stuttgart).

Cameron, Averil (Ed.). 1989. *History as Text. The Writing of Ancient History* (London).

——— (Ed.). 2003. *Fifty Years of Prosopography. The Later Roman Empire, Byzantium and Beyond* (Oxford etc.).

Cancik, Hubert. 1985/86. "Rome as a Sacral Landscape. Varro and the End of Republican Religion in Rome." In *Visible Religion* 4/5: 250–65.

Cannadine, David (Ed.). 2002. *What is History Now?* (Basingstoke).

Cannadine, David, and Price, Simon (Eds.). 1992. *Rituals of Royalty. Power and Ceremonial in Traditional Societies* (Cambridge).

Cape, Jr., Robert W. 2002. "Cicero's Consular Speeches." In May (Ed.), 2002b, 113–158.

Carney, Thomas F. 1973. "Prosopography: Payoffs and Pitfalls." In *Phoenix* 27: 156–79.

Cartledge, Paul. 2002. "What is Social History Now?" In Cannadine (Ed.), 19–35.

———. 2009. *Ancient Greek Political Thought in Practice* (Cambridge).

Casini, Matteo. 1996. *I gesti del principe. La festa politica a Firenze e Venezia in età rinascimentale* (Venice).

Chaplin, Jane D. 2000. *Livy's Exemplary History* (Oxford).

Chartier, Roger. 1992. *Die unvollendete Vergangenheit. Geschichte und die Macht der Weltauslegung* (Frankfurt). Orig. ed. 1989.

Chittolini, Giorgio. 1991. "The Italian City-State and Its Territory." In Molho et al. (Eds.), 1991, 589–602.

Clark, Elizabeth A. 2004. *History, Theory, Text. Historians and the Linguistic Turn* (Cambridge, Mass.).

Classen, Carl Joachim. 1985. *Recht-Rhetorik-Politik. Untersuchungen zu Ciceros rhetorischer Strategie* (Darmstadt).

———. 1986. "*Virtutes Romanorum* nach dem Zeugnis der Münzen republikanischer Zeit." In *MDAI(R)* 93: 257–79 (= idem. 1993. *Die Welt der Römer. Studien zu ihrer Literatur, Geschichte und Religion*, ed. by Meinolf Vielberg et al. [Berlin], 39–61).

———. 1988. "*Virtutes Romanorum*. Römische Tradition und griechischer Einfluß." In *Gymnasium* 95: 289–302 (= idem. 1998. *Zur Literatur und Gesellschaft der Römer* [Stuttgart], 243–54).

————. 2000. "Römische Wertbegriffe im Alltag der Römer." In *AAntHung* 40: 73–86.

Cloud, Duncan. 1994. "The Constitution and Public Criminal Law." In *CAH* 9: 491–530.

Coarelli, Filippo. 1972. "Il sepolcro degli Scipioni." In *DdA* 6: 36–106 (= idem, 1996, 179–238).

————. 1986. 1985. *Il Foro Romano. Periodo arcaico* (second ed.); vol. 2: *Periodo Repubblicano e Augusteo* (Rome).

————. 1996. *Revixit Ars. Arte e ideologia a Roma. Dai modelli ellenistici alla tradizione repubblicana* (Rome).

————. 1997. *Il Campo Marzio, dalle origini alla fine della repubblica* (Rome).

Cohen, David and Müller-Luckner, Elisabeth (Eds.). 2002. *Demokratie, Recht und soziale Kontrolle im klassischen Athen* (Munich).

Colley, Linda. 2002. "What is Imperial History Now?" In Cannadine (Ed.), 132–47.

Connolly, Joy. 2007. *The State of Speech. Rhetoric and Political Thought in Ancient Rome* (Princeton etc.).

Contamine, Philippe. 1997. "Noblesse et service: l'idée et la réalité dans la France de la fin du Moyen Age." In Oexle et al. (Eds.), 299–311.

Conze, Werner and Meier, Christian. 1972. "Adel, Aristokratie." In *GGr* 1: 1–48.

Corbier, Mireille. 1987. "L'écriture dans l'espace public romain." In AA.VV., 1987, 27–60.

————. 1991. "Divorce and Adoption as Roman Familial Strategies (le divorce et l'adoption ,en plus')." In Beryl Rawson (Ed.), *Marriage, Divorce, and Children in Ancient Rome* (Oxford), 47–78.

Cornell, Tim. 1989. "The recovery of Rome; The conquest of Italy." In *CAH* 7.2: 309–50; 351–419.

————. 1995. *The Beginnings of Rome. Italy and Rome from the Bronze Age to the Punic wars (c. 1000–264BC)* (London).

————. 2000. "The *Lex Ovinia* and the Emancipation of the Senate." In Bruun (Ed.), 69-89.

Coşkun, Altay. 2005. "Freundschaft und Klientelbindung in Roms auswärtigen Beziehungen. Wege und Perspektiven der Forschung." In idem et al. (Eds.), 1–30.

Coşkun, Altay, Heinen, Heinz, and Tröster, Manuel (Eds.). 2005. *Roms auswärtige Freunde in der späten Republik und im frühen Prinzipat* (Göttingen).

Cosi, Raffaella. 2002. *Le solidarietà politiche nella Repubblica romana* (Bari).

Coudry, Marianne. 2001. "Camille: construction et fluctuations de la figure d'un grand homme." In eadem et al. (Eds.), 27–46.

Coudry, Marianne, and Späth, Thomas (Eds.). 2001. *L'invention des grands hommes de la Rome antique. Die Konstruktion der großen Männer Altroms* (Paris).

Coulston, Jon, and Dodge, Hazel (Eds.). 2000. *Ancient Rome: The Archaeology of the Eternal City* (Oxford).

Crawford, Michael. 1976. "Hamlet without the Prince" (review of Gruen, 1974). In *JRS* 66: 214–17.

————. 1992. *The Roman Republic*, 2nd edition (London).

Dahlheim, Werner. 1968. *Struktur und Entwicklung des römischen Völkerrechts im dritten und zweiten Jahrhundert v. Chr.* (Munich).

————. 1977. *Gewalt und Herrschaft. Das provinziale Herrschaftssystem der römischen Republik* (Berlin).

————. 1993. "*Se dedere in fidem*: Die Kapitulation im römischen Völkerrecht." In: *RJ* 10: 41–53.

Daniel, Ute. 1993. "'Kultur' und 'Gesellschaft'. Überlegungen zum Gegenstandsbereich der Sozialgeschichte." In *GG* 19: 69–99.

————. 1994. "Quo vadis, Sozialgeschichte? Kleines Plädoyer für eine hermeneutische Wende." In Winfried Schulze (Ed.), *Sozialgeschichte, Alltagsgeschichte, Mikro-Historie* (Göttingen), 54–64.

————. 1997. "Clio unter Kulturschock. Zu den aktuellen Debatten der Geschichtswissenschaft. Teil I-II." In *GWU* 48: 195–219, 259–78.

————. 2001. *Kompendium Kulturgeschichte. Theorien, Praxis, Schlüsselwörter* (Frankfurt).

David, Jean-Michel. 1980. "'*Eloquentia popularis*' et conduites symboliques des orateurs de la fin de la République: problèmes d'efficacité." In *QS* 12: 171–211.

————. 1984. "Du Comitium à la Roche Tarpéienne. Sur certains rituels d'exécution capitale sous la République, les règnes d'Auguste et de Tibère." In AA.VV. *Du châtiment dans la cité. Supplices corporels et peine de mort dans le monde antique* (Rome), 131–75.

————. 1992. "Compétence sociale et compétence oratoire à la fin de la République: Apprendre à rassembler." In Edmond Frézouls (Ed.), *La mobilité sociale dans le monde romain* (Strasbourg), 7–19.

————. 1992. *Le patronat judiciaire au dernier siècle de la République romaine* (Rome).

————. 1993. "Conformisme et transgression: à propos du tribunat de la plèbe à la fin de la République." In *Klio* 75: 219–27.

————. 1996. *The Roman Conquest of Italy* (Oxford).

————. 1997. "La clientèle, d'une forme d'analyse à l'autre." In Bruhns et al. (Eds.), 195–210.

————. 1998. "De l'action exemplaire à la mise en scène des actes, à Rome, aux deux derniers siècles avant nore ère." In *Travail sur la figure, travail de la mémoire*, ed. by Maison des Sciences de l'Homme de Strasbourg (Strasbourg), 5–16.

————. 2000a. *La République romaine de la deuxième guerre punique à la bataille d'Actium (218–31)* (Paris).

————. 2000b. "I luoghi della politica dalla Repubblica all'Impero." In Andrea Carandini (Ed.), *Storia di Roma dall'antichità a oggi* (Rome), 57–83.

————. 2006a. "Rhetoric and Public Life." In Rosenstein et al. (Eds.), 2006, 421–38.

————. 2006b. "Una repubblica in cantiere." In *StStor* 47, 2: 365–76.

————. 2008. "Préface." In Hölkeskamp (2004) 2008, vii–xi.

————. 2009. "L'exercice du patronat à la fin de la République. Entre la compétition des pairs et la hiérarchie des puissances." In Hölkeskamp et al. (Eds.), 73–86.

De Chaisemartin, N. 2003. *Rome. Paysage urbain et idéologie, des Scipions à Hadrien (IIe s. av. J.-C.—IIe s. ap. J.-C.)* (Paris).

Deininger, Jürgen. 1989. "Die antike Stadt als Typus bei Max Weber." In Werner Dahlheim, Wolfgang Schuller, and Jürgen von Ungern-Sternberg (Eds.), *Festschrift Robert Werner zu seinem 65. Geburtstag* (Constance), 269–89.

———. 1998. "Zur Kontroverse über die Lebensfähigkeit der Republik in Rom." In Kneissl, Peter and Losemann, Volker (Eds.), *Imperium Romanum. Studien zu Geschichte und Rezeption. Festschrift für Karl Christ...* (Stuttgart), 123–36.

Dench, Emma. 2005. *Romulus' Asylum. Roman Identities from the Age of Alexander to the Age of Hadrian* (Oxford).

Deniaux, Elizabeth. 1993. *Clientèles et pouvoir à l'époque de Cicéron* (Rome).

———. 1997. "La rue et l'opinion publique à Rome et en Italie (1er siècle avant J.-C.): cortèges et popularité." In Alain Leménorel (Ed.), *La rue, lieu de sociabilité? Rencontres de la rue* (Rouen) 207–13.

———. 2000. "Images de l'orateur au Forum." In eadem (Ed.), 163–75.

———. 2006. "Patronage." In Rosenstein et al. (Eds.), 2006, 401–20.

——— (Ed.). 2000. *Rome antique. Pouvoir des images, images du pouvoir* (Caen).

Deroux, Carl (Ed.). 1978ff. *Studies in Latin Literature and Roman History*, vols. 1 ff. (Brussels).

Dillon, Sheila, and Welch, Katherine E. (Eds.). 2006. *Representations of War in Ancient Rome* (Cambridge).

Dinges, Martin. 2002. "Neue Kulturgeschichte." In Eibach et al. (Eds.), 179–92.

Dittmer, Lowell. 1977. "Political Culture and Political Symbolism: Toward a Theoretical Synthesis." In *World Politics* 29: 552–83.

Döbler, Christine. 1999. *Politische Agitation und Öffentlichkeit in der späten Republik* (Frankfurt).

Dondin-Payre, Monique. 1993. *Exercice du pouvoir et continuité gentilice: Les Acilii Glabriones* (Rome).

Dressel, Gert. 1996. *Historische Anthropologie. Eine Einführung* (Vienna).

Drexler, Hans. 1988. *Politische Grundbegriffe der Römer* (Darmstadt).

Drummond, Andrew. 1989a. "Early Roman *clientes*." In Wallace-Hadrill (Ed.), 1989b, 89–115.

———. 1989b. "Rome in the fifth century II: The citizen community." In *CAH* 7.2: 172–242.

Van Dülmen, Richard. 1995. "Historische Kulturforschung zur Frühen Neuzeit. Entwicklung—Probleme—Aufgaben." In *GG* 21: 403–29.

Duncan-Jones, Richard P. 1984. "The Heritability of the Consulship" (review article on Hopkins, 1983). In *CR* 34: 270–74.

Dupont, Florence. 1985. *L'acteur-roi ou le théâtre dans la Rome antique* (Paris).

———. 1992. *Daily Life in Ancient Rome* (Oxford), original edition: 1989. *La vie quotidienne du citoyen romain sous la République* (Paris).

Duplouy, Alain. 2006. *Le prestige des élites. Recherches sur les modes de reconnaissance sociale en Grèce entre les Xe et Ve siècles avant J.-C.* (Paris).

Earl, Donald C. 1967. *The Moral and Political Tradition of Rome* (Ithaca).

Eck, Werner. 1974. "Beförderungskriterien innerhalb der senatorischen Laufbahn, dargestellt an der Zeit von 69 bis 138 n. Chr." In *ANRW* 2, 1: 158–228 (updated and augmented Italian translation in idem, 1996, 27–83).

———. 1981. "Altersangaben in senatorischen Grabinschriften: Standeserwartungen und ihre Kompensation." In *ZPE* 43: 127–34.

———. 1984. "Senatorial Self-Representation: Developments in the Augustan Period." In Fergus Millar and Erich Segal (Eds.), *Caesar Augustus. Seven Aspects* (Oxford), 129–67.

———. 1993. "Überlieferung und historische Realität: ein Grundproblem prosopographischer Forschung." In idem (Ed.), 365–96.

———. 1996. *Tra epigrafia, prosopografia e archeologia. Scritti scelti, rielaborati ed aggiornati* (Rome).

———. 1999. "Elite und Leitbilder in der römischen Kaiserzeit." In Jürgen Dummer and Meinolf Vielberg (Eds.), *Leitbilder der Spätantike—Éliten und Leitbilder* (Stuttgart), 31–55.

———. 2002. "Imperial Administration and Epigraphy: In Defence of Prosopography." In Bowman et al. (Eds.), 131–52.

———. 2003. "The *Prosopographia Imperii Romani* and Prosopographical Method." In Cameron (Ed.), 11–22.

———. 2005a. "Auf der Suche nach Personen und Persönlichkeiten: *Cursus honorum* und Biographie." In Konrad Vössing (Ed.), *Biographie und Prosopographie. Festschrift für Anthony R. Birley* (Stuttgart), 53–72.

———. 2005b. "Der Senator und die Öffentlichkeit—oder: Wie beeindruckt man das Publikum?" In idem et al. (Eds.), 2005, 1–18.

——— (Ed.). 1993. *Prosopographie und Sozialgeschichte. Studien zur Methodik und Erkenntnismöglichkeit der kaiserzeitlichen Prosopographie* (Cologne etc.).

Eck, Werner, and Heil, Matthäus (Eds.). 2005. *Senatores populi Romani. Realität und mediale Präsentation einer Führungsschicht* (Stuttgart).

Eckstein, Arthur M. 2006a. *Mediterranean Anarchy, Interstate War, and the Rise of Rome* (Berkeley etc.).

———. 2006b. "Conceptualizing Roman Imperial Expansion under the Republic: An Introduction." In Rosenstein et al. (Eds.), 2006, 567–89.

———. 2008. *Rome Enters the Greek East. From Anarchy to Hierarchy in the Hellenistic Mediterranean, 230–170BC* (Oxford).

Edelman, Murray. 1964. *The Symbolic Uses of Politics* (Urbana, Ill.).

Eder, Walter. 1990a. "Der Bürger und sein Staat—der Staat und seine Bürger. Eine Einführung zum Thema Staat und Staatlichkeit in der frühen römischen Republik." In idem (Ed.), 1990b, 12–32.

——— (Ed.). 1990b. *Staat und Staatlichkeit in der frühen römischen Republik* (Stuttgart).

———. 1991. "Who Rules? Power and Participation in Athens and Rome." In Molho et al. (Eds.), 169–96.

———. 1996. "Republicans and Sinners: The Decline of the Roman Republic and the End of a Provisional Arrangement." In Wallace et al. (Eds.), 439–61.

Edwards, Catharine. 1996. *Writing Rome. Textual Approaches to the City* (Cambridge).

———. 2003a. "Incorporating the Alien: The Art of Conquest." In eadem et al. (Eds.), 2003c, 44–70.

Edwards, Catharine, and Greg Woolf. 2003b. "Cosmopolis: Rome as World City." In idem (Eds.), 2003c, 1–20.

——— (Eds.). 2003c. *Rome the Cosmopolis* (Cambridge).

Eibach, Joachim. 2002. "Sozialgeschichte." In idem et al. (Eds.), 9–22.

Eibach, Joachim, and Lottes, Günther (Eds.). 2002. *Kompass der Geschichtswissenschaft. Ein Handbuch* (Göttingen).

Eich, Armin, and Eich, Peter. 2005. "War and State-Building in Roman Republican Times." In *SCI* 24: 1–33.

Eich, Peter. 2005. *Zur Metamorphose des politischen Systems Roms in der Kaiserzeit. Eine Studie über Hierarchie als Strukturprinzip historischer Bürokratien* (Cologne).

———. 2008. "Aristokratie und Monarchie im kaiserzeitlichen Rom." In Beck et al. (Eds.), 2008c, 125–51.

Eigler, Ulrich, Luraghi, Nino, and Walter, Uwe (Eds.). 2003. *Formen römischer Geschichtsschreibung von den Anfängen bis Livius. Gattungen—Autoren—Kontexte* (Darmstadt).

Eilers, Claude. 2002. *Roman Patrons of Greek Cities* (Oxford).

Eisenhut, Werner. 1973. Virtus Romana. *Ihre Stellung im römischen Wertsystem* (Munich).

Emich, Birgit. 2008. "Bildlichkeit und Intermedialität in der Frühen Neuzeit. Eine interdisziplinäre Spurensuche." In *ZHF* 35: 31–56.

Evans, Richard J. 1991. "Candidates and Competition in Consular Elections at Rome between 218 and 49 BC." In *AClass* 34: 111–36.

Evans, Richard J. 1997. *In Defence of History* (London).

———. 2002. "Prologue: *What is History*—Now?" In Cannadine (Ed.), 1–18.

Faber, Karl-Georg, and Meier, Christian (Eds.). 1978. *Historische Prozesse. Theorie der Geschichte: Beiträge zur Historik*, vol. 2 (Munich).

Fantham, Elaine. 1996. *Roman Literary Culture. From Cicero to Apuleius* (Baltimore).

———. 1997. "The Contexts and Occasions of Roman Public Rhetoric." In William J. Dominik (Ed.), *Roman Eloquence. Rhetoric in Society and Literature* (London), 111–28.

———. 2000. "Meeting the People: The Orator and the Republican *contio*." In Lucia Calboli Montefusco (Ed.), *Papers on Rhetoric 3* (Bologna), 95–112.

———. 2004. *The Roman World of Cicero's De Oratore* (Oxford).

Farney, Gary D. 2004. "Some More Roman 'Also-Rans.'" *Historia* 53: 246–50.

———. 2007. *Ethnic Identity and Aristocratic Competition in Republican Rome* (Cambridge).

Fascione, Lorenzo. 1984. Crimen *e* quaestio ambitus *nell`età repubblicana. Contributo allo studio del diritto criminale repubblicano* (Milan).

Favro, Diane. 1994. "The Street Triumphant: The Urban Impact of Roman Triumphal Parades." In eadem, Zeynep Celik, Richard Ingersoll (Eds.), *Streets: Critical Perspectives on Public Space* (Berkeley), 151–64.

———. 1999. "The City Is a Living Thing: The Performative Rôle of an Urban Site in Ancient Rome, the Vallis Murcia." In Bergmann et al. (Eds.), 1999b, 205–19.

Fears, J. Rufus. 1981a. "The Theology of Victory at Rome: Approaches and Problems." In *ANRW* 2, 17/2: 736–826.

———. 1981b. "The Cult of Virtues and Roman Imperial Ideology." In *ANRW* 2, 17/2: 827–948.

Febvre, Lucien (1947) 1953. "Sur une forme d'histoire qui n'est pas la nôtre. L'histoire historisante." In idem. *Combats pour l'Histoire* (Paris), 114–18, first published in *AESC* 2, 1947.

Feinman, Gary M., and Marcus, Joyce (Eds.). 1998. *Archaic States* (Santa Fe).

Feldherr, Andrew. 1998. *Spectacle and Society in Livy's History* (Berkeley).

Ferrary, Jean-Louis. 1997. "*Optimates* et *populares*. Le problème du rôle de l'idéologie dans la politique." In Bruhns et al. (Eds.), 221–31.

Finley, Moses I. 1973. *Democracy Ancient and Modern* (London).

———. (1973) 1999. *The Ancient Economy* (Berkeley etc.).

———. 1977. "The Ancient City: From Fustel de Coulanges to Max Weber and Beyond." In *CSSH* 19: 305–27 (= idem, 1981, 3–23).

———. 1981. *Economy and Society in Ancient Greece*, ed. by Brent D. Shaw and Richard P. Saller (London).

———. 1983. *Politics in the Ancient World* (Cambridge).

———. 1986. "Max Weber und der griechische Stadtstaat." In Kocka (Ed.), 1986, 90–106.

Fischer-Lichte, Erika. 2003. "Performance, Inszenierung, Ritual: Zur Klärung kulturwissenschaftlicher Schlüsselbegriffe." In Martschukat et al. (Eds.), 33–54.

Flaig, Egon. 1993a. "Politisierte Lebensführung und ästhetische Kultur. Eine semiotische Untersuchung am römischen Adel." In *HA* 1: 193–217.

———. 1993b. "Im Schlepptau der Masse. Politische Obsession und historiographische Konstruktion bei Jacob Burckhardt und Theodor Mommsen." In *RJ* 12: 405–42.

———. 1994. "Repenser le politique dans la République romaine." In *Actes de la Recherche en Sciences Sociales* 105: 13–25.

———. 1995a. "Entscheidung und Konsens. Zu den Feldern der politischen Kommunikation zwischen Aristokratie und Plebs." In Jehne (Ed.), 1995c, 77–127.

———. 1995b. "Die *Pompa Funebris*. Adlige Konkurrenz und annalistische Erinnerung in der Römischen Republik." In Otto Gerhard Oexle (Ed.), *Memoria als Kultur* (Göttingen), 115–48.

———. 1997. "Volkssouveränität ohne Repräsentation. Zum *Römischen Staatsrecht* von Theodor Mommsen." In Wolfgang Küttler, Jörn Rüsen and Ernst Schulin (Eds.), *Geschichtsdiskurs 3: Die Epoche der Historisierung* (Stuttgart), 321–39.

———. 1998. "War die römische Volksversammlung ein Entscheidungsorgan? Institution und soziale Praxis." In Blänkner et al. (Eds.), 1998b, 49–73.

———. 1999a. "Kinderkrankheiten der Neuen Kulturgeschichte." In *RJ* 18: 458–76.

———. 1999b. "Über die Grenzen der Akkulturation. Wider die Verdinglichung des Kulturbegriffs." In Vogt-Spira et al. (Eds.), 1999, 81–112.

———. 2000. "Kulturgeschichte ohne historische Anthropologie. Was römische Ahnenmasken verbergen." In *IJCT* 7.2: 226–44.

———. 2003a. "Warum die Triumphe die römische Republik ruiniert haben— oder: Kann ein politisches System an zuviel Sinn zugrunde gehen?" In Hölkeskamp et al. (Eds.), 2003, 299–313.

———. 2003b. *Ritualisierte Politik. Zeichen, Gesten und Herrschaft im Alten Rom* (Göttingen).

———. 2004. "Habitus, Mentalitäten und die Frage des Subjekts: Kulturelle Orientierungen sozialen Handelns." In *HbKW* 3: 356–71.

———. 2005. "Keine Performanz ohne Norm—keine Norm ohne Wert. Das Problem der zwingenden Gesten in der römischen Politik." In Haltenhoff et al. (Eds.), 209–21.

———. 2007. "Roman Gladiatorial Games: Ritual and Political Consensus." In Roth et al. (Eds.), 83–92.

Fless, Friederike. 2004. "Römische Prozessionen." In *ThesCRA* 1: 33–58.

Flower, Harriet I. 1996. *Ancestor Masks and Aristocratic Power in Roman Culture* (Oxford).

———. 2003. "'Memories' of Marcellus. History and Memory in Roman Republican Culture." In Eigler et al. (Eds.), 39–52.

———. 2004a. "Spectacle and Political Culture in the Roman Republic." In eadem (Ed.), 2004b, 322–43. 394.

——— (Ed.). 2004b. *The Cambridge Companion to the Roman Republic* (Cambridge).

———. 2006a. *The Art of Forgetting: Disgrace and Oblivion in Roman Political Culture* (Chapel Hill).

———. 2006b. "Der Leichenzug—die Ahnen kommen wieder." In Stein-Hölkeskamp et al. (Eds.), 2006, 321–37, 752–53.

Forsythe, Gary. 2005. *A Critical History of Early Rome: From Prehistory to the First Punic War* (Berkeley etc.).

Freist, Dagmar. 2005. "Staatsbildung, lokale Herrschaftspraxis und kultureller Wandel in der Frühen Neuzeit." In Asch et al. (Eds.), 2005, 1–47.

Frevert, Ute. 2005. "Neue Politikgeschichte: Konzepte und Herausforderungen." In eadem and Heinz-G. Haupt (Eds.), *Neue Politikgeschichte. Perspektiven einer historischen Politikforschung* (Frankfurt), 7–26.

Freyburger, Gérard. 1986. *FIDES. Étude sémantique et religieuse depuis les origines à l'époque augustéenne* (Paris).

Fried, Johannes. 2001. "Erinnerung und Vergessen. Die Gegenwart stiftet die Einheit der Vergangenheit." In *HZ* 273: 561–93.

Frischer, Bernard. 1982–1983. "*Monumenta et Arae Honoris Virtutisque Causa*: Evidence of Memorials for Roman Civic Heroes." In *BCAR* 88: 51–86.

Fröhlich, Gerhard. 1994. "Kapital, Habitus, Feld, Symbol. Grundbegriffe der Kulturtheorie bei Pierre Bourdieu." In Mörth et al. (Eds.), 31–54.

Fuchs, Dieter. 2007. "The Political Culture Paradigm." In Russell J. Dalton and Hans-Dieter Klingemann (Eds.), *The Oxford Handbook of Political Behavior* (Oxford etc.), 161-84.

Fuhrmann, Manfred. 1983. *Rhetorik und öffentliche Rede. Über die Ursachen des Verfalls der Rhetorik im ausgehenden 18. Jh.* (Constance).

Gabba, Emilio. 1984. "Il consenso popolare alla politica espansionistica romana fra III e il II sec. a.C." In Harris (Ed.), 115–29.

———. 1995. "La concezione antica di aristocrazia." In *RAL* ser. 9, 6: 461–68.

———. 1997. "Democrazia a Roma." In *Athenaeum* 85: 266–71.

Gaertner, Jan Felix. 2008. "Livy's Camillus and the Political Discourse of the late Republic." In *JRS* 98: 27–52.

Galsterer, Hartmut. 1976. *Herrschaft und Verwaltung im republikanischen Italien. Die Beziehungen Roms zu den italischen Gemeinden vom Latinerfrieden 338 v. Chr. bis zum Bundesgenossenkrieg 91 v. Chr.* (Munich).

———. 1990. "A Man, a Book, and a Method: Sir Ronald Syme's *Roman Revolution* after Fifty Years." In Raaflaub, Kurt A. and Toher, Mark (Eds.), *Between Republic and Empire: Interpretations of Augustus and His Principate* (Berkeley), 1–20.

Gardner, Jane F. 1993. *Being a Roman Citizen* (London etc.).

Garnier, Claudia. 2008. *Die Kultur der Bitte. Herrschaft und Kommunikation im mittelalterlichen Reich* (Darmstadt).

Garnsey, Peter and Saller, Richard. 1987. *The Roman Empire. Economy, Society and Culture* (London).

Gärtner, Hans Arnim. 2000. "Politische Moral bei Sallust, Livius und Tacitus." In *AAntHung* 40: 101–12.

Geertz, Clifford. 1973. *The Interpretation of Cultures* (New York, repr. London 1993).

Gehrke, Hans-Joachim. 1993. "Aktuelle Tendenzen im Fach Alte Geschichte." In *GPD* 21: 216–22.

———. 1995. "Zwischen Altertumswissenschaft und Geschichte. Zur Standortbestimmung der Alten Geschichte am Ende des 20. Jahrhunderts." In Schwinge (Ed.), 160–96.

———. 2004. "Die »Klassische« Antike als Kulturepoche—Soziokulturelle Milieus und Deutungsmuster in der griechisch-römischen Welt." In *HbKW* 1: 471–89.

Gelzer, Matthias. 1912. *Die Nobilität der römischen Republik* (Leipzig) (= idem. 1962, 17–135; new edition 1982, ed. by Jürgen von Ungern-Sternberg).

———. 1920. "Die römische Gesellschaft zur Zeit Ciceros." In *Neue Jahrbücher* 23: 1–27 (= idem, 1962, 154–85).

———. 1921. "Die Entstehung der Nobilität." In *HZ* 123: 1–13 (= idem, 1962, 186–95).

———. 1950. "Review of Scullard, 1951." In *Historia* 1: 634–42 (= idem, 1962, 200–10).

———. 1962–64. *Kleine Schriften*, vols. 1–3, ed. by Hermann Strasburger and Christian Meier (Wiesbaden).

Gendre, Marianne and Loutsch, Claude. 2001. "C. Duilius et M. Atilius Regulus." In Coudry et al. (Eds.), 131–72.

Gersmann, Gudrun. 2005. "Adel." In *EnzNZ* 1: 39–54.

Gilcher-Holtey, Ingrid. 1996. "Kulturelle und symbolische Praktiken: das Unternehmen Pierre Bourdieu." In Hardtwig et al. (Eds.), 111–30.

Girardet, Klaus M. 1996. "Politische Verantwortung im Ernstfall. Cicero, die Diktatur und der Diktator Caesar." In Mueller Goldingen, Christian and Sier, Kurt (Eds.). *LENAIKA. Festschrift für Carl Werner Müller* (Stuttgart etc.), 217–51 (= idem. 2007. *Rom auf dem Weg von der Republik zum Prinzipat* [Bonn], 199–234).

Giuliani, Luca. 1986. *Bildnis und Botschaft. Hermeneutische Untersuchungen zur Bildkunst der römischen Republik* (Frankfurt).

Gladigow, Burkhard. 1972. "Die sakralen Funktionen der Liktoren. Zum Problem von institutioneller Macht und sakraler Präsentation." In *ANRW* 1, 2: 295–314.

Göhler, Gerhard (Ed.). 1994. *Die Eigenart der Institutionen. Zum Profil politischer Institutionentheorie* (Baden-Baden).

——— (Ed.). 1997. *Institution—Macht—Repräsentation. Wofür politische Institutionen stehen und wie sie wirken* (Baden-Baden).

Göhler, Gerhard, and Speth, Rudolf. 1998. "Symbolische Macht. Zur institutionentheoretischen Bedeutung von Pierre Bourdieu." In Blänkner et al. (Eds.), 1998b, 17–48.

Golden, Mark and Toohey, Peter (Eds.). 1997. *Inventing Ancient Culture. Historicism, Periodization, and the Ancient World* (London).

Goldmann, Frank. 2002. "*Nobilitas* als Status und Gruppe—Überlegungen zum Nobilitätsbegriff der römischen Republik." In Spielvogel (Ed.), 45–66.

Goltz, Andreas. 2000. "*Maiestas sine viribus*—Die Bedeutung der Lictoren für die Konfliktbewältigungsstrategien römischer Magistrate." In Linke et al. (Eds.), 2000b, 237–67.

Goppold, Uwe. 2007. *Politische Kommunikation in den Städten der Vormoderne. Zürich und Münster im Vergleich* (Cologne etc.).

Gowing, Alain M. 2005. *Empire and Memory. The Representation of the Roman Republic in Imperial Culture* (Cambridge).

Griffeth, Robert, and Thomas, Carol G. (Eds.). 1981. *The City-State in Five Cultures* (Santa Barbara).

Groß, Karl. 1983. "Gravitas." In *RAC* 12: 752–79.

Gruen, Erich S. 1968. *Roman Politics and the Criminal Courts, 159–78 BC* (Cambridge, Mass.).

———. 1974. *The Last Generation of the Roman Republic* (Berkeley), second ed. 1995, with new Introduction, vii–xxi.

———. 1984. *The Hellenistic World and the Coming of Rome*, vols. 1–2 (Berkeley etc.).

———. 1991. "The Exercise of Power in the Roman Republic." In Molho et al. (Eds.), 251–67.

———. 1992. *Culture and National Identity in Republican Rome* (Ithaca).

———. 1996. "The Roman Oligarchy: Image and Perception." In Linderski (Ed.), 215–34.

———. 2004. "Rome and the Greek World." In Flower (Ed.), 2004b, 242–67. 389–90.

Grziwotz, Herbert. 1985. *Das Verfassungsverständnis der römischen Republik. Ein methodischer Versuch* (Frankfurt).

Guarino, Antonio. 1979. *La democrazia a Roma* (Naples).

Haas, Jonathan. 1982. *The Evolution of the Prehistoric State* (New York).

Haltenhoff, Andreas. 2000. "Wertbegriff und Wertbegriffe." In Braun et al. (Eds.), 16–29.

———. 2005. "Römische Werte in neuer Sicht? Konzeptionelle Perspektiven innerhalb und außerhalb der Fachgrenzen." In idem et al. (Eds.), 81–105.

Haltenhoff, Andreas, Andreas Heil, and Fritz-Heiner Mutschler (Eds.). 2003. *O tempora, o mores! Römische Werte und römische Literatur in den letzten Jahrzehnten der Republik* (Leipzig).

———— (Eds.). 2005. *Römische Werte als Gegenstand der Altertumswissenschaft* (Leipzig).

Hampl, Franz. 1977. "Das Problem des Aufstiegs Roms zur Weltmacht. Neue Bilanz unter methodisch-kritischen Aspekten." In idem, *Geschichte als kritische Wissenschaft*, Vol. III, ed. by Ingomar Weiler (Darmstadt), 48–119.

Hansen, Mogens H. (Ed.). 2000. *A Comparative Study of Thirty City-State Cultures* (Copenhagen).

———— (Ed.). 2002. *A Comparative Study of Six City-State Cultures* (Copenhagen).

————. 2006. *Polis. An Introduction to the Ancient Greek City-State* (Oxford).

Hansen, Mogens H., and Thomas Heine Nielsen (Eds.). 2004. *An Inventory of Archaic and Classical Greek Poleis* (Oxford).

Hantos, Theodora. 1983. *Das römische Bundesgenossensystem in Italien* (Munich).

Hardtwig, Wolfgang, and Wehler, Hans-Ulrich (Eds.). 1996. *Kulturgeschichte Heute* (Göttingen).

Harris, William V. 1979, repr. 1985, 1992. *War and Imperialism in Republican Rome, 327–70 BC* (Oxford).

————. 1984a. "Current Directions in the Study of Roman Imperialism." In idem (Ed.), 1984b, 13–34.

———— (Ed.). 1984b. *The Imperialism of Mid-Republican Rome* (Rome).

————. 1990. "On Defining the Political Culture of the Roman Republic." In *CPh* 85: 288–94.

Hatscher, Christoph. 2000. *Charisma und Res publica. Max Webers Herrschaftssoziologie und die römische Republik* (Stuttgart).

Haupt, Heinz-Gerhard, and Kocka, Jürgen. 1996a. "Historischer Vergleich: Methoden, Aufgaben, Probleme. Eine Einleitung." In idem (Eds.), 1996b, 9–45.

———— (Eds.). 1996b. *Geschichte und Vergleich. Ansätze und Ergebnisse international vergleichender Geschichtsschreibung* (Frankfurt).

Hellegouarc'h, Joseph. 1963, repr. 1972. *Le vocabulaire latin des relations et des partis politiques sous la république* (Paris).

Henderson, John. 1997. *Figuring Out Roman Nobility. Juvenal's Eighth Satire* (Exeter).

Heuss, Alfred. 1956. *Theodor Mommsen und das 19. Jahrhundert* (Kiel). Repr. Stuttgart 1996.

————. 1956a. "Review of Scullard, 1951." In *HZ* 186: 593–97 (= idem, 1995, 2, 1557–61).

————. 1963. "Das Zeitalter der Revolution." In idem and Golo Mann (Eds.), *Rom. Die römische Welt, Propyläen Weltgeschichte*, vol. 4 (Berlin), 175–316.

————. 1965. "Max Webers Bedeutung für die Geschichte des griechisch-römischen Altertums." In *HZ* 201: 529–56 (= idem, 1995, 3, 1835–62).

————. 1976, repr. 1998 (Paderborn). *Römische Geschichte* (Braunschweig).

————. 1995. *Gesammelte Schriften*, vols. 1–3 (Stuttgart).

Hinard, François (Ed.). 2000. *Histoire Romaine. Des origines à Auguste* (Paris).

Hingley, Richard. 2005. *Globalizing Roman Culture. Unity, diversity and empire* (London etc.).

Hofmann-Löbl, Iris. 1996. *Die Calpurnii. Politisches Wirken und familiäre Kontinuität* (Frankfurt etc.).

Hölkeskamp, Karl-J. 1987. *Die Entstehung der Nobilität. Studien zur sozialen und politischen Geschichte der Römischen Republik im 4. Jhdt. v.Chr.* (Stuttgart).

———. 1988. "Die Entstehung der Nobilität und der Funktionswandel des Volkstribunats: die historische Bedeutung der *lex Hortensia de plebiscitis.*" In *AKG* 70: 271–312 (= idem, 2004a, 49–83, with Addenda).

———. 1990. "Senat und Volkstribunat im frühen 3. Jh. v. Chr." In Eder (Ed.), 1990b, 437–57 (= idem, 2004a, 85–103, with Addenda).

———. 1993. "Conquest, Competition and Consensus: Roman Expansion in Italy and the Rise of the *Nobilitas.*" In *Historia* 42: 12–39 (= idem, 2004a, 11–48, with Addenda).

———. 1995. "*Oratoris maxima scaena.* Reden vor dem Volk in der politischen Kultur der Republik." In Jehne (Ed.), 1995c, 11–49 (= idem, 2004a, 219–56, with Addenda).

———. 1996. "*Exempla* und *mos maiorum.* Überlegungen zum kollektiven Gedächtnis der Nobilität." In Hans-Joachim Gehrke and Astrid Möller (Eds.), *Vergangenheit und Lebenswelt. Soziale Kommunikation, Traditionsbildung und historisches Bewußtsein* (Tübingen), 301–38 (= idem, 2004a, 169–98, with Addenda).

———. 1997. "Zwischen 'System' und 'Geschichte'—Theodor Mommsens Staatsrecht und die römische 'Verfassung' in Frankreich und Deutschland." In Bruhns et al. (Eds.), 93–111.

———. 1998. "Parteiungen und politische Willensbildung im demokratischen Athen: Perikles und Thukydides, Sohn des Melesias." In *HZ* 267: 1–27.

———. 1999. "Römische *gentes* und griechische Genealogien." In Vogt-Spira et al. (Eds.), 1999, 3–21 (= idem, 2004a, 199–217, with Addenda).

———. 2000a. "The Roman Republic: Government of the People, by the People, for the People?" (Review of Millar, 1998). In *SCI* 19: 203–23 (= idem, 2004a, 257–80, with Addenda).

———. 2000b. "*Fides—deditio in fidem—dextra data et accepta.* Recht, Religion und Ritual in Rom." In Bruun (Ed.), 2000, 223–50 (= idem, 2004a, 105–35, with Addenda).

———. 2000c. "«Senat und Volk von Rom»—Kurzbiografie einer Republik." In Hölkeskamp et al. (Eds.), 2000, 11–35.

———. 2001a. "Capitol, Comitium und Forum. Öffentliche Räume, sakrale Topographie und Erinnerungslandschaften der römischen Republik." In Stefan Faller (Ed.), *Studien zu antiken Identitäten* (Würzburg), 97–132 (= idem, 2004a, 137–68, with Addenda).

———. 2001b. "Fact(ions) or Fiction? Friedrich Münzer and the Aristocracy of the Roman Republic—Then and Now." In *IJCT* 8.1: 92–105.

———. 2002. "*Nomos, Thesmos* und Verwandtes. Vergleichende Überlegungen zur Konzeptualisierung geschriebenen Rechts im Klassischen Griechenland." In Cohen et al. (Eds.), 2002, 115–46.

———. 2003. "Institutionalisierung durch Verortung. Die Entstehung der Öffentlichkeit im frühen Griechenland." In Hölkeskamp et al. (Eds.), 81–104.

———. 2004a. *SENATVS POPVLVSQVE ROMANVS. Die politische Kultur der Republik—Dimensionen und Deutungen* (Stuttgart).

———. 2004b. "Under Roman Roofs: Family, House, and Household." In Flower (Ed.), 2004b, 113–38, 376–79.

————. 2004c. "The Polis and its Spaces—the Politics of Spatiality. Tendencies in Recent Research." In *OP* 3: 25–40.

————. 2005a. "Images of Power: Memory, Myth and Monuments in the Roman Republic" (review of Holliday, 2002). In *SCI* 24: 249–71.

————. 2005b. "Ein 'Gegensatz von Form und Inhalt'. Theodor Mommsens Konzept des republikanischen 'Senatsregiments'—Hindernis oder Herausforderung?" In Nippel et al. (Eds.), 2005, 87–129.

————. 2006a. "Der Triumph—«erinnere Dich, daß Du ein Mensch bist.»" In Stein-Hölkeskamp et al. (Eds.), 2006, 258–76, 745–47.

————. 2006b. "History and Collective Memory in the middle Republic." In Rosenstein et al. (Eds.), 478–95.

————. 2006c. "Rituali e cerimonie 'alla romana'. Nuove prospettive sulla cultura politica dell'età repubblicana." In *StStor* 47, 2: 319–63.

————. 2006d. "Konsens und Konkurrenz. Die politische Kultur der römischen Republik in neuer Sicht." In *Klio* 88, 2: 360–96.

————. 2006 (2007). "Pomp und Prozessionen. Rituale und Zeremonien in der politischen Kultur der römischen Republik." In *Jahrbuch des Historischen Kollegs*: 35–72.

————. 2007. "Herrschaft, Verwaltung und Verwandtes. Prolegomena zu Konzepten und Kategorien." In Rudolf Haensch and Johannes Heinrichs (Eds.). *Herrschen und Verwalten. Der Alltag der römischen Administration in der Hohen Kaiserzeit* (Cologne etc.), 1–18.

————. (2004) 2008. *Reconstruire une République. La «culture politique» de la Rome antique et la recherche des dernières décennies* (Nantes). French edition of *Rekonstruktionen einer Republik*, translated by Claudine Layre and Frédéric Hurlet.

————. 2008. "Hierarchie und Konsens. *Pompae* in der politischen Kultur der römischen Republik." In Arweiler, Alexander and Gauly, Bardo (Eds.). *Machtfragen. Zur kulturellen Repräsentation und Konstruktion von Macht in Antike, Mittelalter und Neuzeit* (Stuttgart), 79–126.

————. 2009a. "Mythos und Politik—(nicht nur) in der Antike. Anregungen und Angebote der neuen 'historischen Politikforschung'." In *HZ* 237: 1–50.

————. 2009b. "Eine politische Kultur (in) der Krise? Gemäßigt radikale Vorbemerkungen zum kategorischen Imperativ der Konzepte." In idem et al. (Eds.), 2009, 1–25.

————. forthcoming a. "Self-serving Sermons. Oratory and the Self-Construction of the Roman Aristocrat." In Smith, Christopher J. and Corvino, Ralph J. (Eds.). *Praise and Blame in the Later Roman Republic*.

————. forthcoming b. "The Roman Republic as Theatre of Power: The Consuls as Leading Actors." In Beck, Hans and Pina Polo, Francesco (Eds.). *Consuls, Consulars and the Constitution of the Roman Republic*.

Hölkeskamp, Karl-J., and Elke Stein-Hölkeskamp (Eds.). 2000. *Von Romulus zu Augustus. Große Gestalten der römischen Republik* (Munich).

Hölkeskamp, Karl-J., Rüsen, Jörn, Stein-Hölkeskamp, Elke, and Grütter, Heinrich Th. (Eds.). 2003. *Sinn (in) der Antike. Orientierungssysteme, Leitbilder und Wertkonzepte im Altertum* (Mainz).

Hölkeskamp, Karl-J., and Müller-Luckner, Elisabeth (Eds.). 2009. *Eine politische Kultur (in) der Krise? Die "letzte Generation" der römischen Republik* (Munich).

Hölscher, Tonio. 1978. "Die Anfänge römischer Repräsentationskunst." In *MDAI(R)* 85: 315–57.

———. 1980. "Die Geschichtsauffassung in der römischen Repräsentations-kunst." In *JDAI* 95: 265–321.

———. 1982. "Die Bedeutung der Münzen für das Verständnis der politischen Repräsentationskunst der späten römischen Republik." In Tony Hackens and Raymond Weiller (Eds.), *Proceedings of the 9th International Congress of Numismatics* 1 (Luxemburg), 269–82.

———. 1984. *Staatsdenkmal und Publikum. Vom Untergang der Republik bis zur Festigung des Kaisertums in Rom* (Constance).

———. (1987) 2004. *The Language of Images in Roman Art* (English translation of *Römische Bildsprache als semantisches System*, AHAW 1987, no. 2).

———. 1990. "Römische Nobiles und hellenistische Herrscher." In *Akten des 13. Internationalen Kongresses für Klassische Archäologie Berlin 1988* (Mainz), 73–84.

———. 1992. "Bilderwelt, Formensystem, Lebenskultur. Zur Methode archäologischer Kulturanalyse." In *SIFC* 3a ser. 10: 460–84.

———. 1995. "Klassische Archäologie am Ende des 20. Jahrhunderts: Tendenzen, Defizite, Illusionen." In Schwinge (Ed.), 1995, 197–228.

———. 1998a. *Öffentliche Räume in frühen griechischen Städten* (Heidelberg).

———. 1998b. *Aus der Frühzeit der Griechen. Räume—Körper—Mythen* (Stuttgart).

———. 2000. "Bildwerke: Darstellungen, Funktionen, Botschaften." In Borbein et al. (Eds.), 147–65.

———. 2001. "Die Alten vor Augen. Politische Denkmäler und öffentliches Gedächtnis im republikanischen Rom." In Melville (Ed.), 2001, 183–211.

———. 2001a. "Vorläufige Überlegungen zum Verhältnis von Theoriebildung und Lebenserfahrung in der Klassischen Archäologie." In Altekamp, Stefan et al. (Eds.). *Posthumanistische Klassische Archäologie. Historizität und Wissenschaftlichkeit von Interessen und Methoden. Kolloquium Berlin 1999* (Munich), 173–92.

———. 2003a. "Körper, Handlung und Raum als Sinnfiguren in der griechischen Kunst und Kultur." In Hölkeskamp et al. (Eds.), 2003, 163–92.

———. 2003b. "Images of War in Greece and Rome: Between Military Practice, Public Memory, and Cultural Symbolism." In *JRS* 93: 1–17.

———. 2004. "Provokation und Transgression als politischer Habitus in der späten römischen Republik." In *MDAI(R)* 111: 83–104.

———. 2006. "The Transformation of Victory into Power: From Event to Structure." In Dillon et al. (Eds.), 27–48.

———. 2009. "Denkmäler und Konsens. Die sensible Balance von Verdienst und Macht." In Hölkeskamp et al. (Eds.), 161–81.

Holliday, Peter J. 2002. *The Origins of Roman Historical Commemoration in the Visual Arts* (Cambridge).

Hope, Valerie. 2000a. "The City of Rome: Capital and Symbol." In Huskinson (Ed.), 2000, 63–93.

———. 2000b. "Status and Identity in the Roman World." In Huskinson (Ed.), 2000, 125–52.

Hopkins, Keith. 1978. *Conquerors and Slaves* (Cambridge).

———. 1983. *Death and Renewal* (Cambridge).

————. 1991. "From Violence to Blessing: Symbols and Rituals in Ancient Rome." In Molho et al. (Eds.), 479–98.

Hopkins, Keith, and Burton, Graham. 1983. "Political Succession in the late Republic." In Hopkins, 31–119.

Howe, Nicholas (Ed.). 2007. *Ceremonial Culture in Pre-Modern Europe* (Notre Dame).

Hunt, Lynn. 1984. *Politics, Culture, and Class in the French Revolution* (Berkeley etc.).

Huskinson, Janet. 2000. "Looking for Culture, Identity and Power." In eadem (Ed.), 3–27.

————. (Ed.). 2000. *Experiencing Rome. Culture, Identity and Power in the Roman Empire* (London).

Inglebert, Hervé (Ed.). 2005. *Histoire de la civilisation romaine* (Paris).

Itgenshorst, Tanja. 2005. *Tota illa pompa. Der Triumph in der römischen Republik* (Göttingen).

————. 2004. "Augustus und der republikanische Triumph." In *Hermes* 132: 436–58.

————. 2006. "Roman Commanders and Hellenistic Kings. On the 'Hellenization' of the Republican Triumph." In *AncSoc* 36: 51–68.

Jaeger, Mary. 1997. *Livy's Written Rome* (Ann Arbor).

Jehne, Martin. 1993. "Geheime Abstimmung und Bindungswesen in der römischen Republik." In *HZ* 257: 593–613.

————. 1995a. "Einführung: Zur Debatte um die Rolle des Volkes in der römischen Politik." In idem (Ed.), 1995c, 1–9.

————. 1995b. "Die Beeinflussung von Entscheidungen durch 'Bestechung': Zur Funktion des *ambitus* in der römischen Republik." In idem (Ed.), 1995c, 51–76.

————. 2000a. "Rednertätigkeit und Statusdissonanzen in der späten römischen Republik." In Christoff Neumeister and Wulf Raeck (Eds.), *Rede und Redner. Bewertung und Darstellung in den antiken Kulturen* (Möhnesee), 167–89.

————. 2000b. "Jovialität und Freiheit. Zur Institutionalität der Beziehungen zwischen Ober- und Unterschichten in der römischen Republik." In Linke et al. (Eds.), 2000b, 207–35.

————. 2001. "Integrationsrituale in der römischen Republik. Zur einbindenden Wirkung der Volksversammlungen." In Gianpaolo Urso (Ed.), *Integrazione, mesolanza, rifiuto. Incontri di popoli, lingue e culture in Europa dall' Antichità all'Umanesimo* (Rome), 89–113 (updated reprint in Hölkeskamp et al. [Eds.], 279–97).

————. 2002. "Die Geltung der Provocation und die Konstruktion der römischen Republik als Freiheitsgemeinschaft." In Vorländer et al. (Eds.), 2002b, 55–74.

————. 2005. "Die Volksversammlungen in Mommsens *Staatsrecht* oder: Mommsen als Gesetzgeber." In Nippel et al. (Eds.), 131–60.

————. 2006. "Methods, Models, and Historiography." In Rosenstein et al. (Eds.), 3–28.

————. 2009. "Caesars Alternative(n). Das Ende der römischen Republik zwischen autonomem Prozeß und Betriebsunfall." In Hölkeskamp et al. (Eds.), 141–60.

————. 2009a. *Der große Trend, der kleine Sachzwang und das handelnde Individuum. Caesars Entscheidungen* (Munich).

———— (Ed.). 1995c. *Demokratie in Rom? Die Rolle des Volkes in der Politik der römischen Republik* (Stuttgart).

Jehne, Martin, and Pfeilschifter, René (Eds.). 2006. *Herrschaft ohne Integration? Rom und Italien in republikanischer Zeit* (Frankfurt).

Julliard, Jacques. 1974. "La politique." In Le Goff et al. (Eds.) 2: 229–50.

Kablitz, Andreas. 2006. "Geschichte—Tradition—Erinnerung? Wider die Subjektivierung der Geschichte." In *GG* 32: 220–37.

Kallet-(= Morstein-)Marx, Robert. 1995. *Hegemony to Empire: The Development of the Roman Imperium in the East from 148 to 62*BC (Berkeley etc.).

Kaschuba, Wolfgang. 1995. "Kulturalismus: Kultur statt Gesellschaft?" In *GG* 21: 80–95.

Keats-Rohan, Katharine S. B. 2007. "Introduction: Chameleon or Chimera? Understanding Prosopography." In eadem (Ed.), 1–32.

———— (Ed.). 2007. *Prosopography. Approaches and Applications* (Oxford).

Keay, Simon, and Terrenato, Nicola (Eds.). 2001. *Romanisation in Italy and the West. Comparative Issues in Romanisation* (Oxford).

Keller, Johannes. 2005. "Über die Bedeutung von Werten in der römischen Republik." In Haltenhoff et al. (Eds.), 175–208.

Kelly, J. M. 1966. *Roman Litigation* (Oxford).

Kierdorf, Wilhelm. 1980. Laudatio funebris. *Interpretationen und Untersuchungen zur Entwicklung der römischen Leichenrede* (Meisenheim).

Kocka, Jürgen (Ed.). 1986. *Max Weber, der Historiker* (Göttingen).

Kocka, Jürgen, and Thomas Nipperdey (Eds.), *Theorie und Erzählung in der Geschichte. Theorie der Geschichte: Beiträge zur Historik,* vol. 3 (Munich).

Kolb, Frank. 1977. "Zur Statussymbolik im antiken Rom." In *Chiron* 7: 239–59.

————. 1982. "Sozialgeschichtliche Begriffe und antike Gesellschaft am Beispiel der Hohen Kaiserzeit." In *Bericht über die 33. Versammlung deutscher Historiker in Würzburg 1980 (Beih. zu GWU)* (Stuttgart), 131–32.

————. 2002. *Rom. Die Geschichte der Stadt in der Antike* (Munich), second edition, revised and updated.

Kondratieff, Eric. 2004. "The Column and Coinage of C. Duilius: Innovations in Iconography in Large and Small Media in the Middle Republic." In *SCI* 23: 1–39.

Konrad, C. F. 1996. "Notes on Roman Also-Rans." In Linderski (Ed.), 103–43.

————. 2006. "From the Gracchi to the First Civil War (133–70)." In Rosenstein et al. (Eds.), 167–89.

Koortbojian, Michael. 2002. "A Painted *Exemplum* at Rome's Temple of Liberty." In *JRS* 92: 33–48.

————. 2008. "The Double Identity of Roman Portrait Statues: Costumes and Their Symbolism at Rome." In Jonathan Edmondson and Alison Keith (Eds.), *Roman Dress and the Fabrics of Roman Culture* (Toronto etc.), 71–93.

Koselleck, Reinhart. 1979. *Vergangene Zukunft. Zur Semantik geschichtlicher Zeiten* (Frankfurt).

————. 1986. "Sozialgeschichte und Begriffsgeschichte." In Wolfgang Schieder and Volker Sellin (Eds.), *Sozialgeschichte in Deutschland. Entwicklungen und Perspektiven im internationalen Zusammenhang* (Göttingen), 1:89–109 (= idem, 2006, 9–31).

————. 2006. *Begriffsgeschichten. Studien zur Semnantik und Pragmatik der politischen und sozialen Sprache* (Frankfurt).

Koselleck, Reinhart, Wolfgang J. Mommsen, and Jörn Rüsen (Eds.). 1977. *Objektivität und Parteilichkeit. Theorie der Geschichte: Beiträge zur Historik*, vol. 1 (Munich).

Koselleck, Reinhart, Heinrich Lutz, and Jörn Rüsen (Eds.). 1982. *Formen der Geschichtsschreibung. Theorie der Geschichte: Beiträge zur Historik*, vol. 4 (Munich).

Köves-Zulauf, Thomas. 2000. "*Virtus* und *pietas*." In *AAntHung* 40: 247–62.

Krasser, Helmut. 2005. Universalisierung und Identitätskonstruktion. Formen und Funktionen der Wissenskodifikation im kaiserzeitlichen Rom." In Oesterle, Günter (Ed.). *Erinnerung, Gedächtnis, Wissen. Studien zur kulturwissenschaftlichen Gedächtnisforschung* (Göttingen), 357–75.

————. 2006. "Individuum und Gesellschaft. Literarische Inszenierungen im Spannungsfeld von Konkurrenz und Konsens." In *AU* 49.1: 4–12.

Krasser, Helmut, Dennis Pausch, and Ivana Petrovic (Eds.). 2008. *Triplici invectus triumpho. Der römische Triumph in augusteischer Zeit* (Stuttgart).

Krischer, André. 2006. *Reichsstädte in der Fürstengesellschaft. Politischer Zeichengebrauch in der Frühen Neuzeit* (Darmstadt).

Kunkel, Wolfgang. 1955. "Bericht über neuere Arbeiten zur römischen Verfassungsgeschichte I." In *ZRG RA* 72: 288–325 (= idem, 1974, 441–78).

————. 1971. "Gesetzesrecht und Gewohnheitsrecht in der Verfassung der römischen Republik." In *Romanitas* 9: 357–72 (= idem, 1974, 367–82).

————. 1972. "Magistratische Gewalt und Senatsherrschaft." In *ANRW* 1, 2: 3–22.

————. 1974. *Kleine Schriften zum römischen Strafverfahren und zur römischen Verfassungsgeschichte* (Weimar).

————. 1984. "Theodor Mommsen als Jurist." In *Chiron* 14: 369–80.

Kunkel, Wolfgang, and Wittmann, Roland. 1995. *Staatsordnung und Staatspraxis der römischen Republik*, Vol. 2: *Die Magistratur* (Munich).

Kuttner, Ann L. 2004. "Roman Art during the Republic." In Flower (Ed.), 2004b, 294–321. 391–93.

Lacey, Walter K. 1986. "*Patria Potestas*." In Beryl Rawson (Ed.), *The Family in Ancient Rome* (Ithaca) 121–44.

Lahusen, Götz. 1999. "Griechisches *Pathos* und römische *Dignitas*. Zu Formen bildlicher Selbstdarstellung der römischen Aristokratie in republikanischer Zeit." In Vogt-Spira et al. (Eds.), 196–222.

Landwehr, Achim. 2003. "Diskurs—Macht—Wissen. Perspektiven einer Kulturgeschichte des Politischen." In *AKG* 85: 71–117.

————. 2008. *Historische Diskursanalyse* (Frankfurt etc.).

Laser, Günter. 1997. Populo et scaenae serviendum est. *Die Bedeutung der städtischen Masse in der späten Römischen Republik* (Trier).

Laslett, Peter. 1956. "The Face to Face Society." In idem (Ed.), *Philosophy, Politics and Society. First Series* (Oxford), 157–84.

Laurence, Ray. 1993. "Emperors, nature and the city: Rome's ritual landscape." In *ARP* 4: 79–87.

————. 1994. "Rumour and Communication in Roman Politics." In *G&R* 41: 62–74.

Le Goff, Jacques and Nora, Pierre (Eds.). 1974. *Faire de l'histoire*, vol. 1: *Nouveaux problèmes*; vol. 2: *Nouvelles approches*; vol. 3: *Nouveaux objets* (Paris).

Lendon, Jon Edward. 1997. *Empire of Honour. The Art of Government in the Roman World* (Oxford).

Lentano, Mario. 2005. "Il dono e il debito. Verso un'antropologia del beneficio nella cultura romana." In Haltenhoff et al. (Eds.), 125–42.

Le Roux, Patrick. 2004. "La romanisation en question." In *AHSS* 59: 287–311.

Lind, L. Robert. 1972. "Concept, Action, and Character: The Reasons for Rome's Greatness." In *TAPhA* 103: 235–83.

———. 1979. "The Tradition of Roman Moral Conservatism." In Deroux (Ed.), 7–58.

———. 1986. "The Idea of the Republic and the Foundations of Roman Political Liberty." In Deroux (Ed.), 44–108.

———. 1989. "The Idea of the Republic and the Foundations of Roman Morality I." In Deroux (Ed.), 5–34.

———. 1992. "The Idea of the Republic and the Foundations of Roman Morality II." In Deroux (Ed.), 5–40.

———. 1994. "Thought, Life, and Literature at Rome: The Consolidation of Culture." In Deroux (Ed.), 5–71.

Linderski, Jerzy (Ed.). 1996. Imperium sine fine. *T. Robert S. Broughton and the Roman Republic* (Stuttgart).

Linke, Bernhard. 2006. "Politik und Inszenierung in der Römischen Republik." In *Aus Politik und Zeitgeschichte* 7: 33–38.

Linke, Bernhard, and Michael Stemmler. 2000a. "Institutionalität und Geschichtlichkeit in der römischen Republik: Einleitende Bemerkungen zu den Forschungsperspektiven." In idem (Eds.), 2000b, 1–23.

——— (Eds.). 2000b. Mos maiorum. *Untersuchungen zu den Formen der Identitätsstiftung und Stabilisierung in der römischen Republik* (Stuttgart).

Lintott, Andrew W. 1987. "Democracy in the middle Republic." In *ZRG RA* 104: 34–52.

———. 1990. "Electoral Bribery in the Roman Republic." In *JRS* 80: 1–16.

———. 1999. *The Constitution of the Roman Republic* (Oxford).

———. 2005. "Die Magistratur in Mommsens *Staatsrecht*." In Nippel et al. (Eds.), 75–85.

Lipp, Carola. 1996. "Politische Kultur oder das Politische und Gesellschaftliche in der Kultur." In Hardtwig et al. (Eds.), 78–110.

Lomas, Kathryn. 1993. *Rome and the Western Greeks. Conquest and Acculturation in Southern Italy* (London).

———. 2004. "Italy under the Roman Republic, 338–31 BC" In Flower (Ed.), 199–224. 386–88.

Löther, Andrea. 1999. *Prozessionen in spätmittelalterlichen Städten. Politische Partizipation, obrigkeitliche Inszenierung, städtische Einheit* (Cologne etc.).

Lottes, Günther. 1996. "'The State of the Art'. Stand und Perspektiven der 'intellectual history'." In Frank-Lothar Kroll (Ed.), *Neue Wege der Ideengeschichte. Festschrift für Kurt Kluxen* (Paderborn), 27–45.

von Lübtow, Ulrich. 1955. *Das römische Volk. Sein Staat und sein Recht* (Frankfurt).

MacKendrick, Paul. 1995. *The Speeches of Cicero. Context, Law, Rhetoric* (London).

Mackie, Nicola. 1992. "*Popularis* Ideology and Popular Politics at Rome in the First Century BC." In *RhM* 135: 49–73.

Magdalino, Paul. 2003. "Prosopography and Byzantine Identity." In Cameron (Ed.), 41–56.

Mann, Michael. 1986. *The Sources of Social Power. A History of Power from the Beginning to A.D.1760* (Cambridge).

Manthe, Ulrich (Ed.). 2003. *Die Rechtskulturen der Antike. Vom Alten Orient bis zum Römischen Reich* (Munich).

Marcone, Arnaldo. 2002. *Democrazie antiche. Istituzioni e pensiero politico* (Rome).

———. 2005. "Tra antico e moderno. Democrazia e democrazie." In Mario Pani (Ed.), *Storia romana e storia moderna. Fasi in prospettiva* (Bari), 85–100.

Marshall, Anthony J. 1984. "Symbols and Showmanship in Roman Public Life: The *fasces*." In *Phoenix* 38: 120–41.

Martin, Jochen. 1965. *Die Popularen in der Geschichte der späten Republik* (Freiburg).

———. 1990. "Aspekte antiker Staatlichkeit." In Eder (Ed.), 1990b, 220–32.

———. 1997. "Zwei Alte Geschichten. Vergleichende historisch-anthropologische Betrachtungen zu Griechenland und Rom." In *Saeculum* 48: 1–20.

———. 2002. "Formen sozialer Kontrolle im republikanischen Rom." In Cohen et al. (Eds.), 2002, 155–72.

Martines, Lauro. 1988. *Power and Imagination. City-States in Renaissance Italy* (Baltimore), first ed. 1979.

Martini, Wolfram. 2008. "Raum und Ritual im römischen Triumph. Die Wegstrecke des Triumphzuges." In Krasser et al. (Eds.), 75–94.

Martschukat, Jürgen and Steffen Patzold. 2003. "Geschichtswissenschaft und 'Performative Turn': Eine Einführung in Fragestellungen, Konzepte und Literatur." In idem (Eds.), 1–31.

——— (Eds.). 2003. *Geschichtswissenschaft und «performative turn». Ritual, Inszenierung und Performanz vom Mittelalter bis zur Neuzeit* (Cologne etc.).

Mattingly, David. J. (Ed.). 1997. *Dialogues in Roman Imperialism: Power, Discourse, and Discrepant Experience in the Roman Empire* (Providence).

May, James M. 1988. *Trials of Character: The Eloquence of Ciceronian Ethos* (Chapel Hill etc.).

———. 2002a. "Ciceronian Oratory in Context." In idem (Ed.), 2002b, 49–70.

——— (Ed.). 2002b. *Brill's Companion to Cicero. Oratory and Rhetoric* (Leiden).

McDonnell, Myles. 1999. "Un Ballo in Maschera: Processions, Portraits and Emotions." In *JRA* 12: 541–52.

———. 2006a. *Roman Manliness. Virtus and the Roman Republic.* (Cambridge etc.).

———. 2006b. "Roman Aesthetics and the Spoils of Syracuse." In Dillon et al. (Eds.), 2006, 68–90.

Medick, Hans. 2001. "Quo Vadis, Historische Anthropologie? Geschichtsforschung zwischen Historischer Kulturwissenschaft und Mikro-Historie." In *HA* 9: 78–92.

Meier, Christian. 1965. "Populares." In *RE* Supplement 10, 549–615.
———. 1966 (repr. 1980 with new introduction). *Res publica amissa. Eine Studie zu Verfassung und Geschichte der römischen Republik* (Wiesbaden etc.).
———. 1968. "Die *loca intercessionis* bei Rogationen. Zugleich ein Beitrag zum Problem der Bedingungen der tribunicischen Intercession." In *MH* 25: 86–100.
———. 1976. "Der Alltag des Historikers und die historische Theorie." In Hans Michael Baumgartner and Jörn Rüsen (Eds.), *Geschichte und Theorie. Umrisse einer Historik* (Frankfurt), 36–58.
———. 1977. "Der Wandel der politisch-sozialen Begriffswelt im 5. Jh. v. Chr." In *ABG* 21: 7–41, revised in: idem. 1980. *Die Entstehung des Politischen bei den Griechen* (Frankfurt), 275–325 (= *The Greek Discovery of Politics*, Cambridge. Mass., 1990).
———. 1978a. "Review of Bleicken, 1975." In *ZRG RA* 95: 378–90.
———. 1978b. "Fragen und Thesen zu einer Theorie historischer Prozesse." In Faber et al. (Eds.), 11–66.
———. 1984a. *Introduction à l'anthropologie politique de l'Antiquité classique* (Paris).
———. 1984b. "Die Ersten unter den Ersten des Senats. Beobachtungen zur Willensbildung im römischen Senat." In Dieter Nörr and Dieter Simon (Eds.), *Gedächtnisschrift für Wolfgang Kunkel* (Frankfurt), 185–204.
——— (Ed.). 1994. *Die Okzidentale Stadt nach Max Weber. Zum Problem der Zugehörigkeit in Antike und Mittelalter* (*HZ*, Supplements, new series, vol. 17) (Munich).
———. 1996. "Aktueller Bedarf an historischen Vergleichen: Überlegungen aus dem Fach der Alten Geschichte." In Haupt et al. (Eds.), 239–70.
Meier, Christian, and Jörn Rüsen (Eds.). 1988. *Historische Methode. Theorie der Geschichte: Beiträge zur Historik*, vol. 5 (Munich).
Melville, Gert. 1992a. "Institutionen als geschichtswissenschaftliches Thema. Eine Einleitung." In idem (Ed.), 1992b, 1–24.
——— (Ed.). 1992b. *Institutionen und Geschichte. Theoretische Aspekte und mittelalterliche Befunde* (Cologne).
——— (Ed.). 2001. *Institutionalität und Symbolisierung. Verstetigungen kultureller Ordnungsmuster in Vergangenheit und Gegenwart* (Cologne).
Mencacci, Francesca. 2001. "Genealogia metaforica e *maiores* collettivi. Prospettive antropologiche sulla costruzione dei *viri illustres*." In Coudry et al. (Eds.), 421–37.
Mergel, Thomas. 2002. "Überlegungen zu einer Kulturgeschichte der Politik." In *GG* 28: 574–606.
———. 2004. "Kulturwissenschaft der Politik: Perspektiven und Trends." In *HbKW* 3: 413–25.
Mergel, Thomas, and Thomas Welskopp. 1997a. "Geschichtswissenschaft und Gesellschaftstheorie." In idem (Eds.), 1997b, 9–35.
Mergel, Thomas, and Thomas Welskopp. (Eds.). 1997b. *Geschichte zwischen Kultur und Gesellschaft. Beiträge zur Theoriedebatte* (Munich).
Meyer, Ernst. 1964. *Römischer Staat und Staatsgedanke*, 3rd edition (Zurich).

Michels, Robert. 1989 [1911]. *Zur Soziologie des Parteiwesens in der modernen Demokratie. Untersuchungen über die oligarchischen Tendenzen des Gruppenlebens* (4th edition, Stuttgart).

Miles, Gary B. 1995. *Livy. Reconstructing Early Rome* (Ithaca).

Miles, Richard. 2000. "Communicating Culture, Identity and Power." In Huskinson (Ed.), 29–62.

Millar, Fergus. 1984. "The Political Character of the Classical Roman Republic." In *JRS* 74: 1–19 (= idem, 2002a, 109–42).

———. 1986. "Politics, Persuasion, and the People before the Social War (150–90BC)." In *JRS* 76: 1–11 (= idem, 2002a, 143–61).

———. 1989. "Political Power in Mid-Republican Rome: Curia or Comitium?" In *JRS* 79: 138–50 (= idem, 2002a, 85–108).

———. 1995a. "Popular Politics at Rome in the late Republic." In Irad Malkin and Zeev W. Rubinsohn (Eds.), *Leaders and Masses in the Roman World. Studies in Honor of Zvi Yavetz* (Leiden), 91–113 (= idem, 2002a, 162–82).

———. 1995b. "The Last Century of the Republic: Whose History?" In *JRS* 85: 236–43 (= idem, 2002a, 200–14).

———. 1998. *The Crowd in Rome in the late Republic* (Ann Arbor).

———. 2002a. *Rome, the Greek World, and the East.* Vol. 1: *The Roman Republic and the Augustan Revolution,* ed. Hannah M. Cotton, Guy M. Rogers (Chapel Hill).

———. 2002b. *The Roman Republic in Political Thought* (Hanover).

Mörth, Ingo, and Fröhlich, Gerhard (Eds.). 1994. *Das symbolische Kapital der Lebensstile. Zur Kultursoziologie der Moderne nach Pierre Bourdieu* (Frankfurt).

Moir, K.M. 1986. "The epitaph of Publius Scipio." In *CQ* n.s. 36: 264–66.

Molho, Anthony, Raaflaub, Kurt, and Emlen, Julia (Eds.). 1991. *City-States in Classical Antiquity and Medieval Italy* (Stuttgart).

Momigliano, Arnaldo. 1940. Review of Syme, 1939. In *JRS* 30: 75–80 (= idem. 1960. *Secondo contributo alla storia degli studi classici* [Rome], 407–16).

Mommsen, Theodor. 1887–1888³. *Römisches Staatsrecht 1–3* (Leipzig).

Moore, Timothy J. 1989. *Artistry and Ideology: Livy's Vocabulary of Virtue* (Frankfurt).

Morgan, Gwyn. 2006. "Some Belated Reflections on Millar's *Crowd.*" In *OP* 5: 173–79.

Morgan, Teresa. 2007. *Popular Morality in the Early Roman Empire* (Cambridge etc.).

Morley, Neville. 1999. *Writing Ancient History* (London).

———. 2004. *Theories, Models and Concepts in Ancient History* (London).

Morstein-Marx, Robert. 1998. "Publicity, Popularity and Patronage in the *Commentariolum Petitionis.*" In *CA* 17: 259–88.

———. 2004. *Mass Oratory and Political Power in the Late Roman Republic* (Cambridge).

——— and Nathan Rosenstein. 2006. "The Transformation of the Republic." In Rosenstein et al. (Eds.), 625–37.

Mouritsen, Henrik. 2001. *Plebs and Politics in the Late Roman Republic* (Cambridge).

Moussy, Claude. 1966. Gratia *et sa famille* (Paris).

Muir, Edward. 1981. *Civic Ritual in Renaissance Venice* (Princeton).

———. 1997. *Ritual in Early Modern Europe* (Cambridge).

———. 2004."Representations of Power." In Najemy (Ed.), 226–45, 290–93.

Muir, Edward, and Weissman, Ronald F.E. 1989. "Social and symbolic places in Renaissance Venice and Florence." In John A. Agnew and James S. Duncan (Eds.). *The Power of Place. Bringing Together Geographical and Social Imaginations* (London etc.), 81–103.

Münzer, Friedrich. 1920 (Repr. 1963. Darmstadt). *Römische Adelsparteien und Adelsfamilien* (Stuttgart). English Translation: 1999. *Roman Aristocratic Parties and Families*. Trans. Thérèse Ridley (Baltimore).

Mutschler, Fritz-Heiner. 2000. "Norm und Erinnerung: Anmerkungen zur sozialen Funktion von historischem Epos und Geschichtsschreibung im 2. Jh. v. Chr." In Braun et al. (Eds.), 87–124.

———. 2003. "Virtus 2002. Zur Rolle der 'römischen Werte' in der Altertumswissenschaft." In *Gymnasium* 110: 363–85.

Nadig, Peter. 1997. *ARDET AMBITUS. Untersuchungen zum Phänomen der Wahlbestechungen in der römischen Republik* (Frankfurt etc.).

Näf, Beat. 2001. "Nobilitas." In *DNP* 15/1: 1070–84.

Najemy, John M. (Ed.). 2004. *Italy in the Age of the Renaissance* (Oxford).

Nichols, Deborah L. and Charlton, Thomas H. (Eds.). 1997. *The Archaeology of City-States: Cross-Cultural Approaches* (Washington, D.C.).

Nicolet, Claude. 1966. *L'ordre équestre à l'époque républicaine*. Tome 1: *Définitions juridiques et structures sociales* (Paris).

———. 1970. "Prosopographie et histoire sociale: Rome et l'Italie à l'époque républicaine." In *AESC* 25: 1209–28.

———. 1977. "Les classes dirigeantes romaines sous la République: ordre sénatorial et ordre équestre." In *AESC* 32: 726–55.

———. 1979. 1978. *Rome et la conquête du monde méditerranéen*. Tome 1: *Les structures de l'Italie romaine*; tome 2: *Génèse d'un empire* (Paris).

———. 1980. *The World of the Citizen in Republican Rome* (Berkeley); French original 1976. *Le métier de citoyen dans la Rome républicaine* (Paris).

———. 1983a. "Polybe et la «constitution» de Rome: aristocratie et démocratie." In idem (Ed.), 1983b, 15–35.

——— (Ed.). 1983b. *Demokratia et Aristokratia. À propos de Caius Gracchus: mots grecs et réalités romaines* (Paris).

———. 1984. "Les ordres romains: définition, recrutement et fonctionnement." In idem (Ed.). *Des ordres à Rome* (Paris), 7–21.

Nippel, Wilfried. 1980. *Mischverfassungstheorie und Verfassungsrealität in Antike und früher Neuzeit* (Stuttgart).

———. 1986. "Die Kulturbedeutung der Antike. Marginalien zu Weber." In Kocka (Ed.), 112–18.

———. 1988. "Sozialanthropologie und Alte Geschichte." In Meier et al. (Eds.), 300–18.

———. 1988a. *Aufruhr und "Polizei" in der römischen Republik* (Stuttgart).

———. 1991. "Introductory Remarks: Max Weber's 'The City' Revisited." In Molho et al. (Eds.), 1991, 19–30.

————. 1995. *Public Order in Ancient Rome* (Cambridge).

————. 1999a. "Einleitung." In idem (Ed.), 1999b, 1–43.

———— (Ed.). 1999b. *Max Weber: Wirtschaft und Gesellschaft. Die Wirtschaft und die gesellschaftlichen Ordnungen und Mächte. Nachlaß* (Max Weber Gesamtausgabe, Abt. 1, Band 22, Teilband 5: Die Stadt) (Tübingen).

————. 2000. "From Agrarian History to Cross-cultural Comparisons: Weber on Greco-Roman antiquity." In Stephen Turner (Ed.), *The Cambridge Companion to Weber* (Cambridge), 240–55.

————. 2004. "Klientel, Gesellschaftsstruktur und politisches System in der römischen Republik." In *Humanistische Bildung* 21–22, 2000–2002 (publ. 2004), 137–51.

————. 2005. "Das *Staatsrecht* in der Diskussion—von 1871 bis heute." In idem et al. (Eds.), 2005, 9–60.

————. 2009. "Gesetze, Verfassungskonventionen, Präzedenzfälle." In Hölkeskamp et al. (Eds.), 87–97.

Nippel, Wilfried, and Seidensticker, Bernd (Eds.). 2005. *Theodor Mommsens langer Schatten. Das römische Staatsrecht als bleibende Herausforderung für die Forschung* (Hildesheim etc.).

Noè, Eralda. 1988. "Per la formazione del consenso nella Roma del I sec. a.C." In *Studi di storia e storiografia antiche per Emilio Gabba* (Pavia), 49–72.

Nörr, Dieter. 1989. *Aspekte des römischen Völkerrechts. Die Bronzetafel von Alcántara* (ABAW, new series 101) (Munich).

Nora, Pierre. 1974. "Le retour de l'événement." In Le Goff et. al. (Eds.), 1:210–28.

North, John. 1981. "The Development of Roman Imperialism." In *JRS* 71: 1–9.

————. 1990a. "Democratic Politics in Republican Rome." In *P&P* 126: 3–21.

————. 1990b. "Politics and Aristocracy in the Roman Republic." In *CPh* 85: 277–87.

————. 2002. "Introduction: Pursuing Democracy." In Bowman et al. (Eds.), 1–12.

————. 2006. "The Constitution of the Roman Republic." In Rosenstein et al. (Eds.), 256–77.

Oakley, Stephen. 1993. "The Roman Conquest of Italy." In Rich et al. (Eds.), 9–37.

————. 2004. "The early Republic." In Flower (Ed.), 2004b, 15–30.

Ober, Josiah. 1989. *Mass and Élite in Democratic Athens. Rhetoric, Ideology, and the Power of the People* (Princeton).

————. 1996. *The Athenian Revolution. Essays on Ancient Greek Democracy and Political Theory* (Princeton).

Oexle, Otto Gerhard. 1990. "Aspekte der Geschichte des Adels im Mittelalter und in der Frühen Neuzeit." In Hans-Ulrich Wehler (Ed.), *Europäischer Adel 1750–1950* (GG Sonderheft 13) (Göttingen), 19–56.

————. 1995. "Nach dem Streit. Anmerkungen über Makro- und Mikrohistorie." In *RJ* 14: 191–200.

————. 1996. "Geschichte als Historische Kulturwissenschaft." In Hardtwig et al. (Eds.), 14–40.

Oexle, Otto Gerhard, and Paravicini, Werner (Eds.). 1997. Nobilitas. *Funktion und Repräsentation des Adels in Alteuropa* (Göttingen).

O'Neill, Peter. 2003. "Going Round in Circles: Popular Speech in Ancient Rome." In *CA* 22: 135–65.

Ozouf, Mona. 1976. *La fête révolutionnaire, 1789–1799* (Paris).

Pani, Mario. 1997. *La politica in Roma antica* (Rome).

Parker, Holt N. 1999. "The Observed of All Observers: Spectacle, Applause, and Cultural Poetics in the Roman Theater Audience." In Bergmann et al. (Eds.), 163–79.

Patterson, John R. 1992. "The City of Rome: From Republic to Empire." In *JRS* 82: 186–215.

———. 2000. *Political Life in the City of Rome* (London).

———. 2006a. "The City of Rome." In Rosenstein et al. (Eds.), 2006, 345–64.

———. 2006b. "The Relationship of the Italian Ruling Classes with Rome: Friendship, Family Relations and Their Consequences." In Jehne et al. (Eds.), 139–53.

Pedersen, Susan. 2002. "What is Political History Now?" In Cannadine (Ed.), 36–56.

Pignatelli, Anna Maria. 2008. *Lessico politico a Roma fra III e II sec. a. C.* (Bari).

Pina Polo, Francisco. 1996. Contra Arma Verbis. *Der Redner vor dem Volk in der späten römischen Republik* (Stuttgart).

———. 2004. "Die nützliche Erinnerung: Geschichtsschreibung, *mos maiorum* und die römische Identität." In *Historia* 53: 147–72.

———. 2005. "I *rostra* come espressione di potere della aristocrazia romana." In Urso (Ed.), 141–55.

Pittenger, Miriam R. Pelikan. 2008. *Contested Triumphs. Politics, Pageantry, and Performance in Livy's Republican Rome* (Berkeley etc.).

Polverini, Leandro. 2005. "Democrazia a Roma? La costituzione repubblicana secondo Polibio." In Urso (Ed.), 85–96.

Pöschl, Viktor. 1980. "Politische Wertbegriffe in Rom." In *A&A* 26: 1–17 (= idem, 1995, 189–208, with additions).

———. 1989. "Der Begriff der Würde im antiken Rom und später." In *SHAW*, no. 3 (= idem, 1995, 209–274, with additions).

———. 1995. *Lebendige Vergangenheit* (*Kleine Schriften 3*), ed. by Wolf-Lüder Liebermann (Heidelberg).

Powis, Jonathan. 1984. *Aristocracy* (Oxford).

Purcell, Nicholas. 1994. "The city of Rome and the *plebs urbana*." In *CAH* 9: 644–88.

Quaß, Friedemann. 1984. "Zum Einfluß der römischen Nobilität auf das Honoratiorenregime in den Städten des griechischen Ostens." In *Hermes* 112: 199–215.

Raaflaub, Kurt. 1984. "Freiheit in Athen und Rom: Ein Beispiel divergierender politischer Begriffsentwicklung in der Antike." In *HZ* 238: 529–67.

———. (1985) 2004. *The Discovery of Freedom in Ancient Greece* (Chicago) (Revised and updated English edition of *Die Entdeckung der Freiheit. Zur historischen Semantik und Gesellschaftsgeschichte eines politischen Grundbegriffes der Griechen* (Munich).

———. (1986) 2005. "From Protection and Defense to Offense and Participation: Stages in the Conflict of the Orders." In idem (Ed.), 1986, 198–243 (= 2005, 185–222).

————. 1990. "Expansion und Machtbildung in frühen Polis-Systemen." In Eder (Ed.), 511–45.

————. 1991. "City-State, Territory, and Empire in Classical Antiquity." In Molho et al. (Eds.), 565–88.

————. 1996. "Born to Be Wolves? Origins of Roman Imperialism." In Wallace et al. (Eds.), 273–314.

————. 2003. "Zwischen Adel und Volk. Freiheit als Sinnkonzept in Griechenland und Rom." In Hölkeskamp et al. (Eds.), 55–80.

————. 2006. "Between Myth and History: Rome's Rise from Village to Empire (the Eighth Century to 264)." In Rosenstein et al. (Eds.), 125–46.

———— (Ed.). 1986. *Social Struggles in Archaic Rome: New Perspectives on the Conflict of the Orders* (Berkeley). Expanded and updated ed. (Malden etc. 2005).

Rainer, J. Michael. 1997. *Einführung in das römische Staatsrecht* (Darmstadt).

————. 2006. *Römisches Staatsrecht. Republik und Prinzipat* (Darmstadt).

Ranouil, Pierre-Charles. 1975. *Recherches sur le patriciat (509–366 avant J.-C.)* (Paris).

Raphael, Lutz. 1994. *Die Erben von Bloch und Febvre. Annales-Geschichtsschreibung und* nouvelle histoire *in Frankreich 1945–1980* (Stuttgart).

————. 2003. *Geschichtswissenschaft im Zeitalter der Extreme. Theorien, Methoden, Tendenzen von 1900 bis zur Gegenwart* (Munich).

————. 2004. "Habitus und sozialer Sinn: Der Ansatz der Praxistheorie Pierre Bourdieus." In *HbKW* 2: 266–76.

Raulff, Ulrich (Ed.). 1987. *Mentalitäten-Geschichte. Zur historischen Rekonstruktion geistiger Prozesse* (Berlin).

Rawson, Elizabeth. 1973. "The eastern Clientelae of Clodius and the Claudii." In *Historia* 22: 219–39 (= eadem, 1991, 102–24).

————. 1977. "More on the Clientelae of the Patrician Claudii." In *Historia* 26: 340–57 (= eadem, 1991, 227–44).

————. 1991. *Roman Culture and Society. Collected Papers* (Oxford).

Rebenich, Stefan. 2005. "Römische Wertbegriffe: Wissenschaftsgeschichtliche Anmerkungen aus althistorischer Sicht." In Haltenhoff et al. (Eds.), 23–46.

Rehberg, Karl-Siegbert. 1998. "Die stabilisierende 'Fiktionalität' von Präsenz und Dauer. Institutionelle Analyse und historische Forschung." In Blänkner et al. (Eds.), 381–407.

Reichardt, Rolf. 1998. "Historische Semantik zwischen lexicométrie und New Cultural History." In idem (Ed.), *Aufklärung und historische Semantik. Interdisziplinäre Beiträge zur westeuropäischen Kulturgeschichte* (ZHF Beiheft 21) (Berlin), 7–28.

Reichardt, Sven. 1997. "Bourdieu für Historiker? Ein kultursoziologisches Angebot an die Sozialgeschichte." In Mergel et al. (Eds.), 71–93.

Reinhard, Wolfgang. 1999. *Geschichte der Staatsgewalt. Eine vergleichende Verfassungsgeschichte Europas von den Anfängen bis zur Gegenwart* (Munich).

Reiter, William. 1988. *Aemilius Paullus. Conqueror of Greece* (London).

Rexroth, Frank. 2009. "Politische Rituale und die Sprache des Politischen in der historischen Mittelalterforschung." In De Benedictis, Angela, Gustavo Corni, Brigitte Mazohl and Luise Schorn-Schütte (Eds.). *Die Sprache des Politischen in actu. Zum Verhältnis von politischem Handeln und politischer Sprache von der Antike bis ins 20. Jahrhundert* (Göttingen), 71–90.

Rich, John. 1989. "Patronage and interstate relations in the Roman Republic." In Wallace-Hadrill (Ed.), 1989b, 117–35.

———. 1993. "Fear, Greed and Glory: The Causes of Roman War-making in the middle Republic." In idem et al. (Eds.), 38–68.

Rich, John, and Graham Shipley (Eds.). 1993. *War and Society in the Roman World* (London).

Richardson, John S. 1991. "*Imperium Romanum*: Empire and the Language of Power." In *JRS* 81: 1–9.

———. 2008. *The Language of Empire. Rome and the Idea of Empire from the Third Century* BC *to the Second Century* AD (Cambridge).

Richardson, Jr., Lawrence. 1991. "Urban Development in Ancient Rome and the Impact of Empire." In Molho et al. (Eds.), 381–402.

Richter, Melvin. 1995. *The History of Political and Social Concepts: A Critical Introduction* (New York).

Ridley, Ronald T. 1986. "The Genesis of a Turning-Point: Gelzer's *Nobilität*." In *Historia* 35: 474–502.

Riggsby, Andrew M. 1999. *Crime and Community in Ciceronian Rome* (Austin).

———. 2002. "The *Post reditum* Speeches." In May (Ed.), 2002b, 159–95.

Rilinger, Rolf. 1982. "Die Interpretation des Niedergangs der römischen Republik durch 'Revolution' und 'Krise ohne Alternative.'" In *AKG* 64: 279–306 (= idem. 2007, 123–50).

———. 1985. "Moderne und zeitgenössische Vorstellungen von der Gesellschaftsordnung der römischen Kaiserzeit." In *Saeculum* 36: 299–325 (= idem. 2007, 153–79).

———. 1991. "*Ordo* und *dignitas* als soziale Kategorien der römischen Republik." In Manfred Hettling, Claudia Huerkamp, Paul Nolte and Hans-Walter Schmuhl (Eds.), *Was ist Gesellschaftsgeschichte? Positionen, Themen, Analysen* (Munich), 81–90 (= idem. 2007, 95–103).

———. 2007. Ordo *und* dignitas. *Beiträge zur römischen Verfassungs- und Sozialgeschichte*. Ed. by Tassilo Schmitt and Aloys Winterling (Stuttgart).

Robert, Jean-Noël. 2008. *Rome, la gloire et la liberté. Aux sources de l'identité européenne* (Paris).

Robert, Renaud. 1998. "Quelques usages romains du portrait peint à l'époque médio-républicaine." In Clara Auvray-Assayas (Ed.), *Images romaines* (Paris), 73–89.

Roddaz, Jean-Michel. 2005. "*Popularis*, populisme, popularité." In Urso (Ed.), 97–122.

Rogers, Guy M. 2002. "Introduction: Polybius Was Right." In Millar, 2002a, xi–xvi.

Rohe, Karl. 1990. "Politische Kultur und ihre Analyse. Probleme und Perspektiven der politischen Kulturforschung." In *HZ* 250: 321–46.

Roller, Matthew B. 2001. *Constructing Autocracy. Aristocrats and Emperors in Julio-Claudian Rome* (Princeton).

———. 2004. "Exemplarity in Roman Culture: The Cases of Horatius Cocles and Cloelia." In *CPh* 99: 1–56.

Rosenstein, Nathan. 2006. "Aristocratic Values." In idem et al. (Eds.), 365–82.

Rosenstein, Nathan, and Morstein-Marx, Robert (Eds.). 2006. *A Companion to the Roman Republic* (Oxford etc.).

Roth, Roman. 2007. *Styling Romanisation. Pottery and Society in Central Italy* (Cambridge).

Roth, Roman, and Keller, Johannes (Eds.). 2007. *Roman by Integration: Dimensions of Group Identity in Material Culture and Text* (Portsmouth, R.I.).

Rubin, Miri. 2002. "What is Cultural History Now?" In Cannadine (Ed.), 80–94.

Runciman, Walter G. 1982. "Origins of States: The Case of Archaic Greece." In *CSSH* 24: 351–77.

———. 1983. "Capitalism without classes: The case of classical Rome." In *BJS* 34: 157–79.

———. 1986. "The Sociologist and the Historian" (review article on Hopkins, 1983). In *JRS* 76: 259–65.

Rüpke, Jörg. 1990. *Domi militiae. Die religiöse Konstruktion des Krieges in Rom* (Stuttgart).

———. 2000. "Räume literarischer Kommunikation in der Formierungsphase römischer Literatur." In Braun et al. (Eds.), 31–52.

———. 2006. "Triumphator and Ancestor Rituals between Symbolic Anthropology and Magic." In *Numen* 53: 251–89.

Rüsen, Jörn, and Karl-J. Hölkeskamp. 2003. "Einleitung: Warum es sich lohnt, mit der Sinnfrage die Antike zu interpretieren." In Hölkeskamp et al. (Eds.), 1–15.

Ryan, Frank. 1998. *Rank and Participation in the Republican Senate* (Stuttgart).

Rykwert, Joseph. 1976. *The Idea of a Town. The Anthropology of Urban Form in Rome, Italy and the Ancient World* (London).

Saller, Richard P. 1982. *Personal Patronage under the Early Empire* (Cambridge).

———. 1994. *Patriarchy, Property and Death in the Roman Family* (Cambridge).

Schäfer, Thomas. 1989. *Imperii Insignia. Sella curulis und Fasces. Zur Repräsentation römischer Magistrate* (Mainz).

Schimank, Uwe. 2004. "Handeln in Institutionen und handelnde Institution." In *HbKW* 2: 293–307.

Schipporeit, Sven Th. 2008. "Wege des Triumphes. Zum Verlauf der Triumphzüge im spätrepublikanischen und augusteischen Rom." In Krasser et al. (Eds.), 95–136.

Schlögl, Rudolf. 2002. "Politik- und Verfassungsgeschichte." In Eibach et al. (Eds.), 95–111.

———. 2004. "Vergesellschaftung unter Anwesenden. Zur kommunikativen Form des Politischen in der vormodernen Stadt." In idem (Ed.), 9–60.

———. 2005. "Interaktion und Herrschaft. Probleme der politischen Kommunikation in der Stadt." In Stollberg-Rilinger (Ed.), 115–28.

———. 2008. "Kommunikation und Vergesellschaftung unter Anwesenden. Formen des Sozialen und ihre Transformation in der Frühen Neuzeit." In *GG* 34: 155–224.

———. 2008a. "Politik beobachten. Öffentlichkeit und Medien in der Frühen Neuzeit." In *ZHF* 35: 581–616.

——— (Ed.). 2004. *Interaktion und Herrschaft. Die Politik der frühneuzeitlichen Stadt* (Constance).

Schmidt, Peter Lebrecht. 2005. "Zwischen Werttheorie, Begriffsgeschichte und Römertum. Zur Politisierung eines wissenschaftlichen Paradigmas." In Haltenhoff et al. (Eds.), 3–21.

Schmitz, Winfried. 2008. "Verpaßte Chancen. Adel und Aristokratie im archaischen und klassischen Griechenland." In Beck et al. (Eds.), 35–70.

Schneider, Wolfgang Christian. 1998. *Vom Handeln der Römer. Kommunikation und Interaktion der politischen Führungsschicht vor Ausbruch des Bürgerkriegs im Briefwechsel mit Cicero* (Zurich).

Scholz, Peter. 2005. "Zur öffentlichen Repräsentation römischer Senatoren und Magistrate. Einige Überlegungen zur (verlorenen) materiellen Kultur der republikanischen Senatsaristokratie." In Tobias L. Kienlin (Ed.), *Die Dinge als Zeichen. Kulturelles Wissen und materielle Kultur* (Bonn), 409–431.

Schorn-Schütte, Luise. 2006. *Historische Politikforschung. Eine Einführung* (Munich).

Schreiner, Klaus. 1997. "Religiöse, historische und rechtliche Legitimation spätmittelalterlicher Adelsherrschaft." In Oexle et al. (Eds.), 376–430.

Schuller, Wolfgang. 2000. "*Ambitus*. Einige neue Gesichtspunkte." In *Hyperboreus* 6.2: 349–61.

Schulz, Raimund. 1997. *Herrschaft und Regierung. Roms Regiment in den Provinzen in der Zeit der Republik* (Paderborn).

Schwelling, Birgit. 2001. "Politische Kulturforschung als kultureller Blick auf das Politische. Überlegungen zu einer Neuorientierung der Politischen Kulturforschung nach dem »cultural turn«." In *ZPW* 11: 601–29.

Schwerhoff, Gerd. 1994. "Das rituelle Leben der Mittelalterlichen Stadt. Richard C. Trexlers Florenzstudien als Herausforderung für die deutsche Geschichtsschreibung." In *Geschichte in Köln* 35: 33–60.

Schwinge, Ernst-Richard (Ed.). 1995. *Die Wissenschaften vom Altertum am Ende des 2. Jahrtausends n.Chr.* (Stuttgart).

Scullard, Howard H. 1980 [1935, 2nd rev. ed. 1951]. *A History of the Roman World, 753–146 BC* (London).

———. 1951, 1973. *Roman Politics, 220–150 BC* (Oxford), with new Foreword 1973: xvii–xxxiii.

———. 1981. *Festivals and Ceremonies of the Roman Republic* (London).

Sehlmeyer, Markus. 1999. *Stadtrömische Ehrenstatuen der republikanischen Zeit. Historizität und Kontext von Symbolen nobilitären Standesbewußtseins* (Stuttgart).

———. 2000. "Die kommunikative Leistung römischer Ehrenstatuen." In Braun et al. (Eds.), 271–84.

Sellin, Volker. 1985. "Mentalität und Mentalitätsgeschichte." In *HZ* 241: 555–98.

———. 1987. "Mentalitäten in der Sozialgeschichte." In idem and Wolfgang Schieder (Eds.), *Sozialgeschichte in Deutschland. Entwicklungen und Perspektiven im internationalen Zusammenhang*, vol. 3 (Göttingen), 101–12.

Settipani, Christian. 2000. *Continuité gentilice et continuité familiale dans les familles sénatoriales romaines à l'époque impériale. Mythe et réalité* (Oxford).

Shatzman, Israel. 1974. "Scaurus, Marius, and the Metelli: A Prosopographical-Factional Case." In *AncSoc* 5: 197–222.

————. 1975. *Senatorial Wealth and Roman Politics* (Brussels).

Shaw, Brent D. 1984. "Among the Believers" (review article on Hopkins, 1983). In *EMC* 28: 453–79.

Sherwin-White, Adrian N. 1980. "Rome the Aggressor?" (review article on Harris, 1979). In *JRS* 70: 177–81.

Sidebottom, Harry. 2005. "Roman Imperialism: The Changed outward Trajectory of the Roman Empire." In *Historia* 54: 315–30.

Sieder, Reinhard. 1994. "Sozialgeschichte auf dem Weg zu einer historischen Kulturwissenschaft?" In *GG* 20: 445–68.

Sikora, Michael. 2001. "Der Sinn des Verfahrens. Soziologische Deutungsangebote." In Stollberg-Rilinger (Ed.), 2001a, 25–51.

Simmel, Georg. 1992. *Soziologie. Untersuchungen über die Formen der Vergesellschaftung, Kritische Gesamtausgabe*, ed. by Otthein Rammstedt, Vol. 11 (Frankfurt).

Simon, Christian. 1988. "Gelzers 'Nobilität der römischen Republik' als Wendepunkt." In *Historia* 37: 222–40.

Smith, Christopher J. 2006. *The Roman Clan. The* gens *from ancient ideology to modern anthropology* (Cambridge).

Smith, R.R.R. 2002. "The Use of Images: Visual History and Ancient History." In Wiseman (Ed.), 2002b, 59–102.

Sordi, Marta. 2005. "*Populus* e *plebs* nella lotta patrizio-plebea." In Urso (Ed.), 63–69.

Spannagel, Martin. 2000. "Zur Vergegenwärtigung abstrakter Wertbegriffe in Kult und Kunst der römischen Republik." In Braun et al. (Eds.), 237–69.

Späth, Thomas. 2001. "Erzählt, erfunden: Camillus. Literarische Konstruktion und soziale Normen." In Coudry et al. (Eds.), 341–412.

Spielvogel, Jörg (Ed.). 2002. *Res publica reperta. Zur Verfassung und Gesellschaft der römischen Republik und des frühen Prinzipats* (Festschrift Jochen Bleicken) (Stuttgart).

Stambaugh, John E. 1988. *The Ancient Roman City* (Baltimore).

Starr, Chester. 1987. *Past and Future in Ancient History* (Lanham).

Staveley, Ernest St. 1972. *Greek and Roman Voting and Elections* (London).

Stein-Hölkeskamp, Elke. 1989. *Adelskultur und Polisgesellschaft. Studien zum griechischen Adel in archaischer und klassischer Zeit* (Stuttgart). Second enlarged ed. (forthcoming).

————. 2003. "Vom *homo politicus* zum *homo litteratus*. Lebensziele und Lebensideale der römischen Élite von Cicero bis zum jüngeren Plinius." In Hölkeskamp et al. (Eds.), 315–34.

————. 2006. "Das römische Haus—die *memoria* der Mauern." In eadem et al. (Eds.), 300–20. 750–1.

Stein-Hölkeskamp, Elke, and Hölkeskamp, Karl-J. (Eds.). 2006. *Erinnerungsorte der Antike: Die römische Welt* (Munich).

Stemmler, Michael. 2000. "*Auctoritas exempli*. Zur Wechselwirkung von kanonisierten Vergangenheitsbildern und gesellschaftlicher Gegenwart in der spätrepublikanischen Rhetorik." In Linke et al. (Eds.), 2000b, 141–205.

————. 2001. "Institutionalisierte Geschichte. Zur Stabilisierungsleistung und Symbolizität historischer Beispiele in der Redekultur der römischen Republik." In Melville (Ed.), 219–40.

Stewart, Roberta. 1998. *Public Office in Early Rome: Ritual Procedure and Political Practice* (Ann Arbor).

Stollberg-Rilinger, Barbara. 2000. "Zeremoniell, Ritual, Symbol. Neue Forschungen zur symbolischen Kommunikation in Spätmittelalter und Früher Neuzeit." In *ZHF* 27: 389–405.

———. 2001b. "Einleitung." In eadem (Ed.), 2001a, 9–24.

———. 2004. "Symbolische Kommunikation in der Vormoderne. Begriffe—Thesen—Forschungsperspektiven." In *ZHF* 31: 489–527.

———. 2005. "Was heißt Kulturgeschichte des Politischen? Einleitung." In eadem (Ed.), 9–24.

———. 2008. *Des Kaisers alte Kleider. Verfassungsgeschichte und Symbolsprache des Alten Reiches* (Munich).

——— (Ed.). 2001a. *Vormoderne politische Verfahren* (Berlin).

——— (Ed.). 2005. *Was heißt Kulturgeschichte des Politischen?* (Berlin)

Stollberg-Rilinger, Barbara, Matthias Puhle, Jutta Götzmann, and Gerd Althoff (Eds.). 2008. *Spektakel der Macht. Rituale im Alten Europa 800–1800* (Darmstadt).

Stone, Lawrence. 1971. "Prosopography." In *Daedalus* 100,1: 46–71.

Sumi, Geoffrey S. 2005. *Ceremony and Power: Performing Politics in Rome between Republic and Empire* (Ann Arbor).

Syme, Ronald. 1939. *The Roman Revolution* (Oxford).

———. 1986. *The Augustan Aristocracy* (Oxford).

———. 1991a. "Oligarchy at Rome: A Paradigm for Political Science." In idem, 1991c, 323–37.

———. 1991b. "Dynastic Marriages in the Roman Aristocracy." In idem, 1991c, 338–45.

———. 1991c. *Roman Papers*, vol. 6, ed. Anthony R. Birley (Oxford), 323–37.

Tan, James. 2008. "*Contiones* in the Age of Cicero." In *CA* 27: 163–201.

Tanner, Jeremy. 2000. "Portraits, Power, and Patronage in the Late Roman Republic." In *JRS* 90: 18–50.

Tatum, W. Jeffrey. 1999. *The Patrician Tribune: Publius Clodius Pulcher* (Chapel Hill etc.).

———. 2006. "The Final Crisis (69–44)." In Rosenstein et al. (Eds.), 190–211.

———. 2007. "*Alterum est tamen boni viri, alterum boni petitoris*: The Good Man canvasses." In *Phoenix* 61: 109–35.

Taylor, Lily Ross. 1966. *Roman Voting Assemblies: From the Hannibalic War to the Dictatorship of Caesar* (Ann Arbor).

Thomas, Yan. 1996 [1986]. "Rom: Väter als Bürger in einer Stadt der Väter." In André Burguière, Christiane Klapisch-Zuber, Martine Segalen, and Françoise Zonabend (Eds.), *Geschichte der Familie*, vol. 1: *Altertum* (Frankfurt), 277–326.

Thome, Gabriele. 2000. *Zentrale Wertvorstellungen der Römer I-II* (Bamberg).

Thommen, Lukas. 1989. *Das Volkstribunat der späten römischen Republik* (Stuttgart).

Torelli, Mario. 1995. *Studies in the Romanization of Italy* (Edmonton).

———. 2000. "*C. Genucio(s) Clousino(s) prai(fectos)*. La fondazione della praefectura Caeritum." In Bruun (Ed.), 141–76.

————. 2006. "The Topography and Archaeology of Republican Rome." In Rosenstein et al. (Eds.), 81–101.

Trexler, Richard C. 1973. "Ritual Behavior in Renaissance Florence: The Setting." In *Medievalia et Humanistica. Studies in Medieval and Renaissance Culture*, n.s. 4: 125–44.

————. 1994 [1980]. *Public Life in Renaissance Florence* (Ithaca).

Twyman, Briggs. 1972. "The Metelli, Pompeius and Prosopography." In *ANRW* 1, 1: 816–74.

Ungern-Sternberg, Jürgen von. 1997. "Forschungen zur Klientel in Rom. Kommentar zum Beitrag von Jean-Michel David." In Bruhns et al. (Eds.), 211–16.

————. 1998. "Die Legitimitätskrise der römischen Republik." In *HZ* 266: 607–24 (= idem. 2006. *Römische Studien. Geschichtsbewußtsein—Zeitalter der Gracchen—Krise der Republik* [Leipzig], 390–404).

————. 2001. "M. Furius Camillus, ein zweiter Romulus?" In Coudry et al. (Eds.), 289–87.

————. 2004. "The Crisis of the Republic." In Flower (Ed.), 2004b, 89–109, 372–76.

————. 2006. "Die *gens Claudia*—Adelsstolz und Republik." In Stein-Hölkeskamp et al. (Eds.), 290–99. 749–50.

Urso, Gianpaolo (Ed.) 2005. *Popolo e potere nel mondo antico. Atti del convegno internazionale, Cividale del Friuli, 23–25 settembre 2004* (Pisa).

Valvo, Alfredo. 2005. "*Populus, nobilitas* e potere a Roma fra III e II secolo a. C." In Urso (Ed.), 71–83.

Van der Vliet, Edward Ch. L. 1990. "Early Rome and the Early State." In Eder (Ed.), 233–57.

Vanderbroeck, Paul J. J. 1987. *Popular Leadership and Collective Behavior in the Late Roman Republic (ca. 80–50 BC)* (Amsterdam).

Van Ooteghem, Jules. 1967. *Les Caecilii Metelli de la République* (Brussels).

Vasaly, Ann. 1993. *Representations. Images of the World in Ciceronian Oratory* (Berkeley).

Vernant, Jean-Pierre. 1982. *Die Entstehung des griechischen Denkens* (Frankfurt). Orig. ed. 1962.

Versnel, Henk S. 2006. "Red (Herring?). Comments on a New Theory concerning the Origin of the Triumph." In *Numen* 53: 290–326.

Veyne, Paul. 1974. "L'histoire conceptualisante." In Le Goff et al. (Eds.), 1:62–92.

————. 1975. "Y a-t-il un impérialisme romain?" In *MEFRA* 87: 793–855.

————. 1976. *L'inventaire des différences (Leçon inaugurale au Collège de France)* (Paris).

————. (1976) 1990. *Bread and Circuses. Historical Sociology and Political Pluralism* (London) (abridged translation of *Le pain et le cirque. Sociologie historique d'un pluralisme politique* [Paris]).

Vigourt, Annie. 2001. "M'. Curius Dentatus et C. Fabricius Luscinus: les grands hommes ne sont pas exceptionels." In Coudry et al. (Eds.), 117–29.

Visceglia, Maria Antonietta. 2002. *La città rituale. Roma e le sue ceremonie in età moderna* (Rome).

Vittinghoff, Friedrich. 1990. "Gesellschaft." In Wolfram Fischer et al. (Eds.), *Handbuch der europäischen Wirtschafts- und Sozialgeschichte*, vol. 1: *Eu-*

ropäische Wirtschafts- und Sozialgeschichte in der römischen Kaiserzeit, ed. by Friedrich Vittinghoff (Stuttgart), 161–369.

———. 1994. "Soziale Struktur und politisches System der Hohen römischen Kaiserzeit." In idem, *Civitas Romana. Stadt und politisch-soziale Integration im Imperium Romanum der Kaiserzeit*, ed. Werner Eck (Stuttgart), 253–71.

Vogt-Spira, Gregor, and Rommel, Bettina (Eds.). 1999. *Rezeption und Identität. Die kulturelle Auseinandersetzung Roms mit Griechenland als europäisches Paradigma* (Stuttgart).

Von Hesberg, Henner. 2005. "Die Häuser der Senatoren in Rom: gesellschaftliche und politische Funktion." In Eck et al. (Eds.), 19–52.

Vorländer, Hans, and Gert Melville. 2002a. "Geltungsgeschichten und Institutionengeltung. Einleitende Aspekte." In idem (Eds.), 2002b, ix–xv.

——— (Eds.). 2002b. *Geltungsgeschichten. Über die Stabilisierung und Legitimierung institutioneller Ordnungen* (Cologne).

Wallace, Robert W., and Harris, Edward M. (Eds.). 1996. *Transitions to Empire: Essays in Greco-Roman History 360–146 BC, in Honor of E. Badian* (Norman).

Wallace-Hadrill, Andrew. 1989a. "Patronage in Roman Society: From Republic to Empire." In idem (Ed.), 1989b, 63–87.

——— (Ed.). 1989b. *Patronage in Ancient Society* (London).

———. 1989c. "Rome's Cultural Revolution (review of Zanker, 1987)." In *JRS* 79: 157–64.

———. 1990. "Roman Arches and Greek Honours: The Language of Power at Rome." In *PCPhS* 36: 143–81.

Walter, Uwe. 1998. "Der Begriff des Staates in der griechischen und römischen Geschichte." In Theodora Hantos and Gustav Adolf Lehmann (Eds.), *Althistorisches Kolloquium aus Anlaß des 70. Geburtstages von Jochen Bleicken* (Stuttgart), 9–27.

———. 2001. "Die Botschaft des Mediums. Überlegungen zum Sinnpotential von Historiographie im Kontext der römischen Geschichtskultur zur Zeit der Republik." In Melville (Ed.), 241–79.

———. 2002. "Der Historiker in seiner Zeit: Ronald Syme und die Revolution des Augustus." In Spielvogel (Ed.), 137–52.

———. 2003. "AHN MACHT SINN. Familientradition und Familienprofil im republikanischen Rom." In Hölkeskamp et al. (Eds.), 255–78.

———. 2004a. Memoria *und* res publica. *Zur Geschichtskultur im republikanischen Rom* (Frankfurt).

———. 2004b. "'Ein Ebenbild des Vaters'. Familiale Wiederholungen in der historiographischen Traditionsbildung der römischen Republik." In *Hermes* 132: 406–25.

———. 2008. "Aristokratische Existenz in der Antike und der Frühen Neuzeit— einige unabgeschlossene Überlegungen." In Beck et al. (Eds.), 2008c, 367–94.

———. 2009. "Struktur, Zufall, Kontingenz? Überlegungen zum Ende der römischen Republik." In Hölkeskamp et al. (Eds.), 27–51.

Ward, Allen M. 1997. "The Roman Republic." In Carol G. Thomas (Ed.), *Ancient History: Recent Work and New Directions* (Claremont, Calif.), 54–78.

———. 2004. "How Democratic Was the Roman Republic?" In *NECJ* 31.2: 101–19.

Weber, Max. 1976. *Wirtschaft und Gesellschaft. Grundriss der verstehenden Soziologie* (5th edition ed. Johannes Winckelmann) (Tübingen).

———. 1999. *Wirtschaft und Gesellschaft. Die Wirtschaft und die gesellschaftlichen Ordnungen und Mächte. Nachlaß.* Teilbd. 5: *Die Stadt.* Ed. by Wilfried Nippel. (Max Weber Gesamtausgabe, Abt 1, vol. 22/5) (Tübingen).

Webster, Jane, and Cooper, Nicholas J. (Eds.). 1996. *Roman Imperialism: Post-Colonial Perspectives* (Leicester).

Welch, Katherine E. 2006. "*Domi Militiaeque*: Roman Domestic Aesthetics and War Booty in the Republic." In Dillon et al. (Eds.), 91–161.

Weller, Thomas. 2006. *Theatrum Praecedentiae. Zeremonieller Rang und gesellschaftliche Ordnung in der frühneuzeitlichen Stadt: Leipzig 1500–1800* (Darmstadt).

Welwei, Karl-Wilhelm. 1996. "Caesars Diktatur, der Prinzipat des Augustus und die Fiktion der historischen Notwendigkeit." In *Gymnasium* 103: 477–97 (= idem, 2004, 196–216).

———. 1999. *Das klassische Athen. Demokratie und Machtpolitik im 5. und 4. Jahrhundert* (Darmstadt).

———. 2001. "Die frührömische Klientel im Spiegel der Überlieferung." In *ZRG RA* 118: 220–233 (= idem, 2004, 34–47).

———. 2002. "Demokratische Verfassungselemente in Rom aus der Sicht des Polybios." In Spielvogel (Ed.), 25–35 (= idem, 2004, 139–49).

———. 2004. *Res publica und Imperium. Kleine Schriften zur römischen Geschichte* (Stuttgart).

Werner, Robert. 1972. "Das Problem des Imperialismus und die römische Ostpolitik im zweiten Jahrhundert v. Chr." In *ANRW* 1, 1: 501–63.

Wieacker, Franz. 1961². *Vom römischen Recht. Zehn Versuche* (Stuttgart).

———. 1988. *Römische Rechtsgeschichte,* Erster Abschnitt: *Einleitung, Quellenkunde, Frühzeit und Republik* (Munich).

Wilentz, Sean (Ed.). 1985. *Rites of Power: Symbolism, Ritual, and Politics since the Middle Ages* (Philadelphia).

Willems, Pierre. 1968. [1878–1885]. *Le Sénat de la République romaine* (Louvain).

Williamson, Callie. 2005. *The Laws of the Roman People: Public Law in the Expansion and Decline of the Roman Republic* (Ann Arbor).

Willke, Helmut. 1976. "Funktionen und Konstitutionsbedingungen des normativen Systems der Gruppe." In *KZSS* 28: 426–50.

Winterling, Aloys. 2001. "'Staat', 'Gesellschaft' und politische Integration in der römischen Kaiserzeit." In *Klio* 83: 93–112.

Wisch, Barbara, and Susan Scott Munshower (Eds.). 1990. *"All the world's a stage…": Art and Pageantry in the Renaissance and Baroque,* Part 1: *Triumphal Celebrations and the Rituals of Statecraft* (University Park, Md.).

Wischermann, Clemens (Ed.). 1996. *Die Legitimität der Erinnerung und die Geschichtswissenschaft* (Stuttgart).

Wiseman, T. Peter. 1974. "Legendary Genealogies in Late-Republican Rome." In *G&R* 21: 153–64 (= idem, 1987, 207–18).

———. (1976) 1987. "Factions and Family Trees." In *LCM* 1: 21–22 (= idem, 1987, 83–85).

———. 1979. *Clio's Cosmetics* (Leicester).

————. 1985a. "Competition and co-operation." In idem (Ed.), 1985, 3–19.

————. 1985b. *Catullus and His World. A Reappraisal* (Cambridge).

————. 1987. *Roman Studies, Literary and Historical* (Liverpool).

————. 2002a. "Roman History and the Ideological Vacuum." In idem (Ed.), 2002b, 285–310.

———— (Ed.). 1985. *Roman Political Life 90BC–A.D. 69* (Exeter).

———— (Ed.). 2002b. *Classics in Progress. Essays on Ancient Greece and Rome* (Oxford).

Wissowa, Georg. 1912. *Religion und Kultus der Römer* (2nd edition, Munich).

Witzmann, Peter. 2000. "Kommunikative Leistungen von Weih-, Ehren- und Grabinschriften: Wertbegriffe und Wertvorstellungen in Inschriften vorsullanischer Zeit." In Braun et al. (Eds.), 55–86.

Woolf, Greg. 1998. *Becoming Roman. The Origins of Provincial Civilization in Gaul* (Cambridge).

Yakobson, Alexander. 1999. *Elections and Electioneering in Rome. A Study in the Political System of the late Republic* (Stuttgart).

————. 2006a. "Popular Power in the Roman Republic." In Rosenstein et al. (Eds.), 383–400.

————. 2006b. "Il popolo romano, il sistema e l' 'élite': il dibattito continua." In *StStor* 47, 2: 377–93.

————. 2009. "Public Opinion, Foreign Policy and 'Just War' in the late Republic." In Eilers, Claude (Ed.). *Diplomats and Diplomacy in the Roman World* (Leiden), 45–72.

Zaccaria Ruggiu, Annapaola. 1995. *Spazio privato e spazio pubblico nella città romana* (Rome).

Zanker, Paul. (1987) 1988. *The Power of Images in the Age of Augustus* (Ann Arbor) (English edition of *Augustus und die Macht der Bilder* [Munich 1987]).

————. 1994. "Nouvelles orientations de la recherche en iconographie." In *RArch* 1994/2 (1995): 281–93.

————. 2000. "Bild-Räume und Betrachter im kaiserzeitlichen Rom." In Borbein et al. (Eds.), 205–26.

Zecchini, Giuseppe. 2006. "In margine a 'Rekonstruktionen einer Republik' di K.-J. Hölkeskamp." In *StStor* 47, 2: 395–404.

INDEX OF NAMES

ANCIENT PERSONS, *GENTES*, AND FAMILIES

Abbreviations: aed.cur. = *aedilis curulis*; aug. = augur; cos.= consul; fl.D. = *flamen Dialis*; m. = married; praet. = praetor; tr.mil.c.p. = *tribunus militum consulari potestate*; tr.pl. = *tribunus plebis*; all dates BC

Acilii Glabriones, 78

Aemilii (Paulli), 84, 85–86, 87, 110

Aemilius Paullus, L. (cos. I 182), 85–86

Aemilius Scaurus, M. (cos. 115), 81–82n25, 110

Atilii (Reguli; Serrani), 80

Augustus, 63, 124

Caecilia Metella (m. M. Aemilius Scaurus; L. Cornelius Sulla), 81–82n25

Caecilia Metella (m. Ap. Claudius Pulcher), 96

Caecilii Metelli, 81–82, 83 (stemma), 84, 95, 96, 118–19

Caecilius Metellus, L. (cos. I 251), 82, 113–14, 118

Caecilius Metellus, M. (cos. 115), 81n25, 119

Caecilius Metellus, Q. (cos. 206), 82, 113

Caecilius Metellus Calvus, L. (cos. 142), 81–82nn25–26

Caecilius Metellus Celer, Q. (cos. 60), 81n25, 96

Caecilius Metellus Denter, L. (cos. 284), 82

Caecilius Metellus Macedonicus, Q. (cos. 143), 81–82nn25–26, 118, 119

Calpurnii (Pisones), 78

Claudii (Marcelli), 95–96

Claudii (Pulchri, Nerones), 84, 96–97, 109, 116, 117

Claudius Marcellus, M. (cos. I 222), 28n11, 95

Claudius Marcellus, M. (cos. 196), 95

Claudius Marcellus, M. (cos. I 166), 95–96

Claudius Pulcher, Ap. (cos. 79), 96

Claudius Pulcher, Ap. (cos. 54), 96

Clodius Pulcher, P. (tr.pl. 58), 80, 96

Cornelii (Scipiones), 84, 86, 87, 88 (stemma), 91–92, 108, 110, 115–16, 122–23

Cornelius Rufinus, P. (cos. I 290), 110

Cornelius Scipio, P. (aug. 180, fl.D. 174?), 86, 87, 122–23

Cornelius Scipio Aemilianus (Africanus minor), P. (cos. I 147), 81, 86, 116, 122

Cornelius Scipio Africanus, P. (cos. I 205), 28–29n11, 86, 116

Cornelius Scipio Asiaticus, L. (cos. 190), 87, 122n42

Cornelius Scipio Barbatus, L. (cos. 298), 91, 92

Cornelius Scipio Hispallus, Cn. (cos. 176), 116n21, 122

Cornelius Scipio Hispanus, Cn. (praet. 139), 108, 115–16

Cornelius Sulla, L. (cos. I 88), 28–29n11, 81–82n25, 110, 127n8

Curius Dentatus, M'. (cos. I 290), 80, 82

Decius Mus, P. (cos. I 312), 28n11

Duilius, C. (cos. 260), 62, 81, 84, 120

Ennius, 121

Fabii (Maximi), 84, 86, 95

Fabius Maximus Aemilianus, Q. (cos. 145), 84, 86

Fabius Maximus Rullianus, Q. (cos. I 322), 28n11, 84

Fabius Maximus Verrucosus, Q. (cos. I 233), 28n11, 84

Fabricius Luscinus, C. (cos. I 282), 80, 84

Fulvia (m. P. Clodius Pulcher etc.), 80

Fulvii (Flacci; Nobiliores), 80

Fulvius Flaccus, Q. (cos. I 237), 80n18

Furii, 85

Furius Camillus, L. (cos. I 338), 85

Furius Camillus, M. (tr.mil.c.p. I 403), 85, 126

MODERN SCHOLARS

INDEX OF SUBJECTS

imperium (*auspiciaque*), 25, 64, 90, 113, 120
'institution,' 'institutionalization' (concept), 15, 17, 67–70, 72, 93, 133; limited degree of, 15, 23, 25, 34
ius publicum, as defined by F. Wieacker, 17–18, 21

landscape, sacral, urban. *See* space, civic, public
laudatio funebris, 113–14, 120. See also *pompa funebris*; rituals, civic
law, statute, 17; rôle of statutory, 17, 21–22
legislation (procedure), 3; importance, 21–22, 103
legitimacy, legitimation, 55, 56, 70. *See also* culture, political
lex, leges: leges de ambitu, 21; *leges annales*, 21; 86–87, 91; *leges de provocatione*, 117; *leges tabellariae*, 21. See law, statute
libertas, 46–47, 117

magistracy, magistrates, 1, 25–26, 32, 102; and assemblies, 19–20, 71, 73; and *mos maiorum*, 18; and senate, 27, 28–29. *See also* aedile, aedileship, curule; consuls, consulship; *cursus honorum*; *honos, honores*; praetor, praetorship; quaestor, quaestorship
memoria, memory (collective, cultural), 65, 66–67, 74–75, 114, 119, 120–21; of *gentes*, 108–9, 116–19; of *populus Romanus*, 111–12, 119. *See also* capital, social/symbolic; theory, theories
'meritocracy' (concept), 1, 93, 99, 103, 105, 107, 108–9, 120, 121–22, 134–35. *See also* aristocracy, Roman; class, political; *nobilitas*; values, value concepts
monuments (types), 27, 61–63, 65, 75, 131; individual: *columna Duilia*, 62, 74, 120; Porticus Metelli, 118; statues, 27, 61–62, 65, 74, 131; tombs (tomb of the Scipiones), 62, 87, 122–23
monuments, monumentalization, 61, 65, 120, 131
morality, collective, 45, 49, 51–52, 53, 63–64, 89–90. *See also* consensus, social; *mos* (*maiorum*); values, value concepts
mos (*maiorum*), 17–18, 20, 26, 29, 52, 69,

70, 80, 106, 121. *See also* consensus, social; morality, collective

nobilitas (Roman concept), 2, 3, 76, 78, 82, 86, 111, 113–14. *See also* aristocracy, Roman; class, political
'nobility' (modern concept), 2–3, 76–77
'nomological knowledge' (concept), 54–55, 70. See also *Begriffsgeschichte*; morality, collective; values, value concepts

officium, officia (concept), 35, 49, 50. See also *beneficium, beneficia*; *gratia*; reciprocity; values, value concepts
oligarchy (concept), 1, 2, 5
optimates, 5, 42
orator, oratory (rôle of), 4, 73, 102–3
'order' (sociological concept), 77–78. *See also* hierarchy, hierarchies

Parteiungen, new concept of. *See* groupings, political
participation, performative dimension of, 60–61. *See also* assemblies, popular; culture, political; procedure, formal; rituals, civic
'party,' political. *See* 'faction'; groupings, political; prosopography
patrician, patriciate, *patricius*, 1–2, 77, 82, 85–86. *See also* 'struggle of the orders'
patronage, patrons (rôles of), 2, 33–35, 102; phases of development, 36–38, 101. See also *clientela*, clients; *fides*
performance, performative practices, 57, 72, 100, 114, 135. *See also* culture, political; participation, performative dimension of; rituals, civic
plebeian, *plebs* (as a social status/'order'), 2, 3, 19, 35, 37, 45, 55, 57, 92, 114, 117; members/families of the political class, 6, 37, 41, 77, 79–80, 82, 84, 91, 95, 106, 115, 116, 118. *See also* 'struggle of the orders'; tribunate, tribunes of the *plebs*
polis. *See* 'city-state'
politics, 'the political' (concept, contents, character in Roman republic): modern concept, 24, 38, 39–41, 44–45, 53–55, 73; traditional concept, 7. *See also* culture, political